Same Circus
Different Clowns

Brent Tyler

Also by Brent Tyler

Cookham To Cannes (book 1 of this series)

www.brenttylerauthor.com

Dedicated to

Pete and Jen Kirwan

Alain Boulitreau and Marie-Hélène Cain,

Brendan Callighan and Beverly Summers

Docteur Cécile De Chaisemartin

Docteur Pauline Ries

and the staff at the Institut Paoli Calmettes, Marseille

Docteur Samy Boussoukaya, Palais Du Grasse

Introduction

A man dies and goes to purgatory. After a short while, he's joined by Saint Peter, who says, 'Welcome, my son, please follow me. I'm going to give you a brief tour of Heaven as, should you make the decision to spend the rest of time there, it's only fair that you see what it's all about first. At the end of your visit I will bring you back here, where you will be collected by the Devil, and he will show you Hell. When you've finished there, you will be brought back to purgatory and you will then decide where you are going to spend eternity.'

'I don't think that's at all necessary,' replied the man. 'My mind's made up. I really don't need to see Hell. Please pass on my apologies to the Devil but...'

'I'm afraid they are the rules,' interrupted Saint Peter. 'Quickly please, we don't have much time.' The two then began to climb a spiral staircase.

At the top, the Pearly Gates opened and in front of the man were rolling hills, lush meadows and people enjoying themselves with picnics. Naturally, there were angels sitting on clouds and soft music was playing in the background.

'I really don't think I need to visit Hell,' said the man. 'I couldn't ask for more.'

'Even so,' replied Saint Peter, who took the man back to purgatory. 'I will see you later.' Soon, the Devil arrived. 'Follow me,' he said, with a broad smile. The two walked down a wooden staircase. At the bottom, a pair of black iron gates opened and the man saw his first vision of Hell. What he saw before him was quite incredible. It was nothing like he had previously imagined. There were long dining tables, on which was every kind of sumptuous dish that a person could dream of. There was caviar, truffles, platters of meat, fish and fresh fruit. At each table was a beautiful wench who was filling wine glasses to the point of overflowing. Laughter and merriment rang throughout the room.

'It is time to leave now,' said the Devil to the man before he could sit down to join the revellers.

Once back in purgatory, the man was visited once again by Saint Peter, who said, 'Well, my son, have you made your mind up?'

'Yes,' he replied, looking a little sheepish. 'I never thought I'd say this but I'm going to join the Devil in Hell – it seems much more fun. That is where I have decided to spend eternity. I'm sorry.'

'It's your decision,' replied Saint Peter, who, disappointed, started to climb the spiral staircase for the final time.

Eagerly, the man began his descent. As soon as he arrived at the bottom of the staircase he banged on the gates of Hell with great enthusiasm.

'Welcome,' said the Devil with a huge smile. 'Do come in.' Just as the man got inside, the gates slammed shut and, for a few brief moments, the room was plunged into darkness. Seconds later, the lights came back on and what was in front of the man was exactly what he had previously envisaged to be Hell. The tables were strewn with rotting carcasses, the wenches had turned into screaming old hags, the wine was rancid and the stench of burning flesh filled the room.

'Wait a minute,' said the man. 'This isn't what I signed up for. When I came here the last time, it was wonderful – more than I could ever have asked for. What you showed me was my absolute vision of paradise. What happened?'

'Ah,' replied the Devil, with a big grin. 'That was the interview – this is the job.'

Chapter 1

It had become our Sunday ritual to go for a walk by the sea in Mandelieu – a town about ten miles from Cannes. We'd park opposite the church and while my wife, Debbie, went to the local bakery and grocery store, I would take Guss, our dog, to the beach. We'd meet up about an hour later at a small café where we'd enjoy a coffee, a croissant and a read of the local paper. On this particular Sunday, just as Debbie was wrapping her scarf around her neck and about to open the car door, her phone rang. She answered and, for a few moments, listened quite intently. I could make out a male voice on the other end but that was all. Taking a piece of scrap paper and pen from her handbag, she wrote 'Charles Robbins.' I shrugged my shoulders. Debbie then wrote down the word *Job*. Thinking that my input was likely not needed at that stage, I got Guss out of the back of the car as quietly as I could, closed the door, waved goodbye to Debbie and headed off towards the beach.

It was April 2013. By then, Debbie and I had been living and working together in the south of France for more than three years. Somehow, along the way we'd been adopted by a mad German Shepherd-Briard cross puppy, who had since grown into a thirty-five-kilo bundle of endless energy. It hadn't been our intention to have a dog when we moved here. In our line of work, primarily live-in housekeeper-cook, gardener-chauffeur, having a dog can be a non-starter when looking for work. Quite often we'd see employment adverts which read, *No pets, no smokers, no dependants*, or '*no life*,' as Debbie used to put it.

Half an hour after leaving Debbie by the church, Guss, soaked to the skin and covered in sand, and I were back. Debbie, who was still in the car on the phone, mouthed, 'Five minutes.' With little else to do I went and gazed at the church noticeboard and tried to translate what the Sunday sermon was going to be all about.

Ten minutes later I was sitting on a small wall next to the car. Debbie unwound the window. 'Any good?' I asked as I took off my shoes and knocked them together to get rid of the sand.

1

'Yes, actually,' replied Debbie, who was looking down at the notes she'd made. 'You remember that job we applied for in Montauroux?'

'The owners that are based in Hong Kong?' I said as I got into the car.

'That's the one. Seems they're ready to go ahead and want to take a couple on sooner rather than later,' replied Debbie, reaching for her seatbelt.

'So, how have you left it?' I asked.

'He's going to get his secretary to ping us an email with some photos, first thing tomorrow,' said Debbie, who was pulling out of the carpark.

'She's going to do what with an email?' I said. 'Why can't she just send it, like everybody else? What a load of...'

'Look, he's the CEO of a big electronics firm,' Debbie interrupted. 'That's the way these people talk. He doesn't mean anything by it. Although, I have to say, finishing every sentence with the word "right" did get a little annoying.'

'I used to get told off at school for doing that.'

'Why?'

'Sounds like an army marching on one leg my teacher used to say. Right, right, right!' Debbie smiled. 'Anyway, if we do take the job and they start "running things up flagpoles," confusing me with an "envelope that needs stretching" or someone tries "reaching out to me," I'm out of there. And I'm certainly not about to "hit the ground running" either. The last time I tried that, it hurt. Besides, aren't you forgetting one minor detail?'

'Which is?' Debbie replied.

'We've already been offered a job in Carpentras. Not only that, it's working for royalty. Got to look better on our CV than working for Microchips Я Us, surely?'

'Look, my love,' Debbie said, 'I know I haven't said this before, but I've always thought that job was always one for the back burner.'

'Really? That's news to me.'

'I know, I'm sorry, but I don't think you'd manage – it's a huge estate.

You've never driven a tractor and you wouldn't know where to begin with all the things that get attached to the back of it. I'd be worried sick. Look what happened to Daniel.'

Daniel, a groundsman with over thirty-five years' experience, who was my predecessor in our first paying job in France, had fallen off a tractor and could have easily been killed. The tractor lost its grip in the wet and rolled down a slope, miraculously bouncing over him. He'd been lucky to escape with his life – very lucky. Maybe Debbie was right. Since living in France, my skills as a gardener had improved immeasurably but not enough to look after several acres of woodland. Sure, I could prune roses, make a garden look pretty and keep most things alive but that wasn't going to be enough in this case – I simply didn't have the experience.

Soon, we were back at our apartment and as I hung my fleece over the hook behind the front door, I shouted to Debbie, who was already preparing lunch, 'The feeding of the five thousand, you know!'

'What about it?' Debbie called back.

'The subject of today's sermon. I read it on the noticeboard,' I answered as I walked into the kitchen.

'One of my favourite miracles,' said Debbie cheerily.

'Well, it would be, wouldn't it?' I replied. 'It involves food.' Debbie laughed. 'Hardly a miracle, though, was it?'

'Hardly a miracle?' said Debbie. 'What would you call the feeding of five thousand people with two fish and five loaves of bread, then?'

'Tapas.'

Over lunch at our cosy apartment in Théoule-sur-Mer, Debbie explained that the villa in Montauroux belonged to an English couple with two young children. They usually only visited for a few weeks in the summer and occasionally at Christmas. Charles, the person who had spoken to Debbie earlier, said that the property was rented out in July and August, which potentially would give us the opportunity to earn some extra cash on top of our salary.

Debbie could make some money by cooking and perhaps offering some additional cleaning, while I could do airport runs and guided tours. Guided tours of quite what, I didn't know at that stage, but I could apparently 'scope' the area to give the clients the opportunity to experience some extra value during their stay.

'OK,' I said at lunch, while plunging my fork into a roasted parsnip, 'but if this place is so fantastic, why are the other people leaving?'

'Actually, it's only one person, and he doesn't know he's leaving yet. Pass the salt, please.'

'He doesn't know he is yet? That's nice, interviewing other people before the chap who's working for him has been told himself – charming. Anyway, I thought they were looking for a couple.'

'They are,' replied Debbie. 'The man who's there now got divorced a while ago and they need a couple. There's quite a large garden, though it's manageable according to Charles, and with five bedrooms there's more than enough to do in the house. They did consider taking on a housekeeper but as Pierre – I think that's his name – doesn't really enjoy gardening and has refused to go on any gardening courses, they haven't been left with much choice. What with that and him trying to rip Charles off...'

'Trying to rip him off? That'd be right. Have you ever known a rich person who hasn't said someone's trying to rip them off?' Debbie smiled. 'Still sounds a bit fishy to me. Anyway, where do we go from here?'

'Well, if we like the photos and are still keen, Charles is going to arrange a Skype interview with him and his wife, Belinda, tomorrow lunchtime. She'll explain my role to me and after that he'll explain yours to you.'

'Wow, that's quick. They don't hang around, do they?'

'Rich people never do. Besides, he said he wants to see us face to face – make sure we don't have two heads and all that.' Debbie laughed. 'He's also asked us to make a list of any additional services that we think we can offer the rental guests to give them a truly hedonistic experience.'

'A what?' I replied. 'This guy sounds a right...'

'Leave it,' Debbie interrupted. 'Come on, put your thinking cap on. We haven't got much time.'

While Debbie assembled menus, wrote down as many ingredients as she could for a luxury picnic hamper and costed a complete laundry service, I pored over a map of the local area to see where I might be able to take guests out for the day. By bedtime, we'd put together about ten pages of notes that Debbie had hoped to have typed up the following morning before our interview.

'These photos are amazing,' shouted Debbie, who was in the lounge and looking at the computer, early the following morning. 'Come on, Brent. Come and see these.'

I opened one eye and picked up my phone. Five-thirty. Had Debbie gone mad? I didn't even realise there *was* a five-thirty in the morning. Dragging myself out of bed, I made my way into the kitchen and reached for the kettle.

'Look at this,' said Debbie, who had pulled up a chair next to her in the lounge. 'It's absolutely beautiful.' As I sipped my coffee, we watched a slideshow of about twenty photographs, each one as stunning as the last. The kitchen was both large and modern. The marble work surfaces were beautifully crafted and lined with expensive gadgets. The bedrooms were painted in pastel colours and looked very comfortable while the lounge, which was pictured with a substantial log fire, was designed for relaxation. In the grounds there was a swimming pool, a games room, a hot tub and a gym. The lawn was lush and the roses looked well cared for. Stone steps led down to a meadow in which there were, I estimated, about forty or fifty olive trees. In amongst those, there were three or four fig and a couple of cherry trees. At the bottom of the meadow, I could just make out the next-door neighbour's house.

'What's that?' I asked, pointing to a tall, thin building on the edge of the lawn.

'That must be the *pigeonnier*,' replied Debbie, who had just brought me a coffee. 'They rebuilt it, you know. Was a ruin when they first arrived.

5

There's a small apartment in there and Sir's wine cellar is in the basement. Oh, must tell you this while I'm thinking about it.'

'Go on.'

'Charles is happy to sell his wine to guests. He doesn't make any profit out of it but it keeps his stock turning over.'

'Sounds very reasonable.'

'Anyway, last summer, one of the guests went over to Pierre's apartment at about nine in the evening and asked to buy a bottle. And you know what? Pierre refused. Said it was too late and firmly closed his front door.'

'No way.' I laughed. 'Not what you'd call a truly hedonistic experience then?'

'No, not really,' said Debbie. 'Neither the customer, who had paid five thousand euros for the week, nor Charles was too pleased.'

'I bet they weren't. Got to laugh though. Anyway, five thousand euros for the week? Bloody hell,' I said, now fully awake. 'Sounds a lot.'

'That's what I thought, but then Charles said that as there are five bedrooms, so potentially ten adults staying there, it only works out at five hundred euros per head for the week. There's also some bunkbeds and cots dotted around the place, so it's not really that expensive and it's not like they have to share the villa with anyone.'

'I suppose,' I replied, scrolling through the photos once more.

'A lot of people rent it for a special occasion,' Debbie said, 'a fiftieth wedding anniversary, that kind of thing, so they bring the whole family. Also, Charles mentioned that when it's rented out to families, they tend to look after the place better – it's like it's their home. Part of the contract – no stag or hen do's, apparently. He said that's just asking for the place to be trashed. Right, I've got to type this lot up,' Debbie said, referring to her notes.

'Lovely to meet you both,' said Belinda, a woman in her late forties and of oriental descent. Charles is running a bit late, so if you don't mind I'll talk to

Debbie first. Is that OK with you, Brent?' She smiled.

While I sat, listened and quite often drifted off into a daydream, the two women spoke for a good hour about what could be done to improve the inside of the villa.

'Sorry Brent,' apologised Belinda at the end of the conversation, 'we haven't got round to you, but that's really Charles's job and he's still not back from work. We'll have to set up a meeting another time but it all sounds very positive. Bye.'

Chapter 2

'Just about sums up our lives,' I said to Debbie as we headed along the autoroute towards Montauroux, which was only an hour's drive from Théoule-sur-Mer.

'What does?'

'The contents of the glove compartment,' I replied as I rooted around for nothing in particular. 'A dog brush, a corkscrew and a bag of travel sweets.' Debbie laughed.

Our Skype call with Belinda had been so positive that only two weeks later we were driving towards Montauroux to begin our new job. Guss was lying on the back seat, sandwiched between two suitcases. There wasn't an inch of room to be had in the boot.

'It is a bit strange, though, don't you think?' I said. Debbie glanced briefly at me. 'We're starting a job in a place we haven't actually visited, and we haven't met the owners in person. Also, I have no idea what kind of reception we're going to get when we get there. If it's anything like those two clowns at Fatso's...' I added, referring to a previous job where we hadn't been made at all welcome by the outgoing guardians.

'A bit late to start worrying about it now,' interrupted Debbie, who was trying to concentrate on what the woman's voice on the GPS was telling her. 'If we get there and it doesn't work out, what have we lost? And besides, Charles said that Pierre is very nice – useless but nice. We'll be fine.'

'Hope you're right.'

Only a few minutes after we had turned off the autoroute we were crossing Lac de Saint-Cassien. The long, straight road ran over the top of the lake and on either side were vast expanses of water as far as the eye could see. Pedalos bobbed up and down along the shore's edge and brightly coloured parasols lined the banks. I could make out one or two wooden huts that I presumed to be snack bars and in amongst the trees I spotted some hikers. A few yards into the lake were plastic climbing frames in the shape of icebergs.

'Blimey, you didn't tell me about this,' I said, excitedly.

'Sorry, forgot. Charles said that it used to hold the world record for the largest carp ever caught – about seventy pounds. Caught by a Brit as well.'

'That's impressive,' I replied, continuing to admire the scenery.

'Fishing rod for Christmas?'

'This is impossible,' complained Debbie, who was trying to negotiate a very steep, narrow track that led up to the villa.

'We're going to burn the clutch out at this rate,' I said as the car performed yet another wheelspin. 'Surely this can't be right?'

'Good grief!' Debbie shouted. 'We're already ten minutes late. I bet it's that sodding GPS. I hate it. You'd better call him. Not what you'd call a good start, is it?' I reached for the phone.

'He said that you can't get through this way. It's blocked a bit further up.'

'Knew it – bastard thing,' scowled Debbie, staring at the little box on the windscreen. 'So, what do we do now?'

'Turn round apparently. He was surprised that we didn't ask Charles for directions. Anyway, we'd better hurry up. He's got to go out in about half an hour and if we don't make it we'll have to let ourselves in.'

'Charming.'

With about ten minutes to spare we arrived at our new employer's villa, the Mas des Collines. As the gates opened, standing in the middle of the courtyard was a man of average height wearing a flying jacket, pale blue jeans and white tennis shoes. Slowly removing a cigarette from the corner of his mouth, he motioned for us to park to our right, next to a brand-new Land Rover that we assumed belonged to Charles. As we got out of the car the man smiled and offered me his hand.

'*Bonjour*,' he said. 'I am Pierre.'

Debbie, who had decided that it was unlikely to be just us who had had enough of the journey, opened the back door of the car. Guss jumped out and went running off into the grounds as fast as his legs would carry him.

9

'Sorry about that,' I said. 'That was Guss, our dog.'

'And that,' replied Pierre as we heard a very loud screech coming from the bushes to our right, 'was Venezuela, my cat.' The screech was followed by a bark and the bark was followed by one very happy dog returning to us and wagging his tail.

'Never mind,' said Pierre, forcing a smile. 'Come on, I'll show you round – your place at least. I'll give you the keys to the villa before I go. You can have a look in your own time and ask questions later or maybe tomorrow.'

'Interesting name for a cat,' I said as we climbed up some steps to the side of the garage.

'Ah, yes, Venezuela,' replied Pierre. 'It's where my son lives with his wife. They emigrated last year,' he continued, opening the door to the apartment. 'It was a present before they left – something to remind me of them. Very nice gesture, but I don't really like cats – too much trouble. I hope he can find a home because I can't take him with me when I go.'

'Where are you going, if you don't mind me asking?' said Debbie, who was studying the kitchen-cum-sitting room that was just inside the front door.

'For now, not far. Right there, actually,' he said, pointing to a large house just over the road. 'I can spy on you from there. Or you can spy on me, if you like!' Pierre smiled. 'It belongs to some very good friends of mine. They live in Paris. They'll be coming down soon. They're very nice. When they get here, I'm going to stay with my sister in Cannes and then we'll see. My sister is allergic to cats, so I can't really take him.' Pierre laughed. 'If you know of anybody who would like a cat, please let me know. Look, I must get on. I'll leave you to explore. Any questions before I go?'

'Just the one, Pierre,' I said. 'What's the wi-fi code?'

'I don't know that. I think it's in one of the draws in the lounge in the villa. If you don't find it, maybe you ask Charles.'

'You don't have it for your rental guests?' asked Debbie, looking quite surprised.

10

'No,' he replied. 'If they don't find it, they usually phone Charles. Actually, they phone him quite a lot,' he mused. 'Bye, bye,' he said as he quietly closed the door behind him and disappeared down the steps and out of the front gate. I watched him as he walked along the narrow lane and into the drive of the house opposite. He opened the garage, took out a deckchair, which he placed in the middle of the field at the front of the house, sat down and started to read a book. Debbie, who was standing over my shoulder, just shook her head.

'This place is filthy,' said Debbie, who was opening all the cupboards and drawers in our one-bedroom apartment above the garage.

'I know, but he's been on his own. Can't have been easy for him,' I replied. 'Lost his job, his home, his wife – got to feel a bit sorry for him.'

'Of course I do, but Charles did say he was being paid to do it – that and some painting. Doesn't look like that's been done.'

Over the next few weeks Pierre would arrive at about ten in the morning, stay for an hour or two and then make an excuse to leave. This usually involved him having to do some work in Cannes but, more often than not, his rental car didn't move out of the drive across the road. Sometimes, when I went to do some shopping I'd see Pierre sitting outside the local *tabac* with a coffee, deep in thought.

Our apartment was quite small and it didn't take long to get it up to scratch. Then we began to get stuck into our respective jobs. I weeded, dead-headed the roses and cut the grass with the help of a sit-down mower. Debbie pulled out every plate, cup and saucer out of the cupboards, which she counted and inspected for damage. She made list upon list of things that she felt needed either buying or replacing in order to turn the villa into a five-star property, which was part of Belinda's brief. At the end of the day, with her head pounding, she typed up her notes which she would then email to our new bosses.

'None of the crockery matches,' said Debbie, 'and a lot of it is chipped. I'll tell you something else – you should see the linen. How they ever managed to do any changeovers I'll never know. There should be at least two sets for each room but it's all over the place. Whenever I look in a draw there's something stuffed at the back of it. God knows how long it had been there.' Debbie laughed. 'And as for the state of it – looks like people have been camping in it. Five-star service? Hardly, Stanley. I'm sure we can do it but looks like we've got our work cut out here. Anyway, how did you get on?'

'Well, Pierre came over this morning and we had a root around the garage. While we were there he tried to sell me his half of the Porsche. Can you believe it?' I laughed.

'Porsche! What Porsche is that then?' asked Debbie.

'The one he went fifty-fifty with Charles on. It's still there and very nice it is too.'

'Really?' replied Debbie, looking quite surprised. 'Must have been some time ago. Not likely to have bought it after what happened.'

'Pierre said they bought it together when he first started - about three years ago, I'm guessing. So, you found out what happened with Pierre, then?'

'Yes. Belinda phoned this morning when you were out. She said that Pierre's wife got herself into trouble with some online gambling. Got into debt to the tune of around twenty K.'

'Wow, that's a lot of bingo.'

'Sure is. Anyway, the story is that Belinda and Charles offered to pay off the debt and said that Pierre could pay them back at five hundred euros per month and with no interest. Obviously, he jumped at the chance.'

'So, what went wrong?'

'Pierre started to fake invoices, apparently. Each month he'd put in an invoice or a series of invoices for about five hundred euros, so he didn't lose out. When Charles realised what was going on, that's when it all went wrong.'

'Well, it would really, wouldn't it? Cheeky bastard!' I said, going over to the fridge. 'Rosé?'

'Yes please. So, Pierre still owes Charles most of that money, which is why he's supposed to be here every day, working off what he owes.'

'Surprised Charles didn't call the police.'

'That's what I said, but he couldn't, could he? As they'd lent the money to Pierre, technically he hadn't stolen it, and Charles couldn't see the police being interested in a few dodgy invoices. Also, if they reported Pierre to the police, they felt they'd have no chance of getting their money back. Difficult to pay off debts when you're in prison. So, there you go.'

'It all happens here,' I said as I passed Debbie a glass of wine.

'Cheers. I take it we haven't bought half a Porsche then?' Debbie asked.

'Not quite. I did say to Pierre that we didn't happen to have a spare seven grand sitting around, so you know what he came back with? Said we could pay it off in instalments!' Debbie laughed. 'Anyway, he said he's going to pick it up tomorrow,' I said.

'In which case, my love, I imagine that's the last Charles will see of the Porsche.'

'Or the money Pierre gets when he sells it,' I replied.

'That's true. Do you think I should let Belinda know?'

'I'd stay out of it if I were you. Nothing really to do with us.'

By the time I got to the garage at eight o'clock the following morning to fetch my gardening tools, the Porsche had gone.

Little by little, Debbie and I got to grips with the villa and the garden. Pierre, who had been tasked with repainting the shutters in the same colour, was having difficulty matching the paint. He spent hour upon hour in the garage looking through box files for a corresponding invoice. The problem was that the shutters hadn't been painted in ten years and there was no filing system – just thirty or so box files full of paperwork. So interested was he in his task that as I walked past the garage I'd often notice that Pierre had nodded off, waking up just in time for lunch. After that we wouldn't see him again until at least the following day. In the end, Debbie decided to look for it herself, but she found nothing either.

'Ah,' said Belinda one afternoon during a Skype call, 'now that I come to think of it, there wasn't an invoice at all. It was a cash job. Monsieur Duval, brilliant painter. Used to live in the village.'

'Shall I try and track him down?' I asked, helpfully.

'Oh, I can track him down all right,' replied Belinda. 'He's in the cemetery. Unfortunately, he died a couple of years ago. The thing is, what we need is for the shutters to look exactly as they are now – distressed but new, if that makes sense. Maybe you could go to the paint shop and see if they can match it. Hope you haven't wasted too much time already – there's so much to do.'

'Haven't wasted too much time already? Only about three days,' said Debbie scornfully, just after the call ended. 'These people really have no idea. They just think everything takes five minutes.'

'Just found these,' said Debbie, who returned to our apartment one lunchtime. In her right hand she had a key fob, on which were two keys.

'They're for?' I asked.

'They're for the *pigeonnier*,' replied Debbie, who was looking rather pleased. 'Pierre said that he thought Charles had taken them with him when he last left. Thought it was a bit odd.'

'So, where did you find them?' I asked.

'Stuffed away at the back of a drawer, like most things in the villa.' Debbie laughed. 'Come on, let's go and have a look.'

At the far edge of the lawn was the entrance. I opened the front door and before us was a kitchen and a dining room table.

'This is where Charles comes to get away from it all,' explained Debbie. To our left was a spiral staircase which led up to a bedroom and bathroom. 'You coming?' I asked.

'Not sure I can. Look at that ceiling,' Debbie replied. 'It's made of glass. You go.' As I stood on the top floor, I could see what she meant. It was a very strange feeling being able to see the floor below.

14

Of course, the glass was very thick, but my mind didn't want to trust it.

'Anyway,' said Debbie, once I'd come back down, 'you'd have to know the people you're with quite intimately.'

'Why so?'

'I wouldn't want to be walking on that top floor wearing a short skirt, with people downstairs!' Debbie laughed.

'I don't know. I can think of a few people we could invite. Ouch!' I groaned as Debbie pinched my arm. 'Let's go and have a look at the wine cellar.'

I closed the front door, turned left and walked down a few steps onto the croquet lawn where there was the rear entrance to the *pigeonnier*. I turned the key in the lock of the heavy oak door and stood there for a few moments, quite taken aback.

'Wow – never seen anything like this, have you?' I asked.

'No,' replied Debbie, who was equally astonished. Inside there was an arched cave, at the back of which was rack upon rack of fine wines. There was an air-conditioning unit and a strip light running across the floor so the clarity of the wines could be checked when held up to it. To the left were some wooden steps which led up to a trap door that, in turn, led to the *pigeonnier* above. Even the steps were full of wine bottles and there were plenty on the floor too. There was a large, old, wooden barrel that served as a table, and four chairs surrounded it.

'If I ever get locked in there by accident,' I said as we left, 'promise not to try and find me for at least a week.' Debbie laughed. As we walked along the croquet lawn which was as flat and as smooth as silk, I turned to Debbie. 'Look, they've got a small wine cellar in the villa and this one here.'

'Your point?'

'If they had all the cheap ones at the villa, the guests could pay for what they use in the evenings and wouldn't have to bother us. Besides, it would also save them having to lug a load back from the supermarket. If they want an expensive bottle or two from the *pigeonnier* they can ask us during the day. What do you reckon?'

15

'Great idea, Baking Powder. Suggest it to Charles, if you ever meet him, that is.' Debbie smiled.

I shrugged my shoulders. We'd been at the property for almost a month and each time I was due to have a Skype call with Charles it was cancelled, and we'd be left with a very apologetic Belinda. He was always dashing off somewhere or other. The previous occasion it was a last-minute trip to Brazil. Eventually, a time was set and, with no sign of a cancellation, I sat nervously in front of my computer screen. At exactly seven o'clock on Wednesday evening, the call came through. Facing me was man in his early forties, wearing an expensive suit and an open-necked shirt.

'Nice to meet you Brent, but got to keep this short. Got a conference call with Japan coming up in ten minutes so let's get to it,' he began. 'Like your ideas, right? There are just one or two things I want to go over. Firstly, it doesn't look like you know anything about bikes, right?'

'That's correct. Haven't ridden a...'

'Not a problem,' Charles interrupted. 'Belinda, I'm pretty sure, has already explained to Debbie that we've got this thing called a Dropbox, right? It's where we can share information between us and what I'm going to do is to give you the full one 'o' one on bike maintenance, so you can get up to speed on that before I get to you, right? I see you know how to use Excel – great. The thing is we didn't get too much information back from Pierre about what he was doing at the villa when we weren't there, which I doubt was much, so I need you to look under the bonnet for me and find out what's been going on. Got it? I need you to keep us updated. The thing is we've got rental guests arriving in three weeks, so we need to have all of our ducks in a row before they get here. Look, I'm sorry but it looks like that call's coming through a bit early but before I go, I wanted to let you know that I've taken on board your idea about giving the rental guests their own wine cellar. I really think we should give that idea some traction. Coming now!' he bellowed, and the line went dead. For a few moments I sat there motionless. Then I suddenly shouted at the top of my voice, 'Debbie, Debbie, get me out of here!'

16

Chapter 3

It was half-term at the schools in Hong Kong, which gave Belinda the opportunity to come and visit us along with her two girls. As I waited at Arrivals and having seen her previously on Skype, I thought that Belinda Robbins was going to be pretty easy to spot. As usual, I was extremely early but better that than being late – one of the things that I had learned since being in France was that rich people don't like being kept waiting.

I was just beginning to think that they'd missed their flight when a diminutive woman stood in front of me, looked up and said, 'Hello Brent.' She smiled and introduced me to her daughters, Zoe and Caroline. Belinda had always looked so large as she filled the screen on my laptop. How could I have got it so wrong?

'I've brought a few things for the villa,' Belinda said. 'I hope there's enough room in the car,' she continued, looking at the two trollies full of luggage. 'It's so much cheaper in Hong Kong.'

'Can't wait to be home,' shouted Zoe, who I assumed to be around eight or nine years old. As young as she was, she also had a voice that could shatter glass. This was going to be a long journey back. While Zoe bounced around on the back seat of the car, occasionally prodding her sister in the ribs, Caroline, who was four or five years her senior, sat quietly staring at her smart phone. *Home?* I said to myself. Surely Hong Kong was home? But no – Belinda explained that although they weren't there very often, Mas des Collines was home, or at least it would be one day. There wasn't much space in Hong Kong, she said, so they could hardly call a three-bedroom apartment half way up a skyscraper home, however much time they had to spend there. One day, sooner rather than later, they hoped that Charles would make enough money to give up work for a couple of years at least and do the things that he really enjoyed, which revolved mainly around keeping fit. Often, while Belinda and the girls would drive fifty kilometres or so to a restaurant, Charles would set off on his road bike and meet them there.

Then, he'd cycle back. Belinda, too, was quite fanatical. Every other day she'd go for a twelve-kilometre run around the Montauroux countryside.

There wasn't a moment of silence to be had during the hour-long return journey. When Zoe wasn't shrieking in the background, Belinda was on the phone, and when text messages weren't coming through, both Zoe and Caroline were forced to count in Chinese. I was very relieved to jump out of the car when we got back, even if there was no offer of help whatsoever with the carrying of any of the luggage.

As Belinda instructed me in which room I should put each case, the children ran onto the lawn, closely followed by Guss. Debbie had prepared an evening meal and what had seemed quite a calm setting up until then soon descended into chaos. By the time the food was on the table, suitcases were empty, clothes were everywhere, iPods, iPads and chargers littered the work surfaces and the sound of a running bath could be heard upstairs.

'Come on you two, you'll have to share tonight!' Belinda shouted. 'Caroline, where's your shampoo? I know I packed it, but it's not here now. Zoe, what have done with Caroline's shampoo? And stop splashing. Thanks Debbie, don't worry, I'll feed them. You get off. Looks like I could be in for a long night. See you in the morning. Zoe, stop it!' Belinda shouted.

'Is the drowning of young children still illegal in France?' Debbie asked as we walked back to our apartment. I smiled.

'Alas, I believe it still is, my love,' I replied. 'How long did you say they were staying?'

'Ten days.'

'Fuck.'

At nine o'clock the following morning Debbie and I went back over to the villa for a meeting with Belinda. As we walked through the front door we were greeted by Zoe, who looked up at Debbie, smiled and said, 'Can I have a cookie please?'

'No, you can't, Zoe!' replied a stern voice from upstairs. 'Debbie, don't give her any. She has had enough sugar as it is.'

18

'Oh Mummy, that's so unfair,' groaned Zoe, who screwed her face up. 'Anyway, I didn't ask you.'

'I am your mother,' came the reply.

'That's not my fault!' Zoe shouted back as she slammed the front door behind her and headed down the steps towards the garden. Debbie and I sat at the dining room table and waited.

'Sorry about that, Debbie,' apologised Belinda, who had come down from the bedroom and was drying her hair with a towel. 'She's been going through a difficult phase. Seems like she's been going through it for the past eight years, if I'm honest,' she mused.

'Could I have a coffee please? Then we'll begin.'

'I'll do it,' I said, wandering the short distance to the kitchen.

As Belinda and Debbie began to discuss all things to do with the house, I stood by the kettle and looked out of the window. Every now and then I'd see Zoe bobbing up and down on a trampoline outside. Guss waited patiently on the grass beside her. Caroline had taken herself off into the lounge and was stretched out on the sofa, reading a book. As the meeting went on, and with each point on the agenda meticulously talked through, I could see that Debbie was becoming quite frustrated with Belinda's answers. It was clear that despite all of my wife's efforts to improve the quality of what was on offer at Mas des Collines, Belinda either couldn't or didn't want to spend much money at all. From what I could hear, it was all beginning to sound very much like 'mend or make do.' I could hear Debbie's voice in my head saying, 'Why the hell have I bothered?' Instead of replacing the quite worn covers for the sun loungers as Debbie had suggested, Belinda had brought bottles of pink and blue dye with her. The badly chipped mugs and plates were to be put in cupboards by the pool and Debbie was due to spend some of the afternoon cutting off the labels attached to the new bed linen and replacing them with some that Belinda had had specially made for her in Hong Kong.

'I'm sure this isn't legal,' said Debbie who was sitting in our apartment with a

19

needle and cotton later that afternoon. 'People aren't that stupid, and I spent ages working on this sodding report,' she continued, throwing it onto the floor. 'And for what? Cheapskates! Anyway, what are you up to?'

'We're all off to Vidauban, apparently,' I said, picking up the keys to the Land Rover.

'Vidauban. Why on earth are you going to Vidauban?'

'Well, you remember I wrote that I thought it would be a good idea to keep chickens? She's gone for it. The hen house arrives this afternoon. All we need now are the chickens. Belinda thinks we might be able to make some money out of selling eggs to the guests.'

'That'd be right. And yet, she won't even fork out for a new kettle. Unbelievable. See you later. Crap, I hate sewing.'

An hour or so later, we were pulling into the car park at a garden centre on the outskirts of Vidauban. Once inside, we saw that at the far end of the building there was a long line of cages, each one housing five or six hens. The girls were tasked with choosing three each while Belinda and I went to look for chicken feed and a water trough. Much against their mother's advice to name the chickens in case one of them got taken by a fox, by the time we got back, Zoe and Caroline had given names to all six.

'There's no way that Mister Fox will get them!' shouted Zoe, once we were in the car. 'I'll fight him with a stick,' she said, prodding her sister quite hard with a biro.

'Get off me!' Caroline shouted. 'Anyway, foxes come in the night, stupid.'

'Well, then I can stay with them at night. Mummy, can I sleep in the…'

'No, you can't,' said Belinda, already worn out by the morning's events.

'Right girls, your nine times table. Caroline, you start.'

We were about to turn off the busy main road and head up to the Mas des Collines when Belinda asked me to stop at the local bakery. Giving me the chance to get out of the car and away from the over-excited girls, I decided to join her.

'We won't be a moment, so behave yourselves,' were the last words that Belinda uttered before closing the car door.

It was only a few moments before all hell broke loose. There were loud screams as the back doors of the Land Rover opened. Three chickens jumped onto the tarmac and made a run for it. They were shortly followed by Zoe, who was finding the whole situation very funny, and Caroline, who just stood in the middle of the car park, staring at her sister with her arms folded. Belinda and I ran out of the shop while an astonished crowd looked on. People at the café momentarily stopped drinking their coffees. The sight of a man, a woman and two young girls chasing some chickens at the side of a busy road was much more interesting.

With the help of a gendarme and one or two friendly locals, the hens were soon rounded up and we were all back in the car. Unfortunately, it wasn't just Belinda's pride that had been damaged.

'Leather seats!' Belinda said angrily. 'Leather fucking seats, and now look at them. Scratched to buggery. Your father's going to go mad. Christ, I'd only been gone a minute...'

'Ewww,' interrupted Caroline. 'Look what I've just put my hand in. That's disgusting. I told you not to open the box, Zoe. That's vile. Has anyone got a tissue? I hate chickens.'

When we got back to the villa, Belinda and the girls took the hens to their new home. I went to see Debbie. 'Last one, thank God,' she said, looking at her thumb, which had become red and slightly swollen. 'Sorry, not quite,' I replied. 'She wants the same doing with these.' I passed Debbie two carrier bags. 'We were about to leave the bakery down the road when Belinda decided to pop into the kids' clothes shop. Bloody hell, that woman buys some rubbish. Anyway, she wants the labels cutting out of those as well and replacing with these,' I said, passing Debbie a small plastic bag of designer labels that Belinda had brought from Hong Kong.

Debbie opened the small bag and raised her eyebrows. She then opened the bigger bag and stared inside.

'As far as I'm aware, the Devil does not wear this shit.' She snorted with laughter as she pulled out a few cheap, small, red fleeces. 'Ha, ha, ha. Not only that, I don't think he makes clothes for children either. What is she on?'

'The next plane out here with a bit of luck.'

'I wish. Is there any wine in the fridge?'

'I'm sorry but can't get the mower down to the olive grove. It's too steep and there doesn't appear to be a strimmer here. How did Pierre manage to keep it down?' I asked Belinda, who was tucking into a bowl of muesli the next morning.

'No, I don't think there is a strimmer here,' Belinda replied. 'Pierre used to let the local shepherdess graze her flock in there. Seemed to do the trick.'

'You're joking!' I laughed.

'I wish I was,' said Belinda. 'Actually, it worked quite well, until the girls got sheep ticks – horrible things. Then we had to have the whole area sprayed – cost us a small fortune. Look, you'd better go and buy a strimmer then. Fifty euros enough?' said Belinda, reaching for her purse. 'And I'll need the receipt. Anyway, where is Pierre?' 'I spoke to him yesterday. Said he was off to Venezuela. Assumed you knew?'

'Hardly likely, is it? That's him sitting in the deckchair, isn't it?' Belinda replied, pointing out of the window. 'Call him for me, would you? I want to know what's going on with these shutters. Girls!' she shouted. 'Come and have your breakfast.'

'I don't want any breakfast!' Zoe screamed back.

'Then, you won't be coming out with Mummy,' replied Belinda.

'Good.'

Pierre's phone seemed to be permanently on divert. I left message after message saying that Belinda wanted to see him, but Pierre had suddenly become extremely elusive. However, the day before Belinda and the girls were due to leave, she took matters into her own hands. Seeing Pierre sitting in the middle of the field over the road, Belinda stormed out. Curious to see what was about to happen, Debbie and I went back to our apartment, opened the kitchen window and waited.

'You useless, lazy, good for nothing bastard,' were Belinda's opening words. 'Brent has been trying for nearly a week now to get hold of you.'

'My phone, it doesn't work,' he replied.

'And, you told him you were going to Venezuela. You're supposed to be here, working for me.'

'I didn't say that at all. I said I was taking Venezuela to the vet.'

'What's happening about the shutters?'

'I don't have any paint.'

'Well, you won't have any, will you, unless you go and buy some. We've got the first rental guests of the season arriving in less than three weeks. Do you actually care?'

'Not really.'

'Oh, for God's sake!' As Belinda walked back down the lane towards our villa, Pierre got up, walked back into the house where he was staying, and wasn't seen again until he was fairly certain that Belinda had left.

Finally, the day arrived for Belinda and the girls to return to Hong Kong. Debbie was left with list upon list of things that we needed to do over the next few weeks. The hens appeared to be quite happy as they were laying five or six eggs a day between them. We tried Belinda's idea of an honesty box outside the front gate. Unfortunately, most of the people who stopped to pick up some eggs didn't seem to be as honest as we had hoped, so the idea was scrapped. The next step was for me to find out if any of the restaurants in the vicinity would be interested in buying them – they weren't. Debbie and I would be allowed a box of six every two weeks. With none of the restaurants taking us up on the offer, Guss was having omelettes for breakfast most mornings. Debbie, who had occasionally volunteered to collect the eggs, went off them completely, while I would offer them to anybody who came to the house, including a bewildered pair of Jehovah's Witnesses.

23

Chapter 4

Part of my daily routine was to walk around the perimeter of the property to make sure there were no holes in the fences. Though I had never seen any foxes since our arrival, I was told by Pierre that there were a lot in the area, as well as *sangliers*, or wild boar, who were becoming more brazen by the minute. They could often be seen strolling around the country lanes in the early hours of the morning, although by dawn they'd usually disappeared. *Les sangliers affolent le Var* (*The wild boar panic the Var*) was the headline on the front page of that week's local newspaper. In the past year they had caused millions of euros' worth of damage. Vines and all manner of crops had been destroyed and several cars had been written off by groups of *sangliers* trying to cross the main roads. Although weighing up to two hundred kilos, these wild pigs can run very fast and they can cover a lot of ground in a very short space of time. Unsurprisingly, due to the hunters, they tended to be quite shy during the day but at night they had recently come into their own.

During my tour, I noticed some remnants of an electric fence that had long since been discarded and although there were no holes in the fences themselves there were some gaps at the bottom where part of the fence had ridden up. With my DIY skills being close to non-existent, I had no idea how to re-attach the fence to the ground, so I blocked the holes with the largest rocks I could find around the estate.

At about eleven o'clock one morning, I was just coming back to our apartment when I noticed Pierre standing at the main gate. He was about to press the buzzer.

'Good morning,' I said to Pierre, who we hadn't seen for over a month. 'Nice to see you. Fancy a coffee?'

'Why not?' he replied, handing me an expensive-looking bottle of rosé. 'This is for you. I'm sorry I haven't been around – I've had a problem with my sinuses. 'Also, I don't think Belinda likes me anymore. She's not here now?' he asked.

'No, she's gone.'

'That's good,' he said, clearly quite relieved.

'Morning, Pierre,' said Debbie, who was in our apartment doing some ironing. She turned off the radio and went to give Pierre a kiss. 'How are you?' she asked.

'I'm good, thank you,' he replied. 'The thing is, I'm leaving in a week's time, so it means I won't have time to paint the shutters before I go, I'm sorry. Maybe you can do it after the summer.' Debbie smiled.

'Pierre, before you disappear, I've got a couple of questions, if you don't mind,' I said.

'OK,' he replied.

'Firstly, you know the robot that goes into the pool to clean the bottom?'

'Yes,' said Pierre, who was slowly stirring his coffee.

'Then, you also know that there's a fifteen-metre pipe that's attached to the side of the pool.'

'I know that too,' Pierre, replied.

'The thing is, Belinda complained about it when she was here. She couldn't unscrew the pipe to take it out and she didn't want me to force it...'
'You won't be able to take it out,' Pierre interrupted. 'I glued it in.'

'You did what?' I laughed, not quite believing what I had just heard.

'The rental guests kept taking it out last year,' replied Pierre, looking a little perplexed.

'Well, they would really, wouldn't they?' I reasoned. 'Apart from getting in everyone's way, the pipe could potentially strangle someone.'

'I don't know about that. Anyway, I am not there to watch them. I told them that the pool needed to be kept clean but they didn't listen.'

'Pierre, there's a pool vac in the control room.'

'I don't know how to use it.'

'Have you ever asked anybody?' I asked.

'No.'

'OK.' I replied. 'How about olive picking? I suggested to Charles that we harvest the olives this year – can you tell me about it?'

'No, I have never done it. I know I'm French, but I know nothing about olives. I know very little about wine and even less about cheese, except that it smells.' Pierre smiled. 'You see, I've spent most of my life out of this country.'

'Really?' said Debbie. 'I didn't know that. What were you doing?'

'I used to be a pilot. I flew all over the world until I got married and then I stopped. And now, I'm divorced.'

'That's a shame. Can't you go back to it?' asked Debbie, who noticed that Pierre's face had suddenly become very sad.

'No,' he replied, with a rueful smile. 'I haven't kept up with the medicals. Anyway, I'm too old to start all that again.'

'So, what are you going to do?' I asked.

'I want to be a house manager,' replied Pierre, putting his empty cup down beside the sink. 'In the meantime, I have some building work to do with a friend in Cannes. It's only two days a week but it's enough for now. Thanks for the coffee.' He smiled. 'Look, if there's anything you need, just call. *A bientôt*,' he said as he left our apartment, gently closing the door behind him.

'Do you think he'll be all right?' I said to Debbie.

'I hope so,' she replied.

In the weeks leading up to his departure we got to know Pierre much better. Not only that, we'd really warmed to him. We'd invite him for lunch at the weekend and talk about anything apart from the villa. I'd given up asking him things about the house as Pierre's standard reply had become, 'I don't know about that, you'll have to ask Charles.' He didn't seem at all jealous of us taking over. He seemed quite content with a book, a deckchair and a bit of sun on his back.

About a week before we were due to receive our first rental guests of the summer, Pierre called to say that the owners of the house where he was staying had recently arrived and that they would like to invite us for coffee. Happily accepting the offer, Debbie, Guss and I made the short journey along the lane.

'Good morning, I am Marie-Hélène,' said a very pretty lady with long blonde hair, who I presumed to be in her early fifties. Dressed in a long, flowing robe and sandals, she continued, 'You can call me Hélène, if you prefer. Most people do.'

'Thank you,' I said, offering my hand. 'Pierre didn't tell us you were English.'

'I'm not,' answered Hélène, who then laughed. 'I'm actually French, but I was brought up in Notting Hill until I was about ten years old. I work in Paris as a translator. Pierre didn't mention it?'

'No, he didn't,' said Debbie. 'Pierre doesn't mention much, if I'm honest.'

Hélène laughed again. 'That sounds about right. Please, sit down,' she said, offering us a seat outside at a large, stone table to the left of the front door. 'I'll get some coffee.' As Hélène disappeared through the front door of the house there was a 'splosh!' to our right. We turned round and noticed four or five toads jumping into a large, rectangular stone pond which was raised two or three feet off the ground. Guss had his paws up on the sides and was wagging his tail. He was finding this new experience fascinating.

'Hélène likes to cool down in there,' said a man, who came out of the kitchen door. '*Bonjour, je suis Alain.* The water is very clear, and the toads don't seem to mind sharing.' He smiled. Alain appeared very relaxed and self-assured and although his English wasn't fluent, it was excellent – much better than our French. Over coffee our hosts told us that they were based in Paris and would usually come down to Montauroux for the summer, quite often at Christmas as well as other holiday times. Hélène was about to retire and said that she wanted to dedicate more time to her pottery. The mugs that we had been drinking out of were all made by her, as was the plate that was piled high with biscuits. After coffee, Hélène gave us a brief tour of her studio, which was on the ground floor of their house, and showed us her work, which was quite stunning. Not only were there, cups, saucers, plates and bowls, there were also beautifully crafted lamps of all different colours.

'I don't make much money,' she said, 'but it pays for the clay, and I have an exhibition in Paris from time to time.' Hélène was a true artisan. Her and Alain's house reflected that. The inside was comfortable and felt very homely. There were armchairs of a bygone age that a person could sink into. Well-worn rugs were dotted around the wooden floors and, in the evenings, an open fire glowed gently in the sitting room. Alain would occasionally take a large, metal hollow pole and gently blow onto the embers. The shelves in the lounge were piled high with classic novels and books about Greek and Roman mythology and ancient history. The house was in complete contrast to the one across the road. This was a place where scholars and fine minds came together to relax and talk about things other than making money.

'I'm sorry about the field,' said Hélène, who was looking at the long grass in front of us. 'It gets like this every summer and I have to pay someone two hundred and fifty euros to come and cut it with his tractor. Only takes a few hours.' She sighed.

'Why doesn't Pierre do it?' I asked. 'We've got a sit-down mower across the road.'

'He's never really offered,' replied Hélène. 'Anyway, I don't think he knows how to use it.'

'Dead easy,' I said. 'If I show you, would you like to borrow it?'

'Really?' replied Hélène, her eyes lighting up. 'Love to.'

The following morning, I drove down the lane on the mower. I gave Hélène the briefest of lessons and she was off, laughing and waving as she went. Alain, in the meantime, was on one of the upper levels of the garden and was strimming around the olive trees. Within an afternoon, the grass was cut and the field, which had looked overgrown and like a jungle, had been transformed into a fabulous lawn.

28

Debbie and I were there one morning when Hélène announced, 'I'm off to the American beach. Would you like to come?'

'Bit of a long way to go,' I replied.

'Don't be silly, it's only just down the road. It's part of *Lac de Saint-Cassien*,' she said. 'Does Guss swim?'

'I don't know,' I said. 'Don't think he's ever really tried.'

'There's only one way to find out.' Hélène smiled. 'Come on, it'll be fun.'

Our villa's guests were out for the day and we were in need of a change of scenery, so Debbie and I took Hélène up on her offer. We jumped in our car and followed our new friend along the main road. What surprised us was that to get to our destination we found ourselves driving through a huge trading estate. We meandered our way between factories and builders' merchants and Debbie and I, for a short while, began to wonder whether we were going in the right direction at all. Then, without warning, we were winding our way along a narrow dirt track that was flanked on either side by pine trees. After about a mile or so we arrived at a clearing, in front of which was a small, wooden snack bar with some tables and chairs dotted around the outside. Just behind that was the water's edge. Several teenagers were sitting on the grass banks and drinking cans of Coke while toying with their smartphones. Hélène changed into her swimming costume and gently lowered herself into the crystal-clear lake. I dipped my hand in the water and quickly removed it.

'Bloody freezing,' I mouthed to Debbie, who had gone to sit at one of the plastic tables.

'Come on, Guss!' Hélène shouted as she swam away from the shore. Guss stood on the bank, rocking back and forth, trying to summon up enough courage to jump in. After a few short moments, there was a loud splash and Guss was swimming towards Hélène. Debbie and I stood on the shore like proud parents and from that moment on, we'd go to the American beach at least once a week.

'Comment of the summer so far!' Debbie said one morning. 'Fucking unbelievable.' She laughed as she opened the fridge in our apartment. An English family of eight adults and four small children had rented the villa.

Debbie was asked by Belinda to do two hours of light cleaning per day, which served two purposes. Firstly, it meant that when changeover day arrived there wasn't an overwhelming amount of work to do, and, secondly, she could make sure that the villa was being properly looked after by the guests. The arrangement was that the guests should keep the property in a similar state to how they found it on their arrival. As she was passing one of the young mothers' bedrooms, Debbie noticed that there were clothes strewn all over the floor, kids' toys everywhere and the beds were not made. The mother walked in from the dining room with a croissant in her hand.

She smiled and promptly announced, 'You can tell we're on holiday. There's no way that if we were at home, my husband would let me keep the place like this.' She then closed the door behind her, fortunately neither waiting for nor hearing Debbie's reply.

During the course of the summer Debbie only exploded once, when she heard one of the guests say to her daughter, who had just spilt coffee over the worksurface, down the dishwasher and onto the floor, 'Don't worry, Debbie will clear it up. That's what she gets paid for.' Debbie then told the woman, in no uncertain terms, that she was the villa's housekeeper and not 'some bloody skivvy' and that if the villa was not kept in a reasonable condition during their stay, the woman could kiss goodbye to her deposit. When the family left the villa the following Saturday, it was spotless.

It was three o'clock one morning when Guss, who doesn't usually disturb us once we've gone to bed, started barking. I rubbed my eyes, looked out of the window and saw that all of the security lights on the lawn had come on. I opened the front door and Guss barged past, shouting as he went. I quickly put on my training shoes, grabbed the nearest thing that resembled a weapon, which happened to be Debbie's mop, and followed my dog. I got to the lawn just in time to see the last of the *sangliers* disappear through the hole in the fence that I thought I had successfully plugged previously. Even so, the security lights continued to flash, revealing two rather unfortunate incidents. Firstly, the croquet lawn, which had up until that time been as smooth as glass, had been rotovated. The *sangliers* had turned something quite beautiful into a small field ready to plant potatoes in a matter of minutes. I couldn't have done a better job if I'd rotovated the lawn myself. Secondly, apart from some shoes and a mop to try and hide behind, I was completely naked. Also, what I had failed to remember at three o'clock in the morning, was that there were guests in the main house. As I began to fully wake up, I noticed that, due to the commotion, lights had started to come on all over the villa and I could hear the sound of windows being opened. As quickly as I could, I made my way back up the stairs to our apartment where Debbie, who had witnessed everything, burst out laughing.

'Are you completely bloody mad?' she said with a huge grin. 'What on earth were you expecting to do with my mop?'

'That's all there was. Anyway, I wasn't really awake.'

'I couldn't believe all of those lights that went on. They were going off like flash bulbs. It was like the paparazzi were following you.'

'Oh, my God. I hope the rentals weren't taking photos!'

'It'll certainly make a memorable holiday for them if they were,' Debbie replied. 'I wouldn't worry my love, unless they've got a telephoto lens – then you might be in a bit of trouble. I'm going back to bed.'

Chapter 5

I was wandering around the bottom level of the meadow when a small but quite robust woman, who I imagined to be in her in her seventies, waved at me over the fence.

'*Coucou*,' she said. As she got closer I could see that she had with blonde bobbed hair and was wearing a pink jumpsuit and yellow Wellington boots. She walked towards me with a broad smile and said, 'I am Juliette, your neighbour.' She leaned over the small gate that joined the two properties, removed her gardening gloves and offered her hand.

'Brent, *enchanté*. Lovely garden,' I replied, admiring the manicured lawn and flower beds that were full of brightly coloured flowers.

'Thank you. Come, I show you,' Juliette said, opening the gate, which was not locked. As we walked around her garden Juliette explained that over the years, she and her husband, Georges, had become good friends with our bosses and had often babysat their two girls. She also said that she was quite glad to see new guardians at Mas des Collines.

'Really, why's that?' I asked

'I think Pierre tries to avoid me,' Juliette replied. 'I don't really know why. I haven't upset him, or at least I don't think I have. The last time I spoke to Pierre was about a year ago. I asked him to help with the olive harvest and that was the last I saw of him. I see him from time to time in the supermarket but I'm sure that when he sees me, he runs the other way.' She laughed. 'I invited him for so many aperitifs, or *apéros* as we call them. Just a few drinks and nibbles. He didn't have to stay long. He always said he would come but he never turned up. Do you believe it? I am well-known for my hospitality.'

'I'm glad you mentioned the olives,' I said. 'You see, the thing is, I mentioned to Charles that we could harvest his olives this year – the trees are full.'

'I know,' she replied. 'They haven't been picked for years. It is so wasteful. Have you done it before?' Juliette asked as she stooped down on the gravel path to pull up a weed.

32

'No,' I said. 'Never really had the opportunity.'

'Then I tell you everything, my darling,' she said as she put her arm in mine. 'There's not that much to know but it's important you get it right. I don't have time now because I have an appointment with the hairdresser. Look, I explain later. Why don't you and your wife come round for drinks tomorrow evening? Say about six o'clock?' she said as we made our way back to the gate.

'I'm with Pierre,' said Debbie. 'I hate those bloody things – French *apéros*. I hate to sound ungrateful but sitting in a room being passed Tuc biscuits, cherry tomatoes, sweaty peanuts and Ritz crackers with God knows what jollop spread on them, is not my idea of fun – it's my idea of hell. I thought all that went out in the seventies and with good reason. And…'

'Look,' I interrupted, 'we might earn ourselves a few brownie points here. They're friends of Charles and Belinda's, so it would be good to have them on our side, and they can tell us all about olive picking. Let's be honest, we know nothing.'

Armed with two bottles of rosé, the following evening my reluctant wife and I wandered down to our neighbours.

'Pretty garden,' said Debbie as we approached the small gate that divided the two properties. 'That's a bit mean, though.'

'What is?'

'Putting a statue of a heron right next to the fish pond. Poor old fish.' She smiled. 'Are there actually any in there?'

'Oh, yes, giant carp.' I was about to continue when an elderly gentleman who was wearing gardening clothes and a white trilby with a black band appeared from the side of the house. He smiled, introduced himself and asked us to follow him. We walked into the conservatory where our host, Georges, began to remove his shoes, so we felt it only polite to follow suit, which was fine until Debbie noticed a rather large hole in one of my socks.

'You are a disgrace,' she whispered. 'Can't take you anywhere.' She sighed.

33

'How was I to know?' I whispered back. 'Shall I check my underpants?'

Georges led us to the lounge. The room was quite modernly decorated and spotlessly clean. The shelves were adorned with ornamental owls of all different shapes and sizes and the parquet floor had been polished to the point of being so slippery it was dangerous.

'Don't worry, you'll get used to it,' said Georges as I held onto the back of the sofa. Sliding our way to the front we sat down. Georges asked what we would like to drink and disappeared into the kitchen. 'I'm not moving,' I said. 'It's like a skating rink in here. The floor's fucking lethal.'

A few minutes later, Georges returned with two enormous glasses of rosé that he passed to Debbie and me. He then went over to the sideboard next to the television and returned with two further glasses and a bottle of Pastis. We were soon joined by Juliette, who assumed that we both spoke French better than we did. I'd managed to speak to her earlier, but it was all small talk and easy to understand. We got the gist of what she was saying and tried to smile in the right places.

'Do you understand me?' she asked.

'Most of it,' I replied. 'A bit too fast, if I'm honest.'

'OK, I'll speak more slowly,' she said, and then she carried on speaking at the same pace as before. I had the feeling that this was going to be a long evening. After about fifteen minutes of monologue, Juliette got up to go to the kitchen. She returned shortly with one of the most bizarre things I have ever seen. Our smiling hostess was carrying a tray and on top of that tray was an enormous watermelon that had been cut in half. Sticking out of the watermelon were nine-inch long wooden skewers, on which were squares of cheese, cherry tomatoes of different colours, olives, gooseberries and cocktail sausages. There were also chunks of cucumber.

'I bet you've never seen anything like this,' beamed our genial hostess.

'You're not wrong there,' I replied. I could feel daggers in the back of my neck coming from my wife's direction.

'It's very traditional in this region,' Juliette explained. 'Visitors are always surprised.'

As we tucked into the strange combination of food that had been offered to us, Debbie's worst fears began to come to realisation – she could smell cooking. There was an unrecognisable aroma coming from the kitchen. I looked at Debbie, who forced a smile that I was pretty sure meant, *I hope that's not for us.*

What followed next was in keeping with the rest of the evening, which was bordering on the surreal. Georges appeared with four plates and on each those plates was a piece of tuna bread that was swimming in a bright yellow mustard sauce. How was I going to get out of this? There's not much I don't like when it comes to food, but mustard is one ingredient that I can't abide.

'I'm sorry, Juliette, but I'm allergic to mustard,' I said.

'That's a shame, but don't worry,' she replied. She got out of her chair and took my plate. 'We have ketchup!' she shouted triumphantly as she went into the kitchen. 'I know how you like ketchup. You have it with everything, no? You English really need to learn to cook.'

As I struggled my way through the plate of tuna bread and tomato sauce, our hosts took us through all there was to know about harvesting olives. We would need several nets that had to be laid out at the bottom of the trees and the meadow would, ideally, have to be mowed the day before. We should buy some long rakes as well as ten large, plastic crates and an aluminium churn that could hold at least thirty litres of oil.

'You will also need a lot of people,' explained Juliette, who was becoming more and more giggly with every sip of Pastis. 'It's very hard work. You must collect two hundred kilos of olives if you want your own oil, not mixed with anyone else's – that is never a good idea. You should see the state of some of the olives that arrive at the mill. They've been left lying around for ages so, by the time they get there, the olives have lost most of their moisture and are all shrivelled. That way you do not get good olive oil. You must pick the olives in two days and get them to the mill on the third, otherwise they go off.'

I'll make the appointment, unless you are prepared to fight.'

'Fight?' I asked. 'Why would I need to fight?'

'All of the olive picking is done over a few short weeks,' Georges explained. 'The problem is that the mills can't cope. Too many olives, not enough mills. People who haven't made an appointment have to wait in line and some are impatient. Then, they try to jump the queue and that is that,' he laughed.

'You must also make sure you go to the right mill. They're not all honest,' added our genial hostess. Then the next bizarre event of the evening took place. As Juliette continued to talk, her legs became further and further apart, causing the hem of her thin black dress to ride up over her knees, revealing her underwear to everyone in the room. I'm not sure if Georges hadn't noticed or if he was used to this – either way he said nothing. As I tried to focus on anything in the room apart from our hostess's legs, Debbie nudged me in the ribs for me to make our excuses to leave.

'Thank you for a lovely evening,' I said, starting to get up.

'I must just finish,' replied Juliette, who started to get up herself and then promptly sat down again. She wagged her finger. 'Never leave your olives with someone overnight. You never know if what you get back is yours. You have to watch them like a hawk. It's big business here. Maybe I'll come with you. We go to Callas. Georges, see Brent and Debbie out, would you? You don't mind if I don't get up? I'm not sure that I can.' Juliette giggled. 'Night, night, darlings.'

'There are some things I just wish you could unsee,' I said to Debbie as we made our way back across the meadow at around eleven o'clock that evening. Debbie laughed.

'I know,' she replied. 'Seemed such a lady too – a proper French Madame. It's amazing how some people change completely after a few drinks – us included.' She laughed. 'Surely she must have noticed?'

'Apparently not,' I replied. 'Either way, it's not an evening I'm likely to forget in a hurry.'

At the end of quite a long Skype call with Charles the following morning that had involved all things garden, bikes, olive picking and pool, Charles enthused, 'I'm bringing a bunch of guys from the Polish office with me for the olive picking, right? They're not really used to physical work, so I've decided to throw a few more bodies at it. I've told them they can bring their partners. Should be about twenty of us in total. You think that'll be enough? Thought so,' he said without waiting for me to reply. 'I've had some wine labels designed, by the way, so I want you to peel off all of the ones on the cheap rosé and put on our own. Got that? I'll bring them down when we come down. Cheaper than posting, right? Look, I know I haven't been easy to get hold of, but I've got you on my radar now.' And then the line went dead.

'How did it go?' asked Debbie.

'Don't really know,' I replied. 'I'm sure the words that came out of his mouth were English, but I haven't a clue about half of what he was saying. He's as nuts as the rest of them. Can only have been on there a minute before he started squaring circles, moving goalposts and kicking some of my ideas into the long grass.' Debbie smiled.

A week or so later I was waiting in Arrivals at Nice airport for Charles, Belinda and the girls to arrive. Debbie had spent her time making the villa looking immaculate and had prepared an evening meal for the ten people who were due to be staying at the villa that night. The remainder of Charles's guests would be with us the following day.

At seven o'clock, Charles burst through the doors. Dressed in a grey designer suit, black shirt and expensive-looking shoes, he started to look around. As I waved, he removed his Ray-Ban Aviator sunglasses from the top of his shaved head, pointed them towards me and shouted, 'Gotcha!' I'd got to know a few of the chauffeurs at the airport over the years and as I briefly looked around, I noticed several of them smiling in my direction. 'You wait here for Belinda and the girls,' Charles instructed while looking at his phone.

'I've got some important calls to make, right? Give me the keys. See you at the car. In the Kiss and Fly?' I nodded my head. 'Nice to meet you in person by the way,' Charles said as he marched out of the airport.

About ten minutes later, the Arrivals doors opened and Zoe came running towards me. She flung her arms around me and shouted excitedly, 'Hello Brent. Look what I can do!' She then began a series of cartwheels just to my left. 'I learned this in my gym class,' she said. 'Miss Robinson is a fab teacher. What do you think?'

'Hello Brent,' said Belinda, who was wearing dark glasses and pushing a trolley stacked high with luggage. Shaking her head, she continued, 'She's been like it for about the last hour. I fell asleep and you know what the cheeky monkey did? Ordered Coke after Coke from the stewardess. 'And you know what Charles did, without telling me until we got to the airport? Booked himself into First Class. We're not important enough, apparently.'

'He didn't say that, surely?' I said, taking the trolley from Belinda.

'No, he didn't, but what a thing to do. I could kill him. Sorry, Brent, I'll be all right when we get back. Had the journey from hell, that's all. Zoe!' Belinda shouted as she glared at her daughter, who was trying to run the wrong way up an escalator. 'Come here now please, or you'll get left behind.'

'Woo hoo!'

'There was a Porsche in here the last time I looked,' said Charles, who I dropped off at the garage on the way up to villa. 'What's happened to it, Brent?' he asked sternly.

'Pierre took it when we first arrived,' I replied.

'You didn't stop him? You're the guardian now, right?'

'He said it was his. At least half of it anyway.'

'Technically, perhaps, but as he still owes me fourteen grand I'd say it was mine, wouldn't you? Look Brent, I don't want to get off on the wrong foot but everything on this property belongs to me. Got it? Nothing leaves here without my say so. You ask me first.

38

Belinda, you'd better go and see if anything valuable's missing when you get up the top. Brent, I see the bikes need dusting and the tyres haven't been pumped up. I'm out first thing in the morning so you'd best do them this evening.'

'I'm helping Debbie with dinner service. I need to be…'

'Don't care when you do it, right? But I need to be out of here by seven in the morning with a clean bike and pumped up tyres.'

'I shouldn't worry about it, my love,' said Debbie, who was busy peeling some potatoes in the villa kitchen. 'He just wants to assert his authority, that's all. Alpha male syndrome and all that. Don't take it personally,' she added, putting her peeler down and walking over to the sink. 'This is all about Pierre. He feels conned and as Charles can't get hold of him, he's looking for another outlet. Unfortunately, that's you. Anyway, I've just seen some more guests arrive,' she said, looking out of the window. 'By the end of the evening, you'll think he's ignoring you. Come on. Forget it. Set the table for me, would you?'

Debbie was right. Over the course of dinner, not only did Charles not say a single word to either of us, he didn't even look in our direction. Even though Belinda and her guests were very appreciative of the meal that they were served, Debbie and I were not acknowledged by our boss at all. If there had been a honeymoon period it was either over or we hadn't noticed it. The wine flowed endlessly, as did Charles's description of each bottle. Before each course, our host stood up and spoke for a full ten minutes about the origin of the wine, the type of grape, the bouquet and the vintage. At the end of each speech, Charles was greeted by a round of applause by everybody – everybody except Debbie, that is, who glared at the food that was turning cold on the plates in front of the diners while he was speaking.

'Never seen anything like it,' said Debbie as I brought back the last of empty glasses into the kitchen. 'Pompous twat!'

'Boring bastard, isn't he? Mind if I go?' I asked.

'Where are you off to?' replied Debbie, who was looking at the enormous pile of washing up that filled the work surfaces.

'The garage. Better sort the bikes out. I'll come back and help when I'm done.'

'See you later.'

Chapter 6

'He's quite a unit,' said Charles, looking at Guss after getting back from his early morning bike ride. 'Think he'd like to follow me one day?'

'I think he'd probably run off, if I'm honest with you. Wouldn't want to risk it.'

'You haven't had him trained, then? That's a shame. Could always do with a buddy on these things. Look, I'm going to get showered and changed and then you need to meet me at the *pigeonnier*. I'm going to grab a bunch of wine to bring back to the villa. I think the guys like learning about wine and I've got some real classics. Can you give these a quick spruce up?' Charles asked, taking off his cycling shoes and putting on his trainers. 'See you in about ten,' and off he sprinted towards the villa.

As instructed, I went down to the wine cellar and when, after twenty minutes, there was no sign of Charles, I sat down on the step and looked at the not-so-perfect croquet lawn. As I was debating whether to go and flatten out some more of the divots caused by the *sangliers*, I heard a voice say, 'Pigs, right? Are the grounds locked down now? No chance of another attack?'

'I wouldn't have thought so,' I replied as I stood up. 'Fences look…'

'You wouldn't have thought so?' Charles scowled. 'Thought so is not good enough. We need to know so. Can't be replacing the lawn every five minutes, Brent. We'd better scope the area after the olive picking. Speaking of which, is everything ready?'

'It is.'

'Good, because I've drawn up a list of teams – ten in total, two people per team,' he said as he unfolded a piece of A4 paper that he'd taken out of his trouser pocket. 'Plus, Georges and Juliette are coming to help from next door. Do you think we should have a prize? Fastest pickers, that kind of thing?'

'That's up to you. I see you haven't got me on the list,' I said, looking over Charles's shoulder.

'You'll be too busy looking after the troops. I thought you'd be best helping Debbie in the kitchen. We're going to need a lot of hot drinks, right? Now where's the Château Lafite? Too good for a prize? What do you reckon? I suppose if I won it,' he said, thinking out loud.

Although I was a bit surprised at not have been included in the harvesting of the olives, as I'd been tasked with organising the event I wasn't at all disappointed. As I walked down to the olive grove, where Charles was lecturing his guests, I could feel the biting wind that was due to last most of the weekend. There were also spots of rain in the air. Clearly unprepared for this kind of weather, one woman was jumping up and down in an attempt to keep warm.

Out of Charles's earshot I heard her say to her husband, 'You told me it was always hot here. Just bring a bikini, you said. We'll be in the pool by the afternoon. Bloody hell. Look at me!' she said, looking at her skimpy blouse and mini skirt. 'Everyone else is wearing body warmers.'

'I'm sorry, my love,' replied her husband. 'But you do look rather fetching…'

'Oh, fuck off, Nigel,' she snapped back, at the same time picking up a rake and attacking an olive branch as if it were her husband.

I was asked to bring some ladders from the garage, which I gave to the guests. As I made my way back and forth to the villa with refreshments, I'd often see Charles in amongst the higher branches and egging the workers on. As the trees hadn't been pruned for a year or two, some of the branches were very high and out of reach. Charles, who was more interested in the olives than the olive trees themselves, cut down those branches with the aid of my pruning saw. By lunchtime, hundreds of loose branches minus the fruit were strewn across the olive grove and the once picture-perfect olive trees had been hacked.

In between running errands, I helped Debbie to set out several trellis tables on the *pétanque* court. There were home-made terrines, salmon en croûte, piping hot soups as well as meat platters, salads and barbecued chicken. Debbie had sourced a few varieties of local cheese, which she accompanied with her own chutney.

For dessert there was a choice of Tarte Tatin or sticky toffee pudding with vanilla ice cream. She'd also brought along a tray of Bloody Mary shots, each containing a raw oyster.

'Better get rid of those after lunch, Brent,' said Charles, who was tucking into a chicken drumstick and pointing at the cut branches. 'Looks a bit of a mess but you can't make an omelette without cracking a few eggs. Isn't that right, Debbie?' he shouted in her direction and then continued to laugh at his own joke. Debbie smiled and, as soon as Charles's back was turned, raised her eyebrows.

As I walked around the tables collecting used plates and cutlery I noticed that the harvest was already taking its toll on some of the guests. Shoulders, from raking the trees, felt as if they'd been pulled out of their sockets and weary helpers were demanding massages from their partners.

'You said this was going to be easy,' I heard one woman complain to her husband. 'Thought we'd be done by now. We need ten crates. I've counted four and a bit. This isn't a weekend break – it's bloody slavery. Bet we don't get to see any of the oil either. I could be sitting at home now, in front of the fire with a good book. Look at me. Freezing bloody cold, in the middle of nowhere and a body that feels like shit. Jesus!'

'You all right, Hannah?' asked Charles, who had heard her cry out.

'I'm fine, thanks,' she replied, forcing a smile. 'Just a bit cold, that's all.'

'Don't worry, you'll warm up once we get going again. One last push. Come on team, back to work!' he bellowed, before disappearing up another tree.

At the end of the afternoon, as I finished dragging the cut branches towards a patch of barren land where I made a bonfire, I noticed that there were only eight full crates of olives. So, it was decided by Charles that those who weren't getting flights back early on the Sunday morning would have to help complete the task the following morning. Charles was quite apologetic but said as a thank you for all of their hard work, he had booked a table at a local restaurant for seven-thirty that evening. Debbie and I were also invited. Debbie declined.

At seven o'clock that evening a large group of us were milling around just inside the front gates. I had the keys to the Land Rover in my pocket and was waiting for instructions. At about five past, Charles came running down the drive.

'Sorry I'm late, folks,' he said. 'Got a bit caught up. Come on, let's go. Brent, you got the clicker?' I opened the gates. 'I'll go on ahead. Make sure they keep our table, right? See you there. You all follow Brent.' Then, he ran off into the darkness.

'We're fucking walking?' I heard one of the wives say. 'Who does he think we are? Do I look like I go to the gym? Nigel, don't answer that.' A few of the group laughed.

What only Charles and I knew at that point, as the party left Mas des Collines, was exactly how steep the hill was that we would have to climb to get to the restaurant in Montauroux. Debbie had long since refused to walk into town except under sufferance. Under normal circumstances the journey on foot would take about fifteen minutes and by the time I reached the town square my calves would be aching. About ten minutes into the journey, those had hadn't stopped for a rest were either bitterly complaining or asking for piggy backs.

'I'm resigning when I get back,' one man shouted.

'If you'd done that a month ago, Henry, we wouldn't be in this fucking mess now. Bastard!' was his wife's reply. Half an hour or so after we began our journey, twenty weary people and Guss walked into the small bistro at the top of the hill.

'Thought you'd got lost,' beamed Charles, who was sitting at the end of a long table, covered with several red and white checked tablecloths. 'See you've brought Guss with you, Brent. For security, right? Like that. Grab a seat, anywhere you like everybody. It's not formal here.'

As we sat down, the heat from the pizza oven to our left began to fill the room and I noticed that some of our party were struggling to stay awake. Many people, including me, soon drifted off into worlds of their own and although I

44

could see Charles's lips moving almost non-stop, I didn't hear any words.

It was at that point that I began to wonder whether Debbie and I had really made the right decision to come to Montauroux.

After about half an hour I heard a voice over my right shoulder say, '*Voici, monsieur.*' As I looked down, I saw that the waiter had placed in front of me a bowl of lamb stew and potatoes.

Debbie had phoned the restaurant a few days earlier and asked for a set menu for twenty people – apparently Belinda wanted to control the budget. As I looked around, several of the group were toying with their food and by the time the waiter came to collect the plates, much of what came out of the kitchen went back untouched. Unfortunately, the lamb was tough and full of gristle and the potatoes were bordering on raw. So, although the staff were extremely friendly and welcoming, it came as no surprise to Debbie and I that only a few weeks later, the bistro shut down.

On the Sunday morning, and much to the relief of the people who had later flights booked, it rained, it rained, and then it rained some more. The harvesting of the olives had ground to a halt.

As I gazed out of the kitchen window in the villa, Charles said, 'You and Debbie will have to finish it on Monday when you get back from taking us to the airport, right? Need to leave here at five-thirty tomorrow morning so you'll have the whole day. Checked the weather forecast – looked OK. I've spoken to Juliette and Georges. They'll help, and I've left a message for Pierre, so there should be at least five of you. I know it's not many but if you give it a hundred percent, we should get two hundred kilos.'

'See you next year,' I said as I helped Charles's guests to load their cases into their hired cars. Most smiled but not one person appeared at all enthusiastic at the prospect of returning the following year.

One of the men that I had become quite friendly with smiled and then said, 'No fucking chance,' while the others just groaned.

'I think they all enjoyed that,' said Charles, who was sipping his coffee in the kitchen. 'Nothing like a bit of team building. Good for company morale, you know. Look, I see it's still raining quite heavily outside, so why don't you and Debbie…'

'Take the day off?' I said, hopefully.

'Start the inventory, I was about to say,' replied Charles, who was looking at me quite sternly. 'I need to know what's in the *pigeonnier*, Brent. We haven't got much time. I know it's the weekend but you're going to be busy over the next few weeks. As soon as Debbie has finished making the beds, I suggest you make a start, right? Have you seen my weather proofs? I'm going for a ride. Belinda!' he bellowed. 'I'm going out.'

Debbie and I spent the rest of the day cataloguing wine in the *pigeonnier*. We wrote down the vineyard, the date, the colour of the wine, the grape and the size of the bottle. Once finished, we were to upload all of the information onto a website so that Charles could see exactly how much wine he had and each time a bottle was sold or drank we were to update the site.

'I don't know why I bothered to suggest this,' I said wearily as I removed a bottle of Château Margaux from the wine rack. 'It seems to me that every time we come up with a small suggestion, Charles and Belinda turn it into a major project. Bastards.'

'I know,' replied Debbie, who had been cursing under her breath almost from the moment we arrived. 'What amazes me is how Pierre got away with it for so long. That's the problem with this job – you show one ounce of initiative and they leap on you. Spreadsheet this, spreadsheet that. I'm supposed to be a housekeeper, you're supposed to be a gardener, and they think we're a couple of octopuses. They're taking the piss. Oh, shit, this bloody pen's just run out. I'm not going back to the house in this,' Debbie said, looking at the rain that was coming down heavily. 'Umbrella or no umbrella, I'm not getting soaked.'

'Don't worry, I'll go.'

At five o'clock the following morning, just as my alarm clock was going off there was a bang, bang, bang on the front door.

Debbie woke up with a start and shouted, 'What the fuck!' I put on my dressing gown and went to our front door, which I opened. On the other side was Zoe, who was full of beans.

'Mummy says you're to come over now.'

'You're not leaving for another hour,' I said, wearily looking at the clock on the kitchen wall.

'Yes, I know, but she wants you to put all of our bags in the car and there are rather a lot of them,' she said. 'Oh, and can I have a cookie please?' My first reaction was to say no but then I remembered how Zoe behaved even after just one biscuit, so I gave her a whole packet of chocolate chip cookies and told her not to tell anyone.

'Is Daddy not able to help with the bags?' I asked as I opened the door for Zoe.

'No. He's got a fuck off conference call with Japan, so you'll have to do it.'

'He's got a what?'

'Bye, Brent,' replied Zoe, who began to run back to the villa, waving as she went. 'Thanks for the cookies.'

'Shhh,' I replied.

'How was it?' asked Debbie when I got back from the airport at about eight o'clock.

'OK,' I replied. 'Zoe was her usual hyper self but apart from that, all right. You OK?'

'Yeah. Woke up fancying a biscuit this morning. Can't find them. Any ideas?'

'You mean these?' I said, producing an empty packet from my coat pocket.

'Exactly those,' said Debbie. 'You didn't?'

'No, I didn't. Zoe did. About half an hour before they left.'

'The whole packet?' replied Debbie, open-mouthed.

'Yeah. I saw her sitting on the garden wall. Wolfed down the lot in about

47

five minutes. Threw the packet on the grass.'

'And you gave them to her?'

'Too right I did. That's going to be one hell of a journey back – all fourteen hours of it.'

'You're a bad man, Brent.' Debbie smiled. 'On the other hand – nice one. Fancy a coffee?'

At nine o'clock Debbie and I made our way back to the olive grove. A few minutes later, we were joined by Juliette and Georges.

'Ooh, la, la,' said Juliette, before putting her hand over her mouth. 'The poor olive trees. What have they done?' she continued, looking up at the trees that had been butchered. 'They were so beautiful. Now look. What a shame. Never mind. Come on. How much more do we have to get?'

'Another two cases,' I replied.

'That should be easy with four of us,' said Georges. 'I take it Pierre isn't coming?' I shook my head.

By five o'clock that afternoon, and only stopping briefly for lunch, we had filled the final crates.

'You had better bring them all round to me,' said Juliette. 'We can put the olives through my machine. It gets rid of all the leaves. Saves time at the mill, and money too.' She smiled. So, I walked around the olive grove and gathered up the ten crates, which I put in the back of my car. I drove round to Juliette, who was waiting for me. As I tipped the contents into the top of a small hopper, I watched as the olives came out of the other end and the leaves and twigs were blown away.

'It doesn't matter that some of the olives are green and the others black?' I asked Juliette as I made my way with her and Georges to the mill at Callas the next morning.

'Not at all,' she replied. 'The black ones are more ripe, that's all. The important thing is that they are still fresh and juicy by the time we get here. You

48

can really taste the difference. Look at those,' she said, pointing to a huge case of olives as we arrived at the mill. 'They are no good.' As I looked down, I could see what she meant. In front of me was a two-hundred-kilo crate of shrivelled, black olives.

'They have been sitting around a long time – they've lost all of their moisture,' Georges explained. 'And look, they haven't been cleaned. They won't taste very nice and the mill won't get many presses either. I am glad we're not mixing them with ours.'

'How many presses do they normally get?' I asked.

'Three, four, five,' replied Juliette, who was watching one of the workers take our crates out of the back of the car.

'And what happens to them?' I said.

'Well,' said Juliette, whose eyes were watching our olives like a hawk. 'The first press, which is what we're interested in, is the extra virgin olive oil. It is the best. It looks a bit cloudy at first but if you leave it for about three months, which nobody ever does, it settles down and then you see the liquid gold.'

'And then?'

'And then, it gets pressed again and is made into soap, then again and is made into candles, and the final press is used as fertiliser. Olives are very versatile. Come on, let's go inside. We can see the oil being produced.'

We sat in a small waiting room along with some other people and looked through a large glass window into the factory. I gave my empty aluminium churn to the receptionist, who took it into the factory and placed it next to one of the three large churns that contained our olives.

'You want to see?' she said, as she heard my English accent. 'Maybe it is your first time?'

'Love to,' replied Juliette, on my behalf. Before I had chance to utter a single word, Juliette was through the joining door and making her way over to the churn, checking each label on the three mills to see which was ours. Once she was satisfied that all was well, we went back to the waiting room, where we were offered coffee and biscuits. An hour or so later we were presented with thirty litres of olive oil and a bill for one hundred and fifty euros.

'That's only five euros a litre,' I said to Georges.

'I know,' he replied. 'You can sell it for twenty euros. I wouldn't tell Belinda if I were you.' He smiled. 'You'll never get to see any of it.'

That evening, Debbie and I went over to see Georges and Juliette, where we enjoyed a glass of champagne and a baguette that we dipped into some truly delicious extra virgin olive oil.

Chapter 7

Soon after our bosses' departure, Hélène and Alain were due to follow suit – they were about to become very busy. As I sat at the table in Hélène's garden, she explained that she and Alain had sold their flat in Paris and were moving to a quieter area. Their new neighbours, who had moved in above them only a year previously, made so much noise that they were left with little choice.

'It's a shame,' Hélène said. 'They're a family with two very young children who scream from the moment they open their eyes to the minute they go to bed. And you know what?' she continued, sipping her coffee in the late November sunshine, 'The floorboards aren't screwed down properly so when they jump up and down, which is quite often, you can't hear yourself think. It's horrible.'

'You haven't complained?'

'Not really,' said Hélène. 'It's not in my nature. I did put a very polite note through their letterbox asking them to keep the noise down a little in the evenings, and you know what happened? They complained to the *mairie* – said I was harassing them. Can you believe it?'

'No way!'

'I'm afraid so. Anyway, it's all finished now, thank God. Where we're moving to, we overlook the Buttes-Chaumont, which is a beautiful park, and we're on the top floor. We also have a small terrace so we're lucky really. I just feel a bit sorry for the couple who have bought our apartment – they haven't met the people upstairs yet. But what can you do? More coffee?' she asked, putting out her cigarette in the stone ashtray.

'Yes please,' I replied, getting up and following her towards the kitchen. 'So, who's going to be looking after here while you're gone?'

'We'll be back for Christmas but, in the meantime, Pierre's coming back. I think he's had enough of staying with his sister and brother-in-law. From the sound of it, I think they've had enough of him too.' Hélène laughed. 'I don't really believe they get along too well, but he's got nowhere else to go.'

'Shame.'

'Yes, but he's not really trying to help himself. He has a friend who keeps offering him jobs in Cannes doing a bit of decorating, but he doesn't really want that. Quite often he doesn't even turn up. Is that enough milk for you?'

'Yes thanks.'

'I think his friend's patience is running out.'

'So, what is he going to do?'

'Well, he's coming back here for a couple weeks when we go, and then he's off to Venezuela for Christmas. His son's bought him a plane ticket. I don't really think Venezuela's my cup of tea. All looks a bit violent if you ask me. Each to their own, I guess. Perhaps that's why he's joined a gun club.' Hélène laughed.

'Seriously?'

'Yes, seriously. Wouldn't have thought he was the type. Who knows what goes on inside that man's head?' said Hélène. 'Anyway, how are you getting on across the road?'

'Not quite how I expected it to be, if I'm honest,' I replied.

'Is that good or bad?' Alain asked.

'Well, I didn't really have much chance to chat with Charles before we started but Belinda seemed quite nice. But now I've met him, I think the man's deranged. He's like the Duracell Bunny – he never switches off.' Hélène smiled. 'And some of the stuff he comes out with is just incredible. I'm sure he stays awake at night thinking up ridiculous phrases that he can throw at me. I love the sound as they whistle straight over my head.'

'For instance?' Hélène asked.

'I suggested in our last meeting that we build a *potager*, a kitchen garden. I costed it out to be around three thousand euros including trellis, raised beds, gravel and plants. You know what he replied? He said, "I'm not quite joining the dots up on that journey."'

'I see what you mean,' said Hélène, who then laughed.

'Even the kids have got it,' I said. 'I was in the olive grove just after the harvest and needed a bit of help folding the nets, so I said to Zoe, "Would you give me a hand folding these?" and you know what she replied? "That's way above my pay grade," and ran off. Can you believe it?'

'Well, they're gone now, so you'll be rid of them for a while.'

'They're coming back for Christmas.'

'Really? Never used to.'

'Told Debbie they did.'

'In the past, perhaps, but not in the last couple of years. Pierre used to make it quite tricky for them. He refused to buy a tree, let alone put it up.' Hélène took out a cigarette from its packet. 'If Charles wanted logs for the fire he had to get them himself. Funny how Pierre used to suffer from chronic back ache around Christmas.' Hélène laughed again. 'After the first year, they gave up. And Debbie's a good cook, is she?'

'Brilliant. Charles and Belinda love her cooking.'

'I bet they do. It means Belinda doesn't have to do it. She hates cooking. Might have been a bit of a mistake telling them that. They'll run Debbie ragged if they haven't done so already. And they'll have you babysitting. They don't care. The way they look at it is that they're only there for a week or two, so you can have the time off in lieu. Pierre didn't fall for that one. At five o'clock he used to shut his door and that was that. He wasn't interested in getting involved at all with the family. In the three years that he was over the road, I don't think Charles went into your apartment once. On the odd occasion that Charles went over there, Pierre used to stand outside the front door. He even put a curtain up so no one could see in.' Hélène laughed.

'Really?'

'Yes, really. Even Zoe tried, and you know how pushy she can be.'

'Indeed, I do.'

'And one other thing,' said Hélène. 'I hope you don't mind me saying but be very careful with what you say to Juliette and Georges. I think they speak to Charles quite a lot. Charles seemed to know a lot more about what was going on down here than Pierre ever used to tell him, and he certainly didn't get it from me. I'd keep them at arm's length if I were you.'

'Thanks for the warning,' I replied, putting down my now empty coffee cup, at the same time wondering if we'd let anything slip at the *apéro* to Georges and Juliette.

'You're welcome.' Hélène smiled. 'Anyway, look, I have to go and pack,' she said, getting up from her chair. 'Alain's driving to Grenoble to see his son on the way back to Paris and I'm getting the train.' I gave Hélène a hug and a kiss before making the short journey across the road to Mas des Collines.

We were going to miss our time spent with Alain and Hélène. Debbie and I had enjoyed our time at their house. The atmosphere they had created was very relaxed – worlds away from the brash, gauche lifestyle that was led by our bosses and their children.

Over the next few weeks, as well as performing our usual duties, Debbie and I wrote down everything that we could think of that needed doing before the following season. This involved quite mundane tasks such as varnishing the outdoor furniture, power washing the terraces, cleaning out the gutters and drains and stocktaking. Debbie had designed a house book for the guests that detailed all of the local attractions, including golf courses, vineyards, cycling routes and restaurants. She'd also included a list of useful phone numbers, such as taxi services, doctors and dentists. Once designed, Belinda was due to have the booklet printed in Hong Kong.

One morning in early December at about nine o'clock, I'd just made a cup of coffee and was standing in our kitchen and looking across the road.

'Morning, sweetie,' said Debbie, who had just come out of our bedroom and was still in her dressing gown.

'Morning,' I replied. 'What do you think that's all about then?' I asked.

'What's what all about?' asked Debbie, trying to suppress a yawn.

'Over the road at Hélène's. Look at the top window. It's wide open and there are no lights on – just a blanket hanging over the edge. And look, I'm not sure if they're medics or firemen,' I said, pointing at some men who were milling about on Hélène's driveway. 'Their uniforms all look the same to me.'

'Oh, yes,' said Debbie. 'What's Pierre done, I wonder?'

'Bet the silly bastard's set fire to the place,' I replied. 'Probably fell asleep with a cigarette in his mouth. Shall I call him?' Just then, my phone rang. I answered.

'Hello Brent, it's Hélène. How are you?'

'I'm fine thanks. And you?'

'OK,' she replied hesitantly. 'Look, I'm sorry, Brent, there's no easy way to say this, so I'll come straight to the point. Not good news I'm afraid,' she said. She took a deep breath. 'Pierre committed suicide last night.'

'He's done what?' I said, scarcely able to believe what I'd just heard. Debbie, who was looking very worried, mouthed, 'What's happened?'

'Hang on a minute Hélène, I'd better tell Debbie. It's Pierre, he's killed himself.' Debbie sat down. Tears began to roll down her face.

'Carry on, Hélène.'

'He bought a gun from the Internet, according to the police. They've got his computer. Anyway, last night he took himself up to our shower and shot himself. My cleaner, Thérèse, found him this morning.'

'Christ, poor woman. Is she OK?'

'She's quite shaken, but look, the ambulance crew are going to be taking the body shortly but I was hoping you could do me a bit of a favour.'

'Sure, but is it all right if I phone you back? There's a *gendarme* at the gate.'

'Of course.' Debbie rushed into the bedroom to get changed out of her dressing gown.

'*Bonjour monsieur*,' said the policeman as he walked into our kitchen. 'Maybe you have already heard what has happened?'

I nodded my head. 'Hélène's just phoned.'

'I don't need to explain then, but I was wondering if you heard anything.'

'Did we hear anything?' I asked. 'Like what?'

'A gunshot maybe?' he replied.

Debbie, who had just come out of the bedroom, shook her head. 'Perhaps,' I replied, 'but then it wouldn't really have registered if I'm honest with you. It's the hunting season and we are so used to hearing gunshots, we've become accustomed to them. I appreciate that it happened at night time, but even so. Sorry.'

'I see what you mean.' The *gendarme* smiled. 'How did he seem to you when you last saw him. Was he any different from usual?'

'I last saw him a few days ago. He didn't seem any different to me. It's a little strange because I thought he was going to Venezuela for Christmas. But no, in answer to your question, he didn't appear to be any different. I guess I just didn't know him that well. Not sure any of us did.'

'Thank you, Monsieur Tyler,' replied the gendarme. 'We are going to take Pierre's body away now. Thank you for your time. *Au revoir.*'

I picked up the phone and dialled. 'Hi Hélène, it's Brent. The *gendarme*'s just been.'

'All OK?' asked Hélène.

'Yes, all OK, but I still can't believe it.'

'Me neither.'

'I was only talking to him the other day. He seemed his usual self. What happened?'

'I don't know, but he used to talk about it every now and then. "What's the point?" he used to say. I don't know if he told you, but he was on anti-depressants, which isn't exactly a surprise after what he's been through, but we never expected this, and in my house too. I'm not really sure I want to come back.' Hélène cried for a moment or two. 'Look,' she said, gathering herself, '*Thérèse*, the lady who comes in to do the cleaning, is over there now. Would you mind giving her a hand to clean up a bit? I think most of it's done but she could probably do with a bit of moral support. Would you mind?'

'Of course not. I can see the ambulance pulling away. I'll go over there now.'

'Thanks, Brent. I'm sorry about this.'

'Not your fault, Hélène. It's the least I can do.'

'I'll give you a call once this has all had a chance to sink in. Thanks again. Love to Debs. Bye.'

I put my jacket on and began the short journey across the road. As I did so, many thoughts flashed through my mind. Pierre was an intelligent man. He spoke two languages fluently and had much to offer so why had he so readily given up? What a waste, I thought. He wasn't ill, not physically anyway. How low must Pierre have felt to let it get this far? His sister and brother-in-law were psychiatrists – could they have helped more? He never seemed at all angry so how could anyone have really known? Then I remembered once reading that depression was just anger without the enthusiasm. It made me laugh at the time but perhaps it was actually true after all. Over the coming days, another misconception of mine was also dispelled. I'd always thought that suicides were somehow spontaneous, that it was a spur of the moment decision, but Pierre had been planning his own death, to some extent, at least. How awful. How terrible, not just for him, but also for the people around him.

'*Bonjour monsieur*,' said Thérèse, who was on her hands and knees and cleaning the floor of the shower.

'Are you OK?' I asked.

'Yes,' she replied. 'Thanks for coming.' I grabbed a cloth and started to help Thérèse remove the blood that was spattered in and around the shower. 'Stupid man,' she continued. 'Why could he not have taken himself off into the woods? He has a car. It is not fair that he did it here. Hélène and Alain have been so good to him.' She shook her head. 'I am sorry – I am not very sympathetic, am I?' she said, continuing to scrub away.

'That's OK,' I replied. 'Must have come as quite a shock to you this morning.'

'I feel so stupid,' she said. 'You don't expect this kind of thing to happen. I walked into the bathroom and I saw Pierre slumped in the shower, fully dressed. There was an empty bottle of whisky next to him, so I thought he was still drunk. I shouted at him and then started to shake him. It was only then that I saw the gun and a pool of blood underneath him, so I screamed.' Thérèse laughed nervously. 'Fucking hell, what a start to the morning.'

'Are you sure you're all right?'

'Yes, I'm fine,' she replied. 'The ambulance crew cleaned up most of the mess when they took Pierre's body away. Anyway, I didn't really know him that well. He hardly ever spoke when I was here. It is Alain and Hélène I feel sorry for. I think we're done now unless you can see any more,' she said, squeezing out her cloth into a bucket and standing up.

'No, all looks good to me.'

'Well, I need to lock up. I have another job to go to and I'm already late – bloody man. Thanks for your help.'

'I didn't really do very much.'

'I know, but you were here. I appreciate that. Perhaps we'll all have coffee when Hélène and Alain come again? Bye Brent.'

I left it a few days and phoned Hélène again. 'How are you?' I asked.

'As good as can be expected,' Hélène replied. 'We've just been getting on with the flat. There's a lot to be done, which is good because it's helped to take my mind off things. And you?'

'We're OK thanks. Same as you, just getting on with it, I guess. I know this might be a bit early but I wanted to ask about the funeral.'

'No idea, I'm sorry. His sister won't speak to me.'

'She won't? After all you did for him? She's not even giving you the chance to say goodbye?'

'Apparently not,' replied Hélène. She sighed. 'The only communication I've had is through the police. They took Pierre's computer and his phone when they left, so I don't even have her number. I've left messages with the police that

I'm told have been passed on, but she doesn't get back to me except to say that they're not bothered about his things – not that there's much.

To be honest with you, Brent, I think that Pierre's sister and brother-in-law saw him as a big disappointment, an embarrassment even. They didn't understand why he lived his life the way he did, and it seems that now they don't want any memories of him either. It's almost as if they're trying to deny he existed at all. It's a shame, but that's people for you.'

'Charming.'

'I know but what can you do? I'm coming down again in a few weeks for Christmas. I've got to face the house sometime. And I've got my brother, Guy, coming over with his Iranian girlfriend. Haven't met her yet.'

'Sounds very exotic.'

'No doubt.' Hélène laughed. 'And my daughter, Judith, is coming over from the States. My son, Samuel, is coming from Paris, so we'll have a house full. I'm sure we'll manage a laugh or two.'

'I'm looking forward to meeting them.'

'You'll like them a lot. Mad as hell but good fun. I have to go now. I'm in the middle of painting the kitchen and I'm supposed to be going out for lunch. I think I've got more on me than I've got on the walls. Look, thanks for phoning, Brent. If anything changes about Pierre, I'll let you know. Love to Debbie. Take care.'

'Bye Hélène.'

Chapter 8

Christmas was only a week away and Charles and his family were about to arrive. It had been just three weeks since the olive harvest and the devastation that went with it. The family arrived late one Friday night and by eight o'clock the following morning I could see Charles pacing up and down on the lawn, looking at his watch.

'You'd better go and see what he's up to,' suggested Debbie.

'Bugger that, I've got watering to do and then I'm mowing the lawn. What he does in his own garden is up to him,' I said as I poured myself a cup of coffee.

'On your head be it,' replied Debbie. Ten minutes later, just as I was putting on my work boots, there was a knock on our front door.

'Hello, Brent,' said a very stern-looking Charles. 'I was wondering what you had planned today.'

'Oh, all of the usual exciting stuff,' I replied cheerily. 'Mowing the lawn...'

'I see,' Charles interrupted. 'I thought I told you that we've got a *restanque* wall to build and I've already been waiting for you for over an hour.'

'You did tell me you wanted to build a wall. You just didn't tell me when.'

'Well, I'm telling you now. You'd better be on the top lawn in ten minutes. I haven't got any more time to waste. Oh, and bring the wheelbarrow,' Charles said before closing the door firmly behind him.

'Cheeky bastard!' I said to Debbie.

'I know. I did try and warn you. Never switches off, that man. Anyway, you'd better go.'

'What the fuck is a *restanque* wall when it's at home?' I asked Debbie.

'I don't know. Hang on a sec, I'll look it up,' she replied as I began to open the front door. Debbie sat at her computer. 'Apparently, it's a dry-stone wall, a bit like Hélène's. Used to prop up levels in the garden so you get terraces.

Come here, I'll show you.' Just then the buzzer went in our apartment. Debbie picked up the receiver and listened. 'That was Belinda. Wanted to know why I'm not there to help with breakfast. She told me never to be at the house before half eight – it's barely a quarter past. What are these people like? This is going to be another long couple of weeks.'

'Merry Christmas,' I said just before popping a piece of toast into my mouth and leaving the apartment.

When I found Charles, he instructed me to walk around the estate and gather as many rocks of a decent size as I could find and bring them back to the top garden.

'You just bring them to me and we'll have it done in no time. I used to play a lot of Tetris, so this should be a breeze. Right, see you in a bit,' he said. *In no time* turned out to be all day and by the time I got back to our apartment in the early evening, I thought I was going to die.

'Any particular reason you're walking like John Wayne?' asked Debbie, who was stirring the contents of a casserole dish.

'Oh, go boil your head,' I replied. 'That man's an animal. Didn't stop all day. Promised me we'd be done by lunchtime.'

'He promised that to the olive pickers too, if you remember. Anyway, how did you get on?'

'Finished it but it's a bit of a mess if you ask me.'

'A mess, how do you mean, a mess?'

'The wall looked quite good until Sir put the cement on top. Pure white, and he didn't bother to smooth it over. Seemed like a very badly iced cake in the end, which is a shame because it could have been great – something to have been proud of. All because he was in a hurry to get off.'

'Don't you think you should get a trowel and tidy it up?'

'No, I'll only have to admit I found his phone then.'

'His phone. What phone?'

'The one that fell out his pocket and landed in the cement just before he ran back to the house. Should be set by now. *Quick drying*, it said. Anyway, I'm going for a bath after I've had a drink,' I said, sitting down and taking off my shoes. Debbie laughed.

'So, what has he got planned for tomorrow? Any ideas?'

'He said he'll have to see which way the mop flops, which I take it to mean he hasn't got a clue.'

'Has that man got an expression for every occasion?' asked Debbie, who handed me a glass of rosé.

'Thanks. Seems like it. How was your day?'

'Same old, same old. Lists of things that need doing but no money to spend on them.'

'I know what Mummy and Daddy have got you for Christmas,' shouted Zoe, who burst through our front door at eight thirty the following morning. She took a huge slurp of her iced lolly and said, 'But I'm not allowed to tell you. Come on, Brent, you're taking me and Caroline to the climbing park in the woods. Mummy's going shopping quickly with Debbie and then she's going for a run.'

'And what's Daddy doing?' I asked.

'He's touching some bases with people in his office. Is that like touching your toes? Look, I can do it. And, I can do this,' she said, jumping up and spinning around. 'Come on, the park opens soon.'

'I'll see you in a minute,' I said to Zoe. 'Off you go.'

Once she'd gone, Debbie said, 'They've got us Christmas presents? Shit. I've got no idea what to get them – have you? I wish people wouldn't do that. We hardly know them.'

'I suppose. At least we've been warned. Could have been embarrassing.'

'And I'm not spending all of Christmas Day with them. We'll just get saddled with amusing Zoe while Charles and Belinda stare into their phones. And what the hell do you get for someone like Zoe? She's got everything.'

'I was just thinking about that. Can't make my mind up between a drum kit and a year's supply of Coke. Better still, both. Come on, let's go.'

A quarter of an hour later, Caroline, Zoe, Guss and I were all in my car and making our way up to the stadium at the top of Montauroux.

'Brent, can I tell you what we've got Debbie?'

'No.'

'Oh, please?'

'No.'

'OK then, but it's pink and she can wear it round her neck.'

'I'm telling,' said Caroline, who looked up from her book.

'I didn't tell him,' said Zoe, who snatched Caroline's book out of her hand.

'Yes you did. And give that back.' There was a loud tear and while Caroline was holding most of the book, Zoe was holding a single page.

'Now look what you've done, you little shit!' screamed Caroline, who started to punch Zoe on the arm. 'That's my favourite book and I've only just bought it. You wait until I tell Mummy.'

'Brent, she's hurting me,' cried Zoe. 'Tell her to get off.'

'Right, we're here now,' I said as we pulled into the car park next to the stadium. 'Come on girls, get out.' To our left was the entrance to the climbing park. Above us were large red and blue nets that were designed for children to run through, aided by some ropes that acted as handrails. In the distance I could hear the sound of some excited youngsters. As I paid the cashier and smiled broadly, it was clear that she'd seen the look on my face many times before – a look that said '*All yours now. Can't wait to get rid of the little buggers.*' I left the woman my phone number in case of an emergency. As Zoe charged past Caroline, screaming as she went, I went back to the car, collected Guss and headed off into the woods.

After an hour or so it was time to return to the climbing park. I found Caroline, who was sitting in the small open-air café, reading her book. Beside her was a roll of Sellotape that had been lent to her by one of the staff. As I looked up towards the red and blue netting that was high up in the trees directly above us, I could see Zoe's bright red leggings and bare feet.

Suddenly, she lay flat on her stomach, poked her nose through the netting and said, 'Hello Brent. We don't have to go yet, do we?'

'No,' I said. 'You can stay for about another half an hour if you want.'

Zoe blew a huge raspberry in Caroline's direction, stood up and said to one of her playmates, 'That's my sister. She's such an arsehole,' and away they ran.

'Does your mother know she speaks like that?' I asked Caroline.

'She's much worse when there are no adults about,' she mused. 'Don't know where she gets her language from. She seems to know much more than me when it comes to swearing. And…'

Caroline was interrupted by the sound of a loud belch and a cackle of laughter from above. 'That's her. And, I was about to say, she has the most appalling manners. Up there for her is about right, along with the rest of the apes. May I have another Coke please?'

'Sure, I was about to order a coffee. Good book?'

'Great. I love David Walliams's books, or at least I did until that little sod tried to destroy it. I hope she falls off.'

It was lunchtime when we arrived back at the villa. I went in search of Debbie, who I assumed to be cleaning one of the bedrooms. Just as I was passing Charles's and Belinda's bedroom, where I could hear a hairdryer whirring away, Zoe burst past me and flung open the door to reveal Belinda, whose hair was covering her face but was otherwise completely naked. Zoe ran into the room, turned round, looked at me completely horrified and quickly shut the door, which I put my ear to.

'Mummy…' Zoe said.

'I've told you before,' interrupted Belinda, 'to knock when you're here.'

'We don't have to in HK,' protested Zoe.

'Yes, but we're not in HK,' replied Belinda. 'What if Brent was outside when you came in?'

'Oh, don't worry about him. He's in the garden. I just saw him there. Can I have a cookie, please?' I smiled.

'No, you're about to have your lunch.'

'I know that, but I have burnt off a lot of energy this morning and now I feel a bit weedy,' Zoe protested.

'The answer's still no,' replied Belinda.

'Don't you sometimes get fed up with saying no? That's all you ever say.'

'No. Zoe, pass me my top, would you?'

'No.'

I tiptoed down the stairs, opened the front door and sat on one of the chairs on the terrace to put my boots on. As I did so, the door opened again and Zoe appeared.

She put her hand in front of her mouth, giggled and said, 'I won't tell anyone if you don't,' and ran off towards the swimming pool.

'How did you get on?' I asked Debbie, who was in our apartment and looking at the computer.

'OK. We weren't out long. We picked up a few Christmas nibbles and came back pretty much straightaway. I think Belinda was desperate to go for a run. Thought I heard her come back just before you. She's doing lunch for the kids for a change. Fancy a sandwich?'

'Sure. Anyway, what are you up to?'

'Applying for our *Cartes Vitales*.'

'Our what?'

'*Cartes Vitales*. Social security cards, essentially. Means we're properly in the system, so we get the same medical rights as everyone else. Also means we don't have to pay much for the doctor or dentist, not that I hope we need them. I've done mine, but you need to think of a password – must have eight characters.'

I thought for a few moments. '"Snow White and the Seven Dwarfs" any good?'

'You worry me sometimes.' Debbie got out of her chair and shook her head. 'Cheese and pickle?'

'Sounds good to me.'

'There's good news and bad news,' Debbie said as she was buttering the bread.

'Here we go.'

'Well, we don't have to cook Christmas lunch for them. Belinda and the girls are doing it.'

'Sounds interesting. Love to be a fly on the wall for that one.'

'And the bad news?'

'Belinda's asked us to babysit, New Year's Eve.'

'What did you say?'

'What could I say? Caught me on the hop a bit, if I'm honest. Besides, it's not like we're doing anything else, is it?'

'Are we getting paid for that?'

'Wouldn't have thought so, would you?'

On Christmas morning, Debbie and I went to the villa as we had been invited to join the family for a glass of Bucks Fizz and a mid-morning snack. We also exchanged presents and, as Zoe had hinted earlier, Debbie received a pink pashmina. I was given a penknife. We gave Caroline some books and Debbie bought Zoe a woolly panda outfit.

'I didn't know you'd got Zoe a onesie,' I said to Debbie as we stood buttering some toast in the kitchen.

'It was the closest thing I could find to a straitjacket,' Debbie replied. 'Take these through, would you?'

'Good thinking, Batman.' I laughed.

'Come on,' whispered Caroline once we'd finished eating. 'We're all going down to the garage. It's Mummy's surprise present. Daddy picked it up yesterday. She's going to be so surprised.'

'Where is Mummy?' I asked.

'Gone to get changed. She's going out for a run before lunch. Right, we must be quiet and that includes you, you little shit,' Caroline said, looking at her sister.

'Um, I'm telling,' replied Zoe, who was looking most indignant.

'Like I care.'

Charles, Debbie, Caroline, Zoe and I were waiting patiently when Belinda came down the drive.

'What's this all about?' she said, looking quite perplexed.

'Surprise!' shouted Charles, who pressed the clicker that opened the garage. As the door opened, it revealed a gleaming, and very expensive-looking, road bike. Bright red and sparkling in the winter sunshine, it was beautiful.

'I didn't think Mummy wanted a bike,' Zoe whispered in my ear as Belinda went to inspect her present. 'I heard her tell Daddy.' Beside the bike there were a pair of cycling shoes that Belinda was asked to put on.

'Light as a feather,' declared Charles, who lifted the bike triumphantly in the air with just one hand. 'And, I've adjusted the saddle for you.' Although he looked extremely happy, I could see from the expression on Belinda's face that she was not at all impressed. 'Put the shoes on and I'll take a photo,' Charles said, taking his phone out of his pocket. Belinda did as she was asked and stood smiling next to the bike. 'Better still, once round the cark park – I can video it.' Belinda reluctantly straddled the bike and clipped her right shoe into the pedal. She pushed down and tried to get her left foot into the one opposite. Unfortunately, she missed. She wobbled and fell off, hitting the concrete beneath her with a bang. She let out a scream, quickly got to her feet, picked up the bike and threw it in Charles's direction.

'I told you I didn't want a fucking bike!' she scowled. 'Don't you listen to anything I say?' she added, changing into her training shoes. 'Brent, open the gate please.' And with that, Belinda ran out of the car park, leaving the four of us standing around looking quite shocked.

'That went well then,' I whispered in Debbie's ear.

'Best leave them to it. Come on.'

'Did you see the state of the bike when Charles picked it up?' I said to Debbie as we walked back up to our apartment. 'Scratched to buggery. She might be small but she's bloody strong.'

'Sorry, no sympathy. She's right. The man doesn't listen. If I've heard her say once, I've heard Belinda say a thousand times, she doesn't like bikes. What part of that does Charles not understand?'

'I know, but it's his passion.'

'Doesn't make it hers though, does it? He's an idiot. Got what he deserved.'

'Expensive way to prove a point. Glad we're not there for lunch.'

'Me too. Would you mind peeling some potatoes. The turkey's about to go in.'

As it rained almost constantly over the next few days I was tasked with making an inventory of everything that was in the garage.

'There are over a thousand ways to rob people,' Charles said to me one morning. Was he referring to me? I hoped not. I counted batteries, light bulbs, electrical fittings, tools and golf clubs. It amazed me how many duplicate items there were – three sandwich toasters, box upon box of dimmer switches, twelve bicycle tyre repair kits and two rusty exercise bikes. There was also an antiquated telephone system complete with handsets, some broken sun loungers and thirty or forty empty Kilner jars that were covered in dust. It occurred to me at that point that the only thing that had been worth stealing was the Porsche, which had long since gone. I smiled as I imagined Pierre handing over the keys to the used-car dealer and being given the cash. I had no doubt that it would have been registered in his name.

'Where are they off to then?' I asked Debbie, who was watching a cookery programme on the afternoon of New Year's Eve.

'Oh, just down the road to Callian,' she replied. 'A masked ball or fancy dress for growed-ups, as Zoe called it. You're to take them at about seven o'clock and they'll be driven back by a proper chauffeur just after midnight.'

'Oh, OK. Hang on a minute, what do you mean a proper chauffeur? What am I supposed to be?'

'Remind me what you were wearing when you picked them up from the airport.'

'Jeans, t-shirt...'

'Which particular t-shirt?'

'I don't know.'

'I do. It was the one with the slogan, *Today I'm Bruce Wayne but tonight I'm Batman.*'

I laughed. 'That's about the smartest thing I've got,' I said, reaching for the kettle. 'What do you expect?'

'It's not what I expect, my love, it's what they expect,' Debbie replied. 'Chauffeurs wear suits and, if my memory serves me correctly, the last time you wore a suit was at our wedding and that was white.'

'There was a good reason for that. We got married on a cruise and, if you don't mind, you chose it. Anyway, whenever I wear a suit I always look like the accused.'

'That may be true, but I can't think that Charles and Belinda are going to want to be picked up by either Batman or John Travolta, do you? Look, I've ironed you a shirt and your black jeans. Hopefully, not many people will see you.'

'Charming.' I laughed.

At seven o'clock, Debbie and I went to the villa along with Guss. Charles came flying down from upstairs, dressed in a tuxedo and his hair still wet from a shower.

'Come on, Belinda,' he shouted. 'Don't want to be late.' Moments later, Belinda arrived from the same direction and was wearing a sparkly, black ballgown. In her right hand she was carrying an evening bag and as I looked down I noticed she was wearing a pair of training shoes. I thought it a little odd but also thought it best not to say anything.

'Let's run,' said Charles. 'Bye kids!' he shouted at Caroline and Zoe, who were sitting by the fire in the lounge. The three of us jumped into the Land Rover and began the four-mile journey to Callian.

'Fuck, fuck, fuck,' said Belinda as I opened the back door for her when we arrived. 'I've left my shoes behind. I can't go in like this. I was going to get changed as we got out of the car.'

'You've what?' asked Charles, who was looking down in horror at Belinda's feet.

'Bloody high heels,' replied Belinda angrily. 'They pinch to buggery, so I was leaving putting them on until the last minute. Bollocks.'

As I looked round the impressive entrance to the mansion of the people that were hosting the party, I noticed one or two smirking chauffeurs. Dressed in designer black suits, white shirts, black ties and brightly polished shoes, they were finding the whole episode highly amusing. As the gravelled drive was floodlit for the occasion, there wasn't really anywhere to hide either the mistake or Belinda's embarrassment.

'You'd better get back to the house quickly, Brent,' said Charles. 'What a fucking disaster. Shit, shit, shit.'

As I slowly drove around the large, stone fountain, I noticed through the windows of the mansion a hundred or so people all holding champagne glasses and chatting away merrily. I watched as Charles and a very sheepish Belinda went to join them. I also noticed a finely decorated long table with silver platters and tureens. Waitresses with black dresses and white pinafores offered canapés while waiters in black suits and open-necked white shirts circled the room, offering refreshments. The drive was lined with life-sized Greek statues and at the entrance to the property there were several thirty-foot tall conifers that had been decorated with twinkling lights and Christmas baubles.

'In here!' shouted Caroline, who was sitting in the lounge and dangling a pair of black, high-heeled shoes in front of her. 'I think she forgot these.' She smiled. 'I would have mentioned it as they were leaving, but they didn't even have the decency to wish us a Happy New Year before they left. Didn't even say goodbye properly for that matter. Hope they weren't too embarrassed.'

'You'll never know,' I said, smiling. Caroline looked very pleased with herself as she went back to her book.

I returned the shoes to the party, ran the gauntlet of smirking chauffeurs and was back at the villa quite quickly.

'This is amaze balls,' said Zoe excitedly, who had opened the bottle of apple champagne that she had been told to leave until midnight. 'Would you like some, Brent?' she asked at the same time as jumping up and down on the sofa.

'No thanks, Zoe. Anyway, weren't you supposed to leave that until later?'

'Don't worry. There's plenty more in the pidge, pidge erm...'

'*Pigeonnier?*'

'Yeah, that's it. Daddy bought loads,' she said, before taking a huge gulp of juice from her glass.

'Where's Debbie, by the way?'

'In the kitchen. Putting a cold flannel on Caroline's eye.'

'Why exactly is Debbie putting a cold flannel on Caroline's eye?' I asked.

'When I opened the champagne, she didn't get out of the way. Happens quite a lot this time of year, Daddy says. What shall we do now?'

'You'd better stay where you are, Zoe. I'll be back in a minute.'

'Is she OK?' I asked Debbie, who was alone in the kitchen and doing some washing up. 'She will be. Bruise, right on her eyebrow. Could have been worse.'

'Where is she now?'

'She went upstairs to read her book. Said she'd be down later – to kill her sister.' I laughed.

'Can we play a game?' asked Zoe as Debbie and I went back into the lounge.

'Like what?' I asked.

'Like Pass the Parcel,' Zoe replied.

'You've already opened all of your presents,' said Debbie.

'I know, but we can wrap them all back up again.'

'No,' Debbie and I said at the same time.

'Let's do something quiet,' I suggested.

'I don't like quiet,' Zoe protested. 'Quiet is boring.' After a few minutes of near silence, she piped up, 'I know. Let's take Guss for a walk.'

'No.'

'Why not?' she asked.

'It's dark,' I replied.

'We can take a torch.'

'We don't have a torch,' said Debbie.

'We can take some carrots. They help you see in the dark and we've got plenty of those. I've seen them in the fridge,' Zoe reasoned.

'What time is it?' I asked Debbie.

'Eight o'clock.'

'Fuck.'

After a game of Monopoly, Mousetrap and Happy Families, each lasting about ten minutes, we persuaded Zoe to watch Cinderella. Half way through, she put her thumb in her mouth and fell asleep.

'I know how she feels,' said Debbie. 'Feeling a bit tired myself.'

'Look, there's no point in us both hanging around,' I replied. 'Why don't you go back? I'll tidy up. You go and get your head down.'

'Are you sure you don't mind?'

'No, I'm not feeling tired at all. Anyway, they'll be back in a couple of hours, so won't be long.'

'What about our champagne?' asked Debbie, who was looking at the bottle that Charles and Belinda had given us.

'We'll have it tomorrow. Off you go. Night, night.'

After I'd finished tidying up, I flicked around the television channels, only to realise there was nothing on – nothing on that interested me, at least. Almost everywhere I looked there were panel shows with trendy comedians who laughed at each other's jokes that weren't at all funny. So, I went to the bookshelf, picked up a copy of The Hobbit and sat down. Midnight came. I raised a glass to everybody that I could think of, including myself, and then carried on reading. At one o'clock there was still no sign of Charles or Belinda. Two o'clock came and went. Finally, at five past three the front door opened very slowly.

'Hello Brent, I'm so sorry,' apologised Belinda, whose hair was soaking wet. Her ballgown was spattered with mud and torn at the bottom. In the distance I could see Charles, who wasn't looking very happy. He disappeared upstairs without saying a word. Belinda said, 'The thing is, we missed the last chauffeur so we had to walk back. Everything OK? Girls all right?'

'Yes, fine thanks.' I explained briefly what had happened with Zoe and Caroline.

'Can be a bit of a handful, that one,' she said, looking at Zoe, who was still asleep on the couch. I'll get Charles to come and get her in a minute. You can go now, Brent. And tell Debbie that she doesn't need to come in later. We'll look after ourselves. Sorry again for being so late.' Belinda smiled and tiptoed up the stairs to her bedroom.

I got up and started to walk towards the kitchen with my empty champagne glass. As I passed the bottom of the stairs I could hear Belinda, who was trying, albeit unsuccessfully, to keep her voice down. 'Look at this dress, Charles,' she said. 'Fifteen hundred quid. Fifteen hundred fucking quid and it's ruined, all because you were too busy kissing Jeremy's arse. Just look at it. Bloody hell.'

'I didn't know that the chauffeurs had all gone.'

'That's because you didn't read the invitation properly. Look,' Belinda said, presumably waving the invitation at him, 'it clearly says here *Carriages at one o'clock. Complimentary Chauffeur service available until 12.30.*'

As quietly as I could, I closed the front door behind me and disappeared with Guss into the morning air. *Happy New Year everybody*, I said to myself. Once back at the apartment I wrote Debbie a note, telling her she didn't need to go to the house, got into bed and didn't surface until eleven o'clock that morning.

'Brunch?' asked Debbie as I walked into the kitchen in my dressing gown. I yawned.

'Sounds like a plan. What have we got?'

'Eggs, bacon, mushrooms, tomatoes and toast. That OK?'

'Start the year as you mean to carry on is what I say. Go for it. Would you put the kettle on please? I'm going to get changed and then, boy, have I got a story for you.'

As we sat down at the table, Debbie listened open-mouthed as I relayed the events of the night before.

'That was one expensive Christmas then,' said Debbie, who was spreading some Marmite on her toast. 'That bike would have cost about the same as Belinda's dress. Add to that the kids' presents, food, shopping trips and everything else, I'd be surprised if they got away with much less than ten grand.'

'And the rest. Anyway, they go back tomorrow. Should be the last we hear from them until Easter.'

'Peace at last.'

'I wouldn't count on it. Belinda is the queen of emails.'

'Oh, you cheery soul. Give me a hand with the dishes, would you?'

We were due to leave for Nice airport at eight thirty on the Sunday morning but, as was usually the case, we were running late. I had long since loaded the family's bags into the Land Rover and was waiting patiently with the engine running. At twenty to nine, Charles strode towards me, followed by Belinda, Caroline and Zoe, who, for a change, was dawdling.

'Come on!' bellowed Charles. 'We'll be late and miss the plane.'

'Good,' replied Zoe. 'I don't want to go back to HK. I want to stay here. Can't I stay here…?'

With that, Charles ran back to Zoe, picked her up, put her firmly in the back seat and buckled her up. During the forty-five-minute journey, hardly a word was spoken. Belinda and Charles tapped away on their phones. Caroline read her book while Zoe stared out of the window until I looked in the rear-view mirror and then she'd poke out her tongue and smile. When we arrived at the Kiss and Fly car park at Terminal 1, the girls were each given two euros and told to go and fetch a luggage trolley. Moments later they were racing towards us, crashing into one another along the way. Belinda and I loaded the trollies while Charles continued to toy with his phone.

'We'd better go,' said Charles. 'Don't want to be late, right? Regards to Debbie. Didn't see her this morning. Tell her I'll catch her on the flip side. Come on gang!' he shouted and off they went. I stood by the side of the Land Rover and watched as Charles and his family walked through the car park. Just as they got to the zebra crossing that led into the terminal, Zoe stopped, turned round and came running towards me. Charles shouted for her to come back but was ignored.

'Brent,' she said, wiping a tear from her eye with her sleeve. 'You are going to miss me, aren't you? I'm going to miss you and Debbie and Guss.'

'Of course we will.'

'Oh, that's all right then,' Zoe said, flinging her arms around me.

'Anyway, you'll be back for Easter. That's not long now,' I said, noticing Charles, whose face had become very red. 'You'd better go now Zoe, otherwise you are going to get seriously grounded, young lady.'

'For the third time this week,' replied Zoe, who then laughed. 'Bye Brent. Give my love to Debbie,' she said as she started to run back across the car park. About half way, she stopped, turned round and shouted, 'I'll buy you an egg.'

'That's nice.' I smiled.

'Will you buy me one?' she asked.

'No.'

'Bet you do.' Zoe laughed and sprinted off, waving as she went, to re-join her not-so-happy-looking parents.

Chapter 9

With the villa being unoccupied, and having some time to ourselves, Debbie and I decided that at the weekends we'd visit one of the local towns or villages. As most of them were in the middle of the countryside, this also suited Guss, as there were numerous new walks to go on and smells for him to discover. After an hour or two of rambling through the woods, we'd wander round the village and then find a small bistro where we'd enjoy a quiet lunch and a glass or two of rosé.

'I've driven past this place on the way to the garden centre,' I said to Debbie as we approached the aerodrome in Fayence one Sunday at about midday. 'The restaurant seems quite popular – always cars parked outside. Shall we give it a go?'

'Let's at least have a look at the menu,' replied Debbie, who was watching a bi-plane taking off in the distance.

Outside was a glass cabinet mounted on a pedestal, inside of which was a menu.

We'd only been there a few moments when the front door opened and a smiling waiter, dressed in black trousers and a white open-necked shirt, came to greet us.

'*Bonjour, monsieur, dame,*' he said. 'Have you made a reservation?'

'No, we haven't,' I said. 'We…'

'Wait a minute, I'll go and see if we have a room,' he replied, and went back inside. Moments later, he returned and said, 'I have just the place for you. He is big, isn't he?' he continued, looking down at Guss. 'I hope he's friendly. Come on, I'll show you.'

'You OK with this?' I asked Debbie as we followed the waiter.

'The menu looked fine and he seems friendly enough. Anyway, we're here now. Let's give it a go.'

As we made our way to the far end of the restaurant, we noticed some worried expressions on the faces of a few of the diners as they saw Guss approaching.

So concerned was one very elegantly dressed woman, she scooped up quite possibly the smallest dog I'd ever seen in my life from the floor and put it into her handbag, which she partially zipped.

'Don't worry, Madame, he's already eaten,' I said. Not seeing the funny side at all at what I had just said, she turned her head away from me and frowned at the other people sitting at her table.

The waiter found us a table in the far corner of the restaurant – a place where Guss could sprawl out without having to be stepped over. The waiter smiled, gave Debbie and I each a menu and went to greet some other guests. In front of us was a huge picture window that looked out onto the airfield and while I watched planes take off and land in the warm sunshine, Debbie kept her eye on the food that was coming out of the kitchen.

'I think I need to go on a drink awareness course,' I said, tapping my fingers on the table.

'Oh, really?' Debbie replied.

'Yeah, people need to be aware when I need a drink.' Debbie laughed. 'We've been here for over twenty minutes now and the last time we saw a waiter was when he brought us to our table.'

'They are busy,' Debbie reasoned.

'I can see that, but they've also put us right out of the way, which is fair, but do you think there's any chance they've forgotten about us? I mean, those people over there,' I said, pointing at some people a few tables to our right, 'arrived after us and they've already been served. *Monsieur, monsieur.*'

'I could get used to this,' said Debbie as she put down her menu. 'Relaxing weekends, no one bothering us, getting on with things at our own pace. Haven't heard from Belinda for almost two weeks. Cheers,' she said, taking a sip from her glass of rosé that had just arrived.

'That's what worries me,' I replied, reaching for an ice cube.

'Worries you? Why?'

'Well, you know what rich people are like. When you don't hear from them, it usually means they're up to something – about to spring some kind of surprise or other. Silence is never a good sign. I can't imagine Charles and Belinda being any different – devious lot.'

'Oh, you're so cynical. You don't trust anybody.' Debbie smiled. 'Come on, give them a chance. They might have started to trust us. Besides, I don't really want to talk about them now. Let's enjoy our lunch.'

'*Oui, monsieur*,' said the waiter, who had come to take our order.

'I'll have the Pizza Reine, please,' I replied, passing the waiter my menu.

'I'm sorry, sir. We don't do pizzas at lunchtime – only the evening.'

'Really? It doesn't say that on your menu. Give us a couple of minutes, would you?' I said, picking up my menu again.

'Of course.'

As the waiter walked away, Debbie said, 'That's a pity, I was about to do the same. There's nothing on the menu that I really fancy. Actually, that's not true. There's quite a lot I fancy but unfortunately what's coming out of the kitchen resembles nothing that's on the menu.' Debbie laughed. 'Have you seen it?'

'Not really. Been too busy pretending I'm Biggles,' I replied, and then I started to hum the Dam Busters tune.

'Look at that lamb – it's swimming in sauce. 'Not only that, it's grey,' she said, looking horrified at the plate that the waitress had just put on the table next to us. 'And those green beans look as though they've been stewing since Christmas. Takes some skill to make food that bad.' I laughed.

'You want to try somewhere else?'

'No, I like it here. What a view – couldn't ask for much more. Besides, it's not just about the food, which is just as well,' Debbie said as she stared suspiciously at another mysterious plate of something or other that was set down at the table opposite. 'Let's just order a couple of steaks. Surely they can't cock those up?'

They did. An hour later, we left the restaurant with one very well-fed dog. He didn't seem to mind the chewy steaks, or the soggy French fries that accompanied them.

'Maybe we should go back one evening – try the pizza,' Debbie said as we drove out of the car park. 'I don't know if you noticed the poster on the wall next to the loos but on the first Tuesday of each month they have a jazz night.'

'Sounds like fun.'

On Monday morning, we began to look through our individual 'to do' lists. Amongst the thirty or so tasks that had been allocated to me were the shutters that still had to be painted, garden furniture that needed varnishing and the perimeter hedges that had to be trimmed. The wine inventory also needed to be double-checked and numerous light bulbs had to be replaced in the villa. I'd looked at the weather forecast and, as no rain was due until at least Wednesday, Guss and I were going to be outside until then. I put on my boots, placed my empty coffee mug into the dishwasher, reached for the front door and was about to say goodbye to Debbie when she looked up from the computer and said, 'At last, we hear from Belinda.'

'Everything OK?' I asked, walking back through the kitchen and looking over Debbie's shoulder.

'I'm not sure really.' Debbie replied. 'Never seen anything quite like this before – not in this job anyway. I think you'd better come and sit down. This is going to need some thinking about.'

'Sounds serious,' I replied, pulling up a chair.

'Well,' began Debbie, 'you know our "to do" lists that we sent her.'

'Yes.'

'The ones that we spent ages doing that she didn't contribute to herself?'

'With you so far.'

'She's turned them into spreadsheets.'

'And how does that make a difference to us?' I asked.

'That makes a difference to us, my love, because what she's actually done is taken the information that I sent her and turned it into a daily planner. This is crazy.'

'How has she managed to do that?' I asked.

'OK, I'll show you. Here's your bit. We've got one each.'

'Aren't we the lucky ones?'

'Got a feeling you won't be saying that in a minute.'

'Sounds ominous.'

'You see these columns?' Debbie said, pointing at the screen. 'So, she wants to know how long it takes you to mow the lawn and how many times a week you do it and on which days. So, let's say you mow the lawn three times a week and it takes two hours each time, that's six hours of your week gone.'

'You got that?' I nodded my head.

'Carry on.'

'They want to know how many times I vacuum and mop the floors, how long it takes and how often I dust each room and how long that takes. And look at this, how long do you spend walking Guss? And she's also asked if we really need a whole hour for lunch. Read this.' Debbie scrolled down the page. *Charles and I need to know if you have any spare capacity.*

'What does that mean? *Any spare capacity.*'

'I'm afraid, my love, exactly what it says. They want to know if we can take on any more work than we've already said we can do. Not only that, they want to know what we're up to every minute of every day between now and Easter. She's even numbered the weeks.'

'They don't trust us.'

'Doesn't look like it,' replied Debbie, who was looking at her own spreadsheet.

'Surprised they haven't asked how long it takes to go for a sh...'

'Exactly,' Debbie interrupted. 'I'm really cross.' She got up from her chair and went to the fridge.

'Apart from the fact we work really hard and do far more hours than's actually in our contract, we're supposed to be a housekeeper and a gardener. This is nuts,' she continued, reaching for a bottle of water and unscrewing the cap. 'This is like time management from the nineteen-seventies. What's up with her? We didn't come here to fill out forms all day. We came here to get away from the corporate world and now look. She doesn't understand the job. No two days are the same, which is something I really like about what we do – that and managing our own time. I can't plan like this. It's ridiculous. I'll never get any work done. I'll be spending all my time filling out bloody spreadsheets, and chasing you is virtually impossible. Can't imagine you writing down everything you do during the day. This is madness – utter bloody madness.'

'You wait,' I said. 'Give it a couple of days and there'll be a couple of stopwatches in the post.'

'That would be quite funny if I didn't think that was a genuine possibility,' Debbie replied as she paced around the lounge. 'Anyway, the bottom line is I'm not going to be micromanaged in this way and you're not capable of being managed in that way. To be honest, you're not really capable of being managed at all.'

'Harsh but fair,' I replied.

'Even so, I can't believe what she's just done. Wow,' Debbie said as she sat down on the sofa, the wind having completely left her sails.

'So, what are we going to do?'

'What can we do? We'll have to try and reason with her. I thought we were doing such a great job – shit!'

'You know what this is all about, don't you?' I said.

'Not really, no.'

'Pierre.'

'Pierre? What's Pierre got to do with things? Can't really blame him. Not now, anyway.'

'I'm not. Look, for the past three years hardly anything was done here, so

82

the place has been let go. Now they want to make up for lost time. They've looked at our 'to do' lists and have wondered why most of it hadn't been done before. So, they're feeling a bit stupid themselves. Should've kept their eye on the ball but, for whatever reason, they didn't and now we're paying for it. Not our fault.'

'I know but I thought we could be really settled here. None of this was mentioned at the interview – pair of bloody control freaks. Anyway, we're going to have to try. What are you up to this morning?'

'I've got a fire to build. Perhaps I should put it right next to the house. See you later,' I said, opening the front door. 'Come on Guss.'

At lunchtime I got back to our apartment, where there was an email from Charles waiting for me. 'Have you seen this?' I asked Debbie, who was ironing some sheets.

'Seen what?'

'This email from Charles.'

'No, haven't looked at the computer since this morning. What does it say?'

'Apparently, Charles wasn't very happy with the wi-fi when he was here.'

'Oh, no? Worked all right over here.'

'I know, but we're on a different network,' I replied. 'Signal's not strong enough. He wants me to try and find someone to sort it out. Could hardly get anything in the *pigeonnier* when he was there.'

'Not a lot of pinging going on then?' Debbie replied.

'Doesn't look like it. Bet that drove him mad.' I smiled.

'Nothing to do with the girls watching films on their phones when they weren't supposed to?'

'I was coming to that. Charles thinks we need more APs around the property.'

'More what?' asked Debbie.

'Just googled it. Access points, apparently. He goes on to say that he doesn't care who does it as long as we don't use that clown from down the road – the one who's got a shop next to the supermarket. Made things worse, apparently. I can understand that. Have you seen Charles's all-singing, all-dancing control room?'

'No. Why?' Debbie asked.

'Looks like a plate of spaghetti – cables everywhere. Every time I go in there to reboot the system, I think I'm going to get zapped. Charles has also asked me to make a drawing of the garden. It doesn't have to be to scale but he wants me to pay particular attention to the flowerbeds, or zones as he's called them. He wants me to send ideas about what should be planted in each one. Once we've agreed on the types of flowers and the quantities required, I'm then to take the short trip across the border to Italy, where plants are apparently around thirty percent cheaper than they are in France. This I can do in a day and I can, time permitting of course, sample a real pizza for lunch while I'm there. The man is mad. I'm not a landscape gardener. There's got to be at least fifteen beds here. Wouldn't know where to start. Even Daniel, who's a proper gardener, gets people in to landscape. What is he on?'

'I don't know, but look,' Debbie replied, 'they don't want to spend the money. They've already made that clear. Have you ever been to Italy, by the way?'

'No, but there's a first time for everything.'

Chapter 10

'That must be the chap for the Internet,' I said to Debbie one February morning. As I looked outside our kitchen window, I could see a small, white van that had just pulled up outside the front gates of the villa.

'See you in a bit,' I said as I left our apartment and went down the stairs to greet our visitor.

As the gates opened, I noticed that the man was on the phone. In the other hand he had a lit cigarette that he occasionally flicked without bothering to open the window. He waved at me, smiled, pointed to the place where he wanted to park and carried on his conversation. A few minutes later, he ended his call and got out to introduce himself.

'Sorry about that,' he said, offering his hand. 'One of my yacht clients. Must phone me about ten times a day. You must be Brent.'

'And you must be Ajantha,' I replied.

'Yeah, but most people call me AJ. It's a bit easier to pronounce than Ajantha. I'm originally from Sri Lanka, or Ceylon as it was called when I was born,' he said, walking round to the back of his van and opening one of the doors.

'There's a few things I need,' he said. 'Now, where are they?' Casually dressed in a black t-shirt, three-quarter length khaki chinos and flip-flops, AJ rummaged through several boxes that were scattered all over the back of his van. He'd pick one up, look it at, mutter to himself and throw it back in amongst the others. I could only guess at how much time he'd waste during the day performing this ritual but to him it obviously seemed quite normal. Every now and then he'd chuckle and say, 'I wondered what had happened to that,' and off he'd go again. Was this really the owner of a high-tech IT company based on the Côte D'Azur? That's what it said on his website. *No job too big or too small – From luxury yachts to fabulous villas we've got it all* was the slogan that I remembered.

Having no idea how long AJ was going to be, I sat on the stone wall that led up to the villa and looked up to our apartment, where I could see Debbie staring out of the window and looking bemused. I shrugged my shoulders. Debbie pointed to her watch and it was only then that I realised that AJ had already been with us for nearly half an hour and we were not much further on from the moment he arrived.

Eventually AJ picked up a toolbox, an electrical test meter, a laptop and some small, white boxes. He walked round to the front of the van and placed all of the items on the bonnet. Opening the driver's door, he said, 'Won't be a sec, Brent. Just got to get my fags.' He then reached for a cigarette packet that was on the passenger seat. As I peered over AJ's shoulder, I could see that the floor was covered in ash, bits of cable, biros and bits of scrap paper. More small, empty boxes were tightly squeezed in behind the seats and several empty drinks cans, as well as crisp packets, surrounded the gear stick. 'I really must get this van sorted out. Just never seem to get the time. Bugger, it's empty,' AJ continued, having found his packet of cigarettes. 'Don't suppose you smoke, Brent?'

'No, sorry AJ.'

'Oh, bollocks. I'd just better nip to the *tabac*. I saw one on the way here. Should've stopped then really. If you wouldn't mind getting the gate for me,' he said, putting everything back into the van that he'd just taken out. He jumped into the driver's seat and turned on the ignition.

'Now where's my wallet? Hang on a sec. You know what, Brent?' AJ said as he wound down his window, leaned over and began to search through a pile of paperwork that was on the passenger seat. 'I once drove all the way to Saint Tropez and went to get my wallet and couldn't find it. So, I turned round, went all the way home, which is about an hour and a half away, and you know where it was? Down the side of the seat in here.' He laughed loudly. 'Landed up having to work until about eight that evening. Wife went mad. Was supposed to be picking the kids up from school.' He laughed again. 'Right, got it,' AJ said, waving his wallet triumphantly in the air. 'Who's this now?' he asked, taking his phone out of his pocket. 'Better take it. I'll be back in a minute. See ya.'

I opened the gates and stood there for a few moments, trying to take in what I had just witnessed.

'That was quick,' said Debbie as she sat on the sofa, lacing up her training shoes. 'Did he actually manage to sort anything out?'

'Didn't even manage to get as far as the villa,' I replied, scratching my head.

'Everything OK?'

'I think so,' I said, and then I burst out laughing.

'What's up?' Debbie asked.

'You've never seen anyone so disorganised in your life. He's worse than me and that's saying something. The state of his van,' I began, and then I laughed again. 'It's like a skip on wheels.'

'He's all right, though?'

'Oh God, yeah. He seems really nice. He makes me laugh, which is much more than some of the other so-and-sos that we've met since we've been here. He's as scatty as they come but I'm sure he'll do a good job – if we ever see him again, that is.'

'What are you up to this morning?'

'I've taken a bit of paint from one of the shutters. I'm going to Zolpan to see if they can match it and then...'

'Zolpan? Weird name for a shop.'

'It's all weird round here. And while I'm there, I'm going to pick up some varnish for the garden furniture. I might even pop into the supermarket. Anything you need?'

'Well,' I replied, 'you could pick up a packet of shallots for me.'

'What? What on earth are you going to do with a packet of shallots?'

'I'm going to cook them. What do you think I'm going to do with them? I'm making a beef bourguignon with a creamy mashed potato, I'll have you know.'

Debbie looked surprised. 'This I've got to see,' she said. 'Anyway, there are already two packets in the fridge.'

'No there aren't. I've already looked.'

Debbie opened the fridge door, took out two packets of shallots and passed them to me. 'Make sure you use the oldest packet first. You see that set of numbers on the bottom? It's called a *sell by date*.'

'Oh, funny.'

'Anything else you need me to find for you before I go?'

'Garlic?'

'In the bowl in front of you – along with the onions. Right, I'm off. Try not to burn the place down while I'm gone. Good luck,' Debbie said as she closed the front door behind her.

Seconds later, my phone rang. 'Hello Brent, it's AJ,' said the voice on the other end. 'Sorry, but I'm going to have to reschedule. Big problem in Grasse with one of Putin's mates. I'm off there now. Don't want to go upsetting the Russians. I'll explain when I see you. That's them now,' he said. 'Got to…' and the line went dead.

'How are you getting on?' asked Debbie, who walked into our apartment a couple of hours later, holding two heavy carrier bags.

'OK, thanks. Think I'm getting there. Would you like a hand with those?'

'No thanks, I think I can man…' A look of horror came over Debbie's face. 'Oh, my God, what have you done to my kitchen?' she shrieked as she put down the bags in front of her.

'What do you mean, what have I done to your kitchen?' I asked, looking around.

'The state of it,' Debbie said, staring at the worksurfaces that were covered in dirty pots and pans.

'As Charles said, you can't make an omelette without breaking a few eggs,' I replied.

'I wish you were making a bloody omelette,' Debbie said. 'Maybe this place wouldn't look like a bomb's hit it. Look at this floor. Onion peel all over it – bits of garlic, and what's this?' she asked, staring at a pool of liquid on the floor next to the cooker.

'I spilt the olive oil, sorry.'

'And you didn't think to clear it up before you slipped over and broke your neck?'

'Apparently not.'

'Oh, and please don't put my best knives in here,' Debbie said, opening the dishwasher door and taking them out. 'They'll get ruined. What's going on here, if you don't mind me asking?' she said, looking at the saucepan on top of the cooker.

'I'm thrash-boiling the spuds.'

'You're doing what?'

'Thrash-boiling the spuds. You see…'

'You've been watching that Jamie Oliver again, haven't you?' Debbie interrupted, turning the gas down.

'Might've been.'

'You'd better watch these,' she said, gazing into the pan. 'Don't want them turning to mush instead of mash. And where's the beef?'

'Festering in the fridge.'

'Festering? Marinating is the word I think you're looking for.'

'They all say that at first. You haven't tried it yet.'

Debbie opened the fridge door. 'Bloody hell, boy, how much red wine did you use?'

'A bottle.'

'A bottle!' Debbie shouted. 'How much did the recipe call for?'

'A generous glug.'

'A generous glug is not a bottle,' Debbie said, closing the fridge door.

'It is in my world.'

89

For a few moments Debbie stood silently in the middle of the kitchen, her hands on her hips and shaking her head. She then said, 'Have you ever seen Jamie's kitchen looking like this?'

'He's got a team of people to clear up for him,' I replied, at the same time turning on the hot water tap.

'I'll wash, you dry,' Debbie said, passing me a tea towel out of the bottom drawer.

'Oh. That's where you keep them. I was wondering.'

Debbie didn't reply.

It was about a week later before we saw AJ again. This time, instead of arriving in his van, he turned up in a bright red Citroën 2CV. Jumping out of the car, he said, 'Morning, Brent. How have you been?'

'Good thanks, AJ. And you?'

'Really busy. Sorry about the delay. Anyway, I thought I'd give her a spin today,' he said, looking with pride at his car. 'Not really practical – it's hardly secure,' he continued, looking at the canvass sunroof. 'It's a bit like opening a sardine can.' He laughed. 'Wouldn't leave it in Nice. Be gone in sixty seconds. Have you seen that film?'

'No.'

'You should, it's great.'

Having only brought the tools that he needed this time and with no phone calls, we were soon at the front door of the villa. AJ kicked off his flip-flops and followed me to the kitchen, where I made some coffee.

'How was Grasse in the end?' I asked.

'Fucking nightmare,' replied AJ, who then burst out laughing. I'd only known him for a brief time but it soon became apparent that the worse a situation became, the funnier AJ found it. It didn't matter whether it was him or someone else that was in trouble, the bigger the disaster, the bigger the laugh.

'My business partner, Graham, has been stung for about two hundred grand.'

90

'Really?' I replied.

'Yeah, really,' AJ said, scarcely beginning to contain himself.

'Two hundred thousand euros. Can you believe it?'

'So, what happened?'

'Well,' AJ began, 'he was doing some work for a Polish contractor to kit out a brand-new villa. They knocked the old one down and started again. Anyway, Graham got the contract to supply all of the IT and the media. Basically, top of the range tellies in every room. At ten grand a pop and all of the cabling to go with it, doesn't take much to rack up two hundred K.'

'What went wrong?'

'The Polish bloke asked for two million euros to be wired to his bank account. Russians didn't bat an eyelid. He's been on the Côte D'Azur for years. Got a good reputation. Nice coffee, by the way,' he said.

'Thanks. And then?'

'And then,' replied AJ, putting his cup down next to the sink. 'And then he buggered off. To be more accurate, he and the money buggered off. It'll be in an off-shore account now. He's disappeared off the face of the planet. Hope for his sake the Russians don't get hold of him. Anyway, they'd only just found out when I was here the last time, so I thought I'd better go and see if there's anything I could do to help Graham.'

'And was there?'

'No, not really.'

'Can't he get his stuff back?'

AJ chuckled. 'They've got some very scary-looking men in sharp suits and dark sunglasses on the gates now. Nothing goes in and out of that place without the boss's permission. The way they see it, they've paid for it and if Graham didn't get any money up front, that's his lookout.'

'So, why didn't he get any money up front?'

'It's all thirty-day accounts,' AJ explained. 'And as I said, the Polish builder's got a good reputation. At least, he did have.'

'You said he was your business partner. Are you owed any money?'

'Nah, thank God. He's not really my business partner. I do quite a lot of work with him but we're not technically partners. Just got away with that one. Right, let's go and have a look at your technical room. Your boss pays on time, does he?' AJ asked as we made our way through the dining room and down the stairs.

'Not really a bad installation,' AJ said as he pulled out one cable after another and then put it back. 'Only thing is, it looks like someone's been fiddling around with it.'

'The boss has spent a lot of time down here. Likes his IT.' I replied.

'That's the problem,' AJ explained. 'A little knowledge is a dangerous thing when it comes to these systems. Easy enough to fuck them up. See this filter? Plugged it into the wrong place, which makes it pretty much useless. Pass me my meter, would you?'

While he poked around in the small cupboard at the bottom of the stairs that Charles called the technical room, AJ continued to tell me more stories about the Russians, of whom it seemed he was extremely wary. He told me about one group who came to Cannes, rented out a luxury villa and in the space of a week had managed to cause one hundred thousand euros' worth of damage.

'What happened?' I asked. 'They just wrote out a cheque and left,' replied AJ. 'Loads of money but couldn't give a shit. Pass me that screwdriver, would you?'

Once he'd finished putting everything back together in the technical room, AJ went to check the wi-fi signal in the rest of the villa.

I went to the kitchen to make more coffee, and every now again AJ would shout, 'Dead spot in here, mate,' or 'Bedroom's all right but that's probably not where you really want it.' Whenever he spoke, most of AJ's comments were usually followed by a burst of laughter. Half an hour or so later, we began to walk through the garden towards the *pigeonnier*.

'You're only getting about three megs at best in the villa,' AJ explained. 'Have you tried contacting France Telecom to see if the line's all right?'

'I have.'

'And what did they say?' asked AJ, who took out his cigarettes from the top pocket of his shirt.

'They said that we were at the end of line – that's why the signal is so weak.'

AJ puffed out some smoke and laughed. 'That old chestnut, eh? Never known a villa that wasn't at the end of the line! I'll give their techy guys a call. They won't be able to pull any wool over my eyes.'

'I thought we were supposed to get ten megs.'

'Up to ten megs.' AJ smiled. 'Don't worry, Brent, they cover themselves all right. It's all in the small print. What the big print giveth, the small print taketh away.'

As I opened the front door to the apartment in the *pigeonnier*, AJ nodded his head with approval.

'Nice, very nice,' he said. 'Mind you, with the thickness of these walls, I'm surprised you get anything at all. Won't help that the router's shoved away in this cupboard,' he said, pulling out a black box next to the fuse board. 'Going to require some thinking about, this one. What's the reception like by the pool?'

'That's another area they've complained about. Hardly any signal down there either. There's supposed to be some gubbins or other in the games room which is supposed to boost the signal by the pool, but I've never seen anything.'

'Gubbins, Brent?' AJ smiled. 'Is that a technical term?'

'About as good as I get, I'm afraid.'

'Come on. Let's go and have a look.'

In the past, I'd looked in all of the cupboards behind the bar and under the sink and traced back every electrical cable that I could see in the hope of finding something that remotely looked like an Internet connection. I'd even looked under both the pool and table tennis tables and in one of my madder moments I'd removed the dartboard from the wall to see if there was anything behind it.

'What's behind that door?' AJ asked.

'The technical room for the swimming pool,' I replied.

'Wouldn't have thought that would be the best place, but let's have a look anyway,' AJ replied.

Inside, two motors were whirring away. There were some large, plastic boxes containing pairs of flippers, goggles, dented table tennis balls, shuttlecocks with broken feathers and semi-deflated beach balls. There was a rusty pool heater that should have been discarded many moons ago and empty buckets of chlorine powder stacked up to one side. There were old biros, waterlogged instruction manuals and partially used rolls of insulating tape on the shelves. In each corner of the floor was a small plastic tray containing pellets of blue rat poison.

'Not too well insulated,' said AJ, who had noticed some water trickling down the back wall.

'No, not really,' I replied. 'They didn't bother to waterproof the terrace above when they built it so now when it rains or I get the power washer out, it comes through. Charles is trying to sue the company that built it, but I don't think waterproofing was on the quote.'

'Can't really sue them then, can he?' AJ said, staring up at a hole in the ceiling. 'But I would get it sorted if I were you, Brent. Water and electricity don't mix too well. Don't want to see flames licking up through the floor when you're tucking into your barbecue.'

'Negligence,' I replied. 'He thinks he can do the company that built it for negligence. Says he's got a strong case.'

'Hope not. Because if he does, half the French workforce will be in trouble.' AJ laughed. As he did so, he put his hand up and reached for a cable that disappeared up through the ceiling.

'Any idea where this goes, Brent? Might be our culprit.'

'No, sorry.'

'Let's go and have a look up top.'

I followed AJ upstairs. I felt certain that there was nothing of interest there. I'd been through the small poolside kitchen and had found nothing.

'Here you go!' shouted AJ, who was by the side of the pool and kneeling down next to what looked like a tiny chimney pot. He managed to squeeze his hand through the hole at the top and, moments later, produced a small box, at the top of which protruded two aerials. 'That won't have helped,' he said, gazing at the object. 'Stuck half way down the chimney. Still looks all right, though. Hang on, I'll just get my laptop. I left it downstairs.' Soon after, he was back. 'Not brilliant,' he said, 'but at least you do have a signal now. That should keep 'em happy.'

Chapter 11

It was just after breakfast on the morning of Good Friday when I opened the front door of the villa and wandered into the kitchen. Charles, who had arrived with his family the week before, was sitting at the dining room table with a cup of coffee and some toast. He was staring at his phone and without looking up, he called out, 'Ah, just the person! Brent, have you got a minute?'

'Sure,' I replied, and stood next to Charles.

'Sit,' he said. As I pulled up a chair he continued, 'Need some ideas, right? We want the girls to earn their Easter eggs this year. Belinda thinks they'll appreciate them much more that way and I agree with her.'

'So, how can I help?' I asked.

'I've seen you do cryptic crosswords, so I thought you could think up a few clues for an egg hunt. Nothing too difficult. You need to think like an eight-year-old girl. Got it?'

'It's a long time since I was one of those, Charles, but I'll see what I can do.' Debbie, who was loading the dishwasher, smiled.

'Look, I've bought a bunch of cream eggs, thirty of them to be precise. You need to mark them up. Write 'C' on the first fifteen and 'Z' on the second. You put one of each in a hiding place. You following?' I nodded my head. 'The girls can only collect their own eggs, otherwise they'll be disqualified. Here you go,' Charles said, passing me two boxes. 'You can show me the clues tomorrow. Thanks.'

'Bouncy chicken,' said Debbie as we walked back to our apartment a few minutes later.

'I'm sorry?' I replied, reaching for a piece of A4 paper that was in the printer.

'Bouncy chicken.' Debbie smiled. 'We should put a couple on the trampoline.'

'That'll do. Only another fourteen to go,' I said, sitting down on the sofa and stretching out.

'Would you pass me a felt-tip please?' I asked. 'Got to label these up.'

'Sure, would you like me to peel you a grape at the same? Give you a foot massage – that kind of thing?' Debbie replied. Then she passed me the pen.

The next day, just before lunch, I went to look for Charles.

'He's in the *pigeonnier*,' Debbie said as she picked up a cardboard box full of bottles. 'Couldn't give me hand with these before you go, could you?'

'Sure, where are we off to?' I asked.

'Not far. Just to their private room. They don't want the rental guests using their ingredients while they're away.'

'Does that mean they're not coming back until after the summer? Woo hoo!' I said, a little too loudly for Debbie's liking.

'Shhh, they'll hear you,' she replied. 'Looks that way. Grab that one, would you?' Debbie said, pointing to a large box.

'Bloody hell, how much have you got in here?'

'Oh, come on.' replied Debbie, 'What are you, a man or a mouse?'

'Neither. An eight-year-old girl, apparently.'

When I found Charles, he seemed to have lost interest in the Easter egg hunt.

'You'd better deal with Belinda on this one,' he said. 'It's more her pay grade, really.' I was about to open the door to leave when Charles said, 'Oh, I can't remember if we've told you already but we're having a meeting, ten o'clock Monday. You, me, Belinda and Debbie in the kitchen, right?' I was just about to ask whether we needed to bring anything with us when a text message came through on Charles's phone. For a few moments, he stared intensely and then looked at me. 'Any idea what time it is in Japan, Brent? No, of course you haven't. Why would you?' He sighed. 'Never travel anywhere without a fucking secretary,' he said, quite unashamedly. 'If you see Belinda,' Charles piped up, 'ask her to come over, would you? Think I'm going to need some help here.' And then his phone rang. 'Shit!' he groaned, getting out of his chair. Charles took the call.

'Mister Yakamoto, good afternoon,' he began. 'Or should I say *konnichiwa?*' Charles waved me away and motioned for me to close the door behind me.

'Grovelling little fuck,' I muttered as I made my way out.

On Saturday evening, while Debbie cooked supper for the girls, I walked around the grounds with my list of clues and hid most of the cream eggs. Debbie also had a few to hide in the villa. The plan was, after breakfast on the Sunday morning, Belinda would give a list each to the girls and off they'd go, which would hopefully keep them busy until about lunchtime. Once back, the eggs would be counted, the winner declared, and the family would sit down and enjoy a roast turkey and trimmings that had been prepared by Debbie. Instead of dessert, if the girls preferred, they could each have a cream egg.

On Sunday morning at about six o'clock, I went into the kitchen because I was feeling thirsty. I opened the fridge door, took out a bottle of water and unscrewed the lid. As I shut the door, I noticed something out of the corner of my eye. In the courtyard, which was partially lit by a streetlamp as well as the moon, I could see the figure of a small person who was squatting down and shining a torch.

'Jesus, you made me jump!' I said to Debbie, who had just taken the bottle of water out of my hand.

'Sorry,' replied Debbie. 'This is nice and cold,' she said, having taken a mouthful of water. 'Anyway, what are you doing staring out of the window at this time in the morning?'

'Look down there. You know who that is?'

'I can't really see. I haven't got my contacts in.'

'That's Zoe. She's just found clue fourteen. See this?' I said, picking up the list of clues. 'Under Popeye's girlfriend, next to the front gate.'

'Sorry,' Debbie yawned. 'You'll have to tell me. I'm not properly awake yet.'

'Popeye's girlfriend, Olive. Under the olive tree, next to the gates,' I explained.

'Not as daft as she looks,' replied Debbie. 'Not sure I would've got that one.' As I looked through the window I watched Zoe, who was rummaging around the grass at the bottom of the tree.

'The thing is,' I said, 'if she's done them in order, which, if the amount of eggs in that basket is anything to go by she has, she's nearly got the lot. What baffles me is how she's got the list already?'

'I left them on the dining room table for Belinda to keep until the morning,' Debbie said.

As we watched, Zoe retrieved two eggs, which she examined with her torch. She carefully placed one of them inside the wicker basket beside her and threw the other one over the fence into the field opposite.

'I take it that was one of Caroline's.' I laughed. Zoe then put her hand into her dressing gown pocket and pulled out a piece of paper, which she began to examine with the help of the torch. For a few moments, she stood, deep in thought. She then put her hand in front of her mouth and giggled. I worked out that if she had been following the list in order, her next stop would be at the games room. Zoe began to head that way when next door's cockerel crowed.

Zoe's face turned to panic as she looked up at the sky, which was just beginning to come out of darkness. I watched her mouth the word 'Shit,' before she ran up the driveway towards the villa. As she did so, two or three eggs fell out of the basket and rolled down the drive. Not bothering to retrieve them, Zoe ran back up the drive towards the villa. Momentarily, she disappeared out of sight. Intrigued, I rushed to the back door of our apartment, flung it open and walked to the far end of our small garden. After a few seconds I saw a light come on in one of the bedrooms – Zoe's. As quickly as the light was switched on, it went off.

'That was eventful,' I said to Debbie, who was just coming out of the bathroom. 'What shall we do now?'

'What shall we do now? I don't know about you but it's only half past six. I'm going back to bed. I think that's quite enough excitement for one morning, don't you?' Debbie smiled.

At eight o'clock, Debbie, who was already dressed, said, 'Right, I'm going over to the villa to start the breakfast. There's a couple of Easter eggs that I bought for the girls in the cupboard. Would you bring them over in about half an hour? Might be nice to wish everyone a happy Easter.'

'Sure.'

When I arrived at the villa, Caroline was sitting at the dining room table and poring over her list of clues while toying with her bowl of cornflakes. Belinda was standing at the centre console in the kitchen and pushing down the plunger of a cafetière that had recently been filled.

Still in her dressing gown, she yawned and said, 'Good morning, Brent. Don't usually see you in here this time of day. Everything OK?'

'Great thanks. Just brought these for Caroline and Zoe,' I replied, putting the eggs down next to her.

'Oh, thank you, that's kind. Thanks Debbie.' Belinda smiled. 'Oh, and thanks for organising the egg hunt. I think the girls are really looking forward to it. Mind you, if Zoe's not down soon, she won't get any at all. That's unlike her – she loves chocolate. Caroline, where's the other list? I'm sure there were two. You did print two, didn't you, Brent?'

'I did,' I said as I helped Debbie set the table.

'Caroline, any ideas?'

'No. There was only one on the table when I came down this morning.'

'Are you sure you haven't hidden it from her?'

'Yes,' replied Caroline, 'I'm sure. I'm not that desperate. If I'm honest, I'd much rather be reading a book.'

'Which is one of the reasons we're doing it in the first place. You don't get anywhere near enough exercise, young lady.'

'Zoe gets enough for both of us, the little shit.'

'Do you mind!' snapped Belinda. 'That's your sister you're talking about.'

'I know.'

'Maybe Dad's got it. Zoe, will you get down here now, please?' Belinda shouted from the bottom of the stairs. 'Come on, Caroline's ready to go.' Caroline raised her eyebrows, put the list down and started to eat her cornflakes.

'I'm not going. I'm not feeling very well,' Zoe shouted back.

'Why, what's wrong with you?' asked Belinda, who was beginning to climb the stairs.

As Belinda opened the bedroom door, I heard Zoe say, 'My tummy hurts.'

For a brief moment there was silence, and then Belinda said, quite angrily, 'Oh, my God, Zoe, what have you done?'

'Nothing.'

'It doesn't look like nothing to me, my girl,' Belinda replied. 'There's chocolate all over the bed sheets. What have you been up to? Charles! Charles! I think you'd better come in here,' Belinda called out. 'Let's see what your father has to say about this.'

'Mummy, Mummy,' Zoe cried. 'I think I'm going to be si…' And she was.

'That's my new dressing gown,' Belinda shouted. 'Happy fucking Easter,' I heard her say as one door slammed after another.

Thinking that I was probably much better off away from the situation, slowly I edged my way to the front door, which I opened very quietly. Closing it behind me, I put my shoes on and headed off to visit the chickens at the far end of the olive grove.

At about eleven o'clock, I went back to our apartment, where Debbie was ironing some of Charles's shirts.

'How did it go up there?' I asked.

'Where did you get to?' Debbie replied.

'"Let's hear what your father has to say" was the last thing I remember Belinda saying. Bet he went mad.'

'No, quite the opposite in fact. He said that he was quite proud of her for having taken the initiative, although that's not quite how he put it. "Always pays to be one step ahead of the competition, Zoe. Just disappointed you blew all of the profits the minute you got them." And that was that.'

'Not quite the reaction Belinda was expecting then?'

'That's a bit of an understatement.' Debbie laughed. 'She followed Charles back into their bedroom and shut the door. There was a lot of shouting, mainly from Belinda, but I couldn't really tell what was being said. I can imagine, though. Charles has got a bit of a blind spot when it comes to Zoe.'

'I had noticed. And Caroline?'

'Caroline's Caroline. Couldn't care less. She was just happy to have solved all the clues. When I left, she was in the lounge with a Harry Potter book.'

After breakfast on Monday morning, I went to the villa. Just inside the front door were a dozen or so suitcases that had been left for me to load into the Land Rover. One by one I wheeled them through the gravelled, top car park and began to lift them into Charles's car, in readiness for the family's departure. As I did so, Zoe came running up to tell me that she was much better now and that she was never going to eat another piece of chocolate as long as she lived. She also asked if she could have a cookie.

I'd just finished putting the suitcases into the back of the car when I heard Charles shout, 'Brent! Brent! Where are you, Brent?' And then he whistled. With that, Guss, who had been foraging in amongst the hydrangeas, came skidding past me and belted along towards the villa. He arrived at the front door with his coat and nose covered in pink petals. Charles, who was not looking at all impressed, cupped his hands and was just about to shout for me again when he saw me. 'Come on, Brent,' he said, frowning. 'Meeting at ten o'clock. Where have you been?'

'Loading your car,' I replied. As Charles flung the front door open, I looked at my watch. It was only five to ten but, clearly, Charles was in a hurry.

'Right,' he said as I sat down next to Debbie. There was no sign of Belinda.

'Need to get this out of the way quickly. Got a plane to catch.' He looked at Debbie and me. Picking up a piece of paper that I recognised to be Debbie's weekly report, Charles said, waving it in the air, 'This isn't working. Can't tell anything from this.' He threw it dismissively onto the dining room table.

'That's not true,' replied Debbie, who was looking quite angry. 'It tells you exactly what Brent and I have been doing and what jobs have been completed.'

'I can see that,' snapped Charles, 'but there's nothing here that tells me how much capacity you have left. I don't know from this whether you're working twenty hours a week or fifty. I want to know what you're doing every minute of every day when I'm not here.' Debbie and I looked at each other. 'And I've looked through this several times and there's not one mention of you having gone to Italy, Brent. Why is that?'

'I phoned them,' I replied. 'They weren't any cheaper. They also said...'

'I don't care what they said,' snapped Charles. 'You have clearly disobeyed one of my orders. What's the point in having soldiers if they don't do as they're told?'

'You are joking, Charles?' I said.

'Do I look like I'm joking?' he replied. 'Face to face, you might have got a deal. Use your charm. Schmooze them. I do it all the time. The point is, as you've refused to fill out Belinda's spreadsheet we have no idea where we are, and that makes me mad.'

'I'm sorry, Charles. We've already told you we can't work this way,' said Debbie. 'We're not soldiers. You employed us as a housekeeper and a gardener...'

'I know that,' said Charles, 'but you two are capable of much more and that's what I want, much more. This is not helping me,' he continued, picking

Debbie's report up again. 'But I think we need more boots on the ground, so this is what we're going to do. We've got two Danish friends, Magnus and Frida, who live in the village. When they get back off holiday in two weeks' time, they'll be coming to help out until the start of the season – maybe longer.

And as you're so reluctant to fill out Belinda's spreadsheet, they're going to do it for you. That way, we'll know exactly what's happening here.' Charles's phone rang. He picked it up, answered it and started to walk around the kitchen.

'He's a fucking nut case,' I whispered in Debbie's ear. 'What was that all about?'

Debbie shook her head. 'I don't know but doesn't look good. We'll speak when you get back.'

Hurriedly, and with me in the driver's seat, the family got into the Land Rover. As we left Mas des Collines, Charles's phone rang. Before answering it, he asked everybody to keep quiet. From the conversation it soon became apparent that Charles had been waiting for news of a big deal that he was trying to secure with a company in Japan.

After about ten minutes, Charles put his phone down and shouted, 'Got it! We've got it!' he said, punching the air. 'Thirty million quid. That…'

'Daddy, do you mind if I ask you a question?' Caroline interrupted from the seat behind me.

'Sure, go ahead.'

'Daddy, why are you always talking about money? It can't buy you happiness, you know.'

'I know that, sweetie,' Charles replied, 'but it's more comfortable to cry in a Mercedes than it is on a bicycle. You should never forget that.'

Chapter 12

'So, what do you think, then?' I said to Debbie as soon as I got back from the airport.

'What I think, my love,' she replied, 'is that, unfortunately, this is the beginning of the end.'

'Really?'

'Yes, really,' said Debbie, who was sitting at the computer. 'They're bringing people in over our heads and, as Charles is getting them to report directly to him, I would be surprised if we hear from either Charles or Belinda directly again. Sorry to say, I think we're about to become *personae non gratae*, if we're not already, that is.'

'That's ridiculous. Pierre got away with doing nothing for three years. We've hardly been here any time at all and we've done loads.'

'I know,' said Debbie. 'They've got a real bee in their bonnet about spreadsheets and that is that.'

'So, what are we going to do?' I asked.

'I'm doing it,' she replied. 'I'm looking for another job. I just can't believe this is happening after all we've done for them. Bastards. I've made a list of agencies. If there are any you think I've missed,' said Debbie, passing me a piece of paper, 'let me know.'

Over the coming days, Debbie and I spent most of our time trawling the Internet for *gardiennage* jobs, but there were very few.

When we first arrived in France there were plenty of positions advertised for people who wanted our skills, or Debbie's at least. As one employment agent put it to me, 'You are the oily rag in this arrangement, you know. Anyone can dig a hole in the ground and stick a plant in it. But when it comes to cooking and making sure that the guests are comfortable, that's a different story.'

But then, the jobs started to dry up. Due to the French taxes, a lot of wealthy people had either left France or were thinking about doing so.

They were buying homes in countries such as Croatia, where they could enjoy the same sun, sea, Mediterranean climate and food for about half the price. Even Italy and Spain were reducing taxes to try and attract more visitors, whereas it seemed that the French government's answer to a shrinking economy was to increase revenue by taxing the rich and the businesses more heavily. In the UK the jobs were plentiful, hundreds in fact, but we didn't want to go back. Whether it was due to some sense of misguided loyalty or the fact that we had fallen in love with the south of France and its quirkiness I'm not sure, but we were determined to hang on for as long as we could.

So, we set about applying for the few jobs that were advertised, and one sunny afternoon we were contacted by a very pleasant-sounding chap called Mike. He and his wife, June, were the managers of a property in Noves, a small town about a hundred and twenty-five miles west of Montauroux. They'd been there for a few years but were leaving to complete renovations on a house that they'd bought in the Dordogne a few years previously.

We planned to set off from Mas des Collines early on Thursday morning. That way we'd give ourselves a chance to have a look around Noves before our interview at midday. We also thought that if things went well, we'd find a small *auberge* in which to stay that night and could explore the area further on the Friday. The only problem that we envisaged was the mistral, which was due to blow solidly during the time that we would be there.

'Eighty-kilometre-an-hour winds,' I said to Debbie as I packed our suitcase into the car.

'Oh, good,' she replied. 'You know how I hate the autoroutes. Bloody scary at the best of times. Don't mind if I drive, do you? I think I'd be better that way.'

'No, you go ahead,' I said, passing her the keys to the car. By the time we got to Aix-en-Provence, about an hour and a half away, we could feel the wind picking up. Curtain-sided lorries were swaying under the force of the mistral.

Debbie was driving in the slow lane and breathed a huge sigh of relief every time a heavy goods vehicle got past us. Far from being protected from the elements, as there were vast swathes of open land on either side of the autoroute we were being buffeted from side to side.

'Thank God for that,' Debbie said as we pulled into a small car park next to the town square.

'We're very early,' I replied, looking at my watch. 'It's only half ten. Shall we stop for coffee?'

'After that journey, I'd settle for a large brandy, right now,' said Debbie, who then smiled.

As we got out the car, leaves from the avenue of plane trees that lined the road began to swirl round our feet. People fought against the strong wind that was blowing. Dressed in heavy coats, boots and scarves, the townsfolk of Noves fought their way along the main street. We looked in a few shop windows and then went in search of a café.

'Ouch, Shit!' I shouted.

'What's up?' asked Debbie, who was looking concerned.

'I'll tell you what's up,' I said, pointing at a large, stone ashtray that was lying next to my feet. 'That fucking thing just hit me on the head.'

'Where the hell did that come from?' Debbie replied.

'That's where it came from,' I said, glaring up at the window ledge of a terraced house. 'You'd think they'd know, wouldn't you? I suppose at least it wasn't that bloody flowerpot. Someone could get seriously hurt round here. Bastard place.'

Debbie laughed. 'Shall I call an ambulance?'

'Thank you, Florence Nightingale. No, I don't think so.'

As we sat in a small local café, Debbie said as she peered out of the window, 'Looks a bit desolate here. Not like there's much happening. Most of the shops are shut. Not really what we're used to, is it? Not quite the Côte D'Azur.'

She looked at the chipped paint on the walls and the dated, wooden furniture.

'Supposed to be really popular in the summer,' I said, 'which is just as well – it's like a ghost town now.'

'You have arrived at your destination,' the woman's voice on our GPS declared as we arrived at the entrance to La Grande Bastide, about two miles out of town. We'd driven along several country roads that were flanked by both olive groves and vines. Every now and then we'd see a sign for home-made honey and fresh garden produce. We stopped in front of the main gates and I got out of the car. As I did so, I noticed a bit further down the lane in a ditch a small, white van with a baguette painted on the outside.

'Hello, mate. I'm Mike. Park over there next to the gardeners' truck, if you don't mind,' said a stocky man in his forties as we drove through the villa's gates. 'They'll be off to lunch in a minute. Yep, here they come,' he continued as three men approached from the left of the drive. Mike smiled and waved as they got into their truck. 'Bit windy for them today. Spent most of the morning tidying up,' he explained. 'Good lads, though. We don't really have very much to do with them. They let themselves in and out, which suits me. They're here five days a week. Mrs Pryce, the owner, really likes her garden. She's also got a soft spot for the owner, which is probably why he now drives a Porsche.' He laughed.

Debbie, who had parked the car, walked towards us. Holding tightly onto her scarf with one hand and holding a folder in the other, she struggled against the biting wind.

'Let's go inside,' suggested Mike, who was jumping up and down in an attempt to keep warm. 'Bloody mistral – never got used to it. That's one thing I won't miss when we go. Come on, I'll show you round – after you've met June, that is. You're a good-looking boy,' he said to Guss, who had taken himself off into a bush and returned with a tennis ball that he dropped at my feet. Inside the front door of the villa was a large lobby with a stone floor. Several umbrellas sat in a stand. Wellington boots were alongside them, and raincoats as well as

Barbour jackets were on hooks. To our right was an ornate staircase leading up to a landing where it trailed off to both sides. To the left was a partially open wooden door, through which I could see the kitchen and a woman who was standing at the sink.

'Is that you, Mike?' shouted the woman.

'I hope so. If not, we've got fucking burglars.' He laughed.

'Hello, I'm June,' said a very thin, nervous-looking woman who was drying her hands with a tea towel. 'I wish he wouldn't do that,' she continued, looking at Debbie. 'He knows what I'm like. I'm on pills for my nerves but it doesn't seem to make any difference.' Mike, who had gone to put the kettle on, ignored her. 'I hope you don't mind it quiet,' June said. 'The thing is, sometimes you hardly see a soul for days, except for the gardeners and they don't speak any English and I don't speak any French. Not ideal, is it? I find this place a bit scary, if I'm honest with you. It's so big and there's only two of us here, except when the owners come down. You could be murdered here and no one would know for weeks.' She laughed nervously. 'I haven't put you off, have I?' Debbie shook her head. 'Sorry, I talk too much, don't I? Mike, would you like a hand?' June said, before going over to help her husband with the coffees.

'So,' Mike began as he stood with his feet wide apart and leaning against the glass door that led to the garden, 'best tell you a bit about the job. The owners, Mr and Mrs Pryce, are really nice people. They've got one or two strange habits, but I'll come on to those later. Like all the rich – a bit odd, right? Don't live in the same world as us, do they? But at the end of the day, if you're good to them, they'll really look after you, which is what it's all about. The Pryces are mega rich,' Mike said, proudly. 'Don't know how much they've got but I do know he made his money in South Africa – diamonds, I think. How the other half live, eh? They get private planes everywhere and they take their dog, Scooter, with them wherever they go. Nothing's too good for him, so I hope your dog gets on with other dogs. Where is he, by the way?'

'He's outside, exploring,' I replied. 'Scooter, that's an interesting name for a dog. What breed is it?'

109

'Rat on a string,' said Mike, who then laughed.

'No, it's not,' June snapped. 'It's a Miniature Pinscher.'

'Yeah, and it pinches my arse every time it sees me, the little sod.'

'He knows you don't like him,' June replied.

'Feeling's mutual, my love. Anyway, I digress. The point is, Mr and Mrs Pryce follow the sun. They've got houses all over the world and as soon as the weather starts to turn bad, they're off. So, you should only see them for about three months of the year – if that. They plan well in advance, so I can even give you the dates they'll be here this year. About twelve weeks in total,' Mike said, before slurping a mouthful of coffee. 'When they are here, it's really full-on, but you can make up for it when they go. You don't have to do any gardening, Brent, but your days are going to be pretty long. You've got all of the terraces to keep clean and part of your job is to close all of the shutters at night but not till it gets dark. That can be about ten o'clock. Don't try it before. I did it once. Mrs Pryce went fucking mad. I think Mr Pryce was all right but like many women in this industry, she rules the roost, especially when it comes to the house. Apart from that and doing the odd airport run – oh, and looking after the tennis court, that's about it.'

'Debbie, I understand you're a good cook,' June said.

'I like to cook,' Debbie replied. 'It's a passion of mine.'

'Thing is, Mrs Pryce is very particular about the way she wants certain things done in the kitchen.'

'Go on,' said Debbie, who picked up her notepad and pen from the kitchen table.

'Well, there's a few things, but let's start with breakfast. She likes her grapefruit cut up into segments. They must all be perfect. If you damage one, you mustn't serve it to her. She likes boiled eggs that you must bring up to the boil and leave for two minutes and twelve seconds.' Debbie raised her eyebrows. 'The first few times you do it, she'll be watching you. She likes a new pack of butter every morning and Brent has to collect two fresh baguettes from the boulangerie at seven-thirty. They must be served warm, along with two croissants. They don't eat the croissants, but they do like the smell. Now, lunch…'

Just then, Guss, who had been exploring the grounds, scratched on the glass door behind Mike. 'I'll go and have a look round, if you don't mind,' I suggested.

'Of course,' replied Mike as he opened the door. 'Sooner you than me, mate. Looks a bit blowy out there. Good luck!'

It came as no surprise that the garden was as beautiful as it was extensive. The topiary was perfectly shaped, the lawns were lush-green and there was hardly a weed to be found. There were two life-sized sculptures of horses, which Guss was very wary of and wouldn't approach. There was also one of a wild boar, at which he growled. I found the tennis court, which had rows of seating at either end, and a bit further along I came across the twenty-metre swimming pool that was still heated, even though there were no guests at the villa. As I put my hand in to test the water, I thought that it was hot enough for the average bath. Must cost a small fortune, I thought.

'Heated all year round,' explained Mike once I'd got back to the house. 'Oil, you know. Costs about five grand every three months but they keep it that way in case their daughter wants to come down. She never does, but it's their money, I guess.'

'Anything else you'd like to know, Debbie?' June asked.

'No, I think that's it,' she replied, and then she puffed out her cheeks.

'Sorry, she is quite demanding,' apologised June. 'Takes a bit of getting used to, but I managed it, somehow. Still haven't put you off, have we?'

'Not yet,' said Debbie, who was looking through her notes.

'You got any questions, Brent?'

'Just the one. Not really anything to do with the job but I did notice a van in the ditch opposite when we arrived. What's that all about?'

111

'Oh, that.' Mike laughed, loudly. 'That belongs to Gaston, the baker. Likes the odd Pastis or six. Drove into the ditch on Friday night.

There was a terrible bang, but he was all right. I went out to investigate. He said the steering had failed. Bloody piss head. Can you believe it?'

'And the *gendarmes* didn't do anything?' Debbie said.

'Don't be daft,' Mike replied. 'A *gendarme* round here? You must be joking. Anyway, he's the only baker in town. Needs to drive for his work, and you know what the French are like for their baguettes in the morning. If he lost his job, there'd be a riot. He's also the mayor's son, so that helps. Van'll be gone tomorrow. Basically, it never happened. Anything else, Brent?'

'No, I think you've covered everything pretty well,' I said. 'So, what's the next step?'

'Well,' said Mike. 'We need to speak to the owners. You seem perfectly OK to us. Agreed, June?' She nodded her head. 'We'll be back to you as soon as we can.'

Debbie picked up her notepad and car keys from the kitchen table and was about to say goodbye when June whispered something into Mike's ear. Mike nodded and puffed out his cheeks.

'Everything OK?' I asked.

'Look, Brent, Debbie – there is one thing you should know. Not sure if this is going to make a difference to you but we might as well tell you now,' Mike said. 'The thing is, Mrs Pryce likes to sunbathe naked on the top terrace.'

'Is that it?' I laughed. 'Not a problem. I'll just keep out of her way. I don't want…'

'That's the problem,' Mike interrupted. 'You can't.'

'What do you mean, I can't?' I replied.

'She likes butler service when she's up there. Actually, to put it more precisely, she'll want you to bring her a gin and tonic at about eleven o'clock.'

'Blimey,' I said. 'And you do this, do you?'

'I do,' replied Mike. 'It was a bit odd at first, but I don't really think about it now. There's not much of Mrs Pryce that I haven't seen.' Mike laughed. 'I'm sure you'd get used to it, Brent. And another thing,' he said enthusiastically, 'she would've seen more of me if she'd had the chance. After the first few times I'd done it, and she could see I was more comfortable with the situation, she said I could serve her naked if I wanted to. I politely declined. Not really my sort of thing, but just be aware, in case she asks you.'

'How old is she?' asked Debbie.

'She's in her early seventies,' replied June, 'but you wouldn't know it.'

'And what about Mr Pryce?' said Debbie. 'Does he do the same thing?'

'Not quite,' June said, awkwardly. 'He erm…'

'Go on,' said Mike, who was trying to make light of the situation. 'Spit it out.'

'Well,' said June, 'he likes me to wash his back when he's in the bath. And the thing is, he's not at all shy.'

'Really?' said Debbie, who was looking decidedly uncomfortable. 'How do you mean he's not at all shy?'

'Well, let's just say he doesn't bother with bubble bath. And,' continued June, 'he likes you to rub him down afterwards.'

'Is that all you do for him, June?' Mike asked, sniggering.

'It is,' June replied, firmly. 'That is all I do for him, Mike.'

'Mind you, I was wondering why we got such large tips at the end of the season.' Mike laughed again. 'A couple of grand last year. Anyway, we thought we should let you know. Can't see them changing now.'

'And if we refuse?' asked Debbie, whose mood was clearly worsening. 'What then?'

'Well,' answered Mike, 'I'll explain it to you the way it was explained to us when we arrived. Mrs Pryce will ask you if you have any problem with her sunbathing naked, and if you do she's happy to cover up when you bring her a drink. Mr Pryce will just ask you outright, Debbie. They will both be very polite but if you do refuse that'll be the end of you. Don't forget you're on a three-month trial period and they could come up with any number of reasons why you're not suitable. Not that they need to give you a reason at all.

Of course, they'd never tell you why they really got rid of you. They can't, can they?'

Debbie shook her head in disbelief. 'I'll be back in a minute,' she said, reaching for the side door that led to the car park. As I looked through the kitchen window, I saw that Debbie had found Guss and was standing next to the car.

'She's not looking too happy,' remarked June, who was looking very agitated.

'Not surprised, are you?' I replied. 'Not exactly what we were expecting. In fact, had we known…'

'I guess you won't be taking this any further, then?' Mike interrupted.

'You guess correctly,' I said, and went to join Debbie, leaving Mike and June standing in the middle of the kitchen.

'Bunch of weirdos.' Debbie said as I put my arm round her. 'What a waste of fucking time. Is there anyone who's actually normal in this business? Brent, let's get out of here before I scream. Who the hell do they think they are? And, no, I'm not saying goodbye. Give me the car keys, would you? Come on Guss. Time to go.'

The three of us jumped into the car and Debbie turned on the ignition. She put the car into reverse and wheel span for a metre or two. In the rear-view mirror, I watched as a cloud of dust came up from the gravel. Mike, who was now standing next to his wife, June, in the car park, reached into his pocket and took out the remote control for the gates, which began to slowly open. June, I could see, began to raise her right arm. She was about to wave goodbye but, instead, put her hand over her mouth. As I looked at Debbie I could see tears rolling down her face.

'Are you…?'

'Please don't speak to me, Brent,' Debbie interrupted. 'I just can't. I am so angry. People, fucking people,' she said, and put her foot down.

Chapter 13

'I'm not lazy, I'm useless – there is a difference,' I said to Debbie the following morning over breakfast. She laughed.

'Meaning?' Debbie replied, while buttering some toast.

'I reckon Charles doesn't think I do anything in the garden when he's not here, so he's now bringing in Hans Christian Andersen to give me a hand. Cheeky sod. What do the Danes know about gardening? The country's full of bloody snow!'

'Charles went mad because you didn't go to Italy. He doesn't think you're useless. He wanted you to get some prices so he and Belinda could decide what to put in the beds. So now he's bringing in one of his friends to do it. He's also not happy with me for not sending him any spreadsheets. The man is a control freak – they both are, in fact, so we've got to keep looking.'

As promised, one Monday morning, Magnus and Frida arrived at the front gates. They drove up to the villa, parked and started to unload some suitcases. I said hello and offered my hand but was ignored.

'You're staying here?' I asked.

'Yes,' replied Magnus, quite sternly. 'Didn't Charles tell you?'

'No, he didn't,' I said, quite surprised at what I'd just been told. 'I thought you lived in the village.'

'We do,' said Frida, 'but Charles has asked us to stay until…' And then she stopped.

'Until?' I asked.

'Just until,' said Magnus, who was glaring at his wife. 'Help us with the bags please, Brent.'

Half an hour later, I was back at our apartment. 'You look like you've just seen a ghost. Are you all right, my love?' Debbie asked.

'No, not really,' I said, and then I explained what had just happened.

'Bastards. Fucking bastards,' snapped Debbie. 'They want us out, now. They know that they can't just get rid of us without any warnings, so they're going to make it as uncomfortable as possible for us so we walk out. Did they say anything else?'

'Only that they want the keys — all of them except to our apartment. Other than that, we're to carry on as normal.'

'Carry on as normal?' Debbie replied. 'How are we supposed to do that with those two looking over our shoulders? This is ridiculous. They've been sent here to push us out and if we don't go they're going to try and dig some dirt up on us. They'll be watching our every move, so from now on we need to be on our guard.'

We continued to work as usual over the coming days, although Debbie now had to ring on the bell of the villa to gain access. Sometimes Magnus and Frida would leave the property in the evenings and not return until the following day. As they didn't inform us of their movements, we were never sure who was staying at the villa at night. Charles and Belinda had severed all lines of communication with us. Despite Debbie and I sending several emails and leaving messages on their phones to ask what was going on, we were being ignored.

'They can't force you out just like that,' said Hélène, who had just returned from Paris and was sitting with me in her garden. 'The *Prud'homme* would have a field day.' She laughed, before taking a sip of her coffee. 'We have rules over here, you know. France is a republic — we don't tolerate bullies. We used to cut their heads off for doing exactly that!' Hélène laughed again, this time more loudly. 'We've toned things down a bit now, but we still don't like bullies.'

'The *Prud'homme*, who is he?' I asked.

'It's not really a he,' replied Hélène, who lit a cigarette. 'It's a government body that Charles really doesn't want to mess with. They have enormous powers and they, more often than not, come down on the side of the employee. Can take years to get rid of someone and, even when they do, it can cost the employer a fortune. There was a famous case a long time ago when the owner of a large

116

château came back one day unexpectedly and found his maid in bed with the gardener. He wouldn't have minded but it was the owner's bed that they were in.'

'No way,' I replied.

'Seriously,' Hélène said.

'So, what happened?'

'Being French, she told the owner to get out. Not only that, she tried to sue the owner for invading her privacy. I don't think she won but it took the man years to get rid of her. Cost him a fair bit too, so I shouldn't worry if I were you. With French bureaucracy it'll take them forever to get the paperwork together. Just dig your heels in, is my advice. Stay put, but be careful they don't change the locks on you when you go out.'

Over the next few weeks various workmen of all descriptions came to the property. Magnus would go down to the front gate, greet them and then show them up to the villa. Lorryloads of plants and trees began to arrive. Electricians and plumbers, not previously known to Debbie and I, had also been called.

'Let them get on with it,' Debbie said, as she could see me shaking my head.

'He's taken my job,' I replied. 'We were told they were here to help, not...'

'We were told a lot of things, my love. Charles is full of crap. We know that. Come on, we'll be all right. Do me a favour, would you? Get my stockpot out of the garage. I can't really go and use theirs now.'

'Sure.'

I went downstairs, took out the remote control from my trouser pocket and aimed it at the garage. Nothing happened. The light was green but, just in case, I went back upstairs to get the spare one. Still nothing – the door simply wouldn't open. So I went to search for Magnus, who I found on his hands and knees in the middle of a flowerbed.

'There's a problem with the garage door, Magnus,' I said. 'It won't open.'

117

'There's nothing wrong with the garage,' Magnus replied, a broad grin spreading over his face. 'Charles asked me to change the frequency. He has some valuable things in there that he doesn't think you need to have access to.'

'But our stuff is in there, Magnus. Our belongings,' I said, angrily. 'You can't just kidnap our belongings. That is not legal.'

'We are not kidnapping your belongings,' said Magnus, who was continuing to make a hole in the ground with a trowel. 'If you want something you must ask and then I'll come with you. If this is not convenient, perhaps you should move your goods elsewhere.'

'For example? We haven't been sacked, so why should we move it?' Magnus didn't reply. 'Anyway, we need something now, please.'

'Then, you'll have to wait until lunchtime. Can't you see I'm busy now? Shall we say twelve o'clock?'

When I got back to our apartment, Debbie was sitting on the sofa. I noticed that she had been crying. On the coffee table in front of her was a red plastic basket which was full of dirty laundry.

'What's up?' I asked.

'Bastards, utter bastards,' replied Debbie. 'When you left, I went down to put some washing on and they've changed the lock on the laundry room door. I can't believe it. What are we supposed to do?'

'Have you spoken to Frida?'

'Too right I have. Bitch.'

'She wasn't nasty to you, was she?'

'Oh no. She took great delight in telling me that it was nothing to do with either her or Magnus. They are just following orders, apparently, and if I wanted to take it any further I'd have to speak to either Charles or Belinda.'

'Who aren't talking to us.'

'Correct.'

'Hang on a minute. I'll be back,' I said, reaching for the handle of the front door.

'You're not going to do anything stupid, are you?' Debbie said.

'No, but I have got an idea. See you later.'

'Before you go, did you manage to get my stockpot?'

I turned round, went and sat next to Debbie and explained.

Soon after, I went over the road and explained the situation to Hélène, who had very kindly said that we could use her washing machine. She also said that she had contacted the local *mairie* who had sent her a list of local arbitrators who would be very happy to explain to Charles and Belinda the implications of not abiding by the laws of France when it came to employment.

'This could get nasty,' said Hélène, who was taking some dinner plates out of her kiln. 'Actually, it's beginning to sound like it already has,' she mused. 'You might also want to go to the local police and make a complaint there. Don't think there's much they can do but at least they'll have it on record? How's Debbie?'

'She's OK. Tougher than she looks, that one.' I smiled.

'Looks like she's going to need to be. These things can take months to resolve, so prepare yourselves. Anyway, there's always a bed for you here if you need it. Would you like me to contact an arbitrator for you?'

'That's very kind of you,' I replied, 'but we haven't been sacked yet.'

'Not on paper, maybe,' Hélène said, 'but I think you're going to need all the help you can get. I'll call a few of them for you this afternoon. What do you think of these?' she asked, arranging four or five beautifully decorated plates on the stone table outside.

'Magnificent,' I replied. 'Really magnificent.'

Hélène laughed. 'You would say that whatever they were like, wouldn't you? Not really a boy's thing is it? Ask Debbie to come over later. She'll tell me honestly. And besides, it's been a while since we had a chat. Right, must put the lunch on.'

119

'Great, what have we got?' I asked jokingly as I got up to leave.

'Rabbit stew,' Hélène replied, just before giving me a kiss on the cheek. 'Alain's favourite. He especially loves the head.'

'Right, that's it. I'm off. See you later.'

Over the coming days, any possibility of Debbie and I being able to carry out our duties began to fade. One morning, I went to the pool room to do my weekly checks but, once again, the lock had been changed. Debbie would often go over to the villa at half past eight, complete with her cleaning bucket, only to find that there was nobody there and she had no keys to get in. We desperately wanted to leave but where to? If we walked out, we would have no chance of being paid and, as it was now October, the chances of us finding any work before Christmas were extremely remote.

Then, one sunny morning, Hélène phoned to say that Madame Lefèvre, a former judge from the court of industrial tribunals, was coming to see us on the following Friday. She wanted details of our employment contracts, our salary slips and copies of any written warnings, if we had them. This could not have been better timed as a few days later Debbie and I each received a letter from Charles, sent recorded delivery, stating that our employment had been terminated forthwith and that we had one month to vacate the apartment.

'That's not even his signature,' I said to Debbie as I studied the letter. 'And look, he's managed to post it from France,' I examined the envelope. 'Is there nothing straight about that man?'

'Apparently not,' replied Debbie, who was looking quite shocked. 'What are we going to do?'

'Sit tight. It's all we can do.'

That evening we sat out on the terrace with a pen, paper and a bottle of rosé. With the wood burning stove to keep us warm, we started to make plans, as best we could. We talked about everything from going back to the UK, to housesitting, to maybe trying to find work in either Italy or Spain. Just as we were beginning to get into the flow of things we heard some rustling in the bushes. Guss, who had been lying next to my feet, got up and began to wag his tail. I pulled back one of the branches.

'What the fuck are you doing?' I shouted at Magnus, who was crouched down and holding a small voice recorder.

'I am listening to what you have to say,' he replied, quite unapologetically.

'You're what?' I said.

'Yes, Charles told me to record everything you have to say. You are on his property, so he has a right to know.'

With that, I snatched the recorder out of Magnus's hand, opened the cassette drawer, threw the cassette onto the ground and stamped on it.

'Give me the recorder back!' Magnus snapped.

'Fetch,' I replied, and hurled the recorder as far as I could towards the villa. Both Guss and Magnus went in pursuit. A few minutes later, Guss was back, with the recorder. By midnight, the recorder was sitting at the bottom of the swimming pool.

'This is incredible,' said Debbie. 'All this for not filling out a spreadsheet? The man's deranged, completely bloody deranged. He should be certified. He's seriously worrying me now. Are there no lengths that he won't go to get rid of us? Are you sure we're safe?'

'He's nuts but he's not stupid. We'll be fine, but we need to get this sorted sooner rather than later.'

'You're right there,' Debbie replied. 'We need to be gone before Christmas. I don't think I can stand much more.'

'Well,' said Madame Lefèvre, 'here's a pretty kettle of fish.' She smiled. 'It is an English expression, no? I like English expressions – they make me laugh. We have some of our own but not as good as yours. Please sit down.'

We'd decided to have the meeting at Hélène's, away from prying eyes. As we all gathered around the stone table outside, Madame Lefèvre explained.

'We see this type of thing every day. It is very unfortunate, but you are not alone. Part of the problem is that in the industry in which you work, the employers think that they own you and they can treat you how they like. All it takes is one disagreement and that is the end. Your boss is not much different, except that he appears to be particularly mean. I have spoken to him and…'

'You've spoken to him?' I interrupted.

'Yes, I have spoken to him. I need to hear from both sides.'

'What did he say?' asked Debbie.

'Oh, he gives me the poppycock. I have heard it all before. He says that you have had warnings but when I asked him for them, he can't find them. *Il me prend pour une dinde.*'

Alain and Hélène burst out laughing. Debbie and I looked at each other. Seeing the look of confusion on our faces, Madame Lefèvre explained, 'He takes me for a turkey.' We initially thought that the expression was to do with a turkey being an object of ridicule. It was only much later that I was to discover that the origin was from a turkey being stuffed in the rear. That, according to Madame Lefèvre, was exactly what Charles was trying to do to her, and she wasn't having any of it. 'My advice is that you try and settle this before it gets to court,' she said. 'Although there is no doubt in my mind that you would win, it can take years for your case to come up. It can also be very expensive. You will need a lawyer and the funds to pay for one. I will write to Monsieur Robbins when I get back and explain in no uncertain terms the consequences of the court ruling against him.'

'Which are?' I asked.

'I know one case where the employer was fined one hundred thousand euros, numerous where bank accounts have been frozen and others where the employer's house was seized. I think that will focus his mind, don't you?' Debbie and I smiled.

'Thank you so much,' Debbie said with a tear in her eye. 'I can't tell you how much you being here today has meant to us.'

'It's my pleasure,' replied Madame Lefèvre, who reached into her handbag for her car keys.

122

'It might not seem like it now, but you'll be fine, you'll see. You're not the first and you certainly won't be the last. I think I'm busier since I retired.' She laughed. 'If there's anything you need, just give me a call but I don't think this is going to go on for very long.'

'You think it will be settled before Christmas?' Debbie said, hopefully.

'What are we now?' Madame Lefèvre replied. 'The middle of October. I would have thought so. I'm sure he'll try and wriggle for a bit but if he's got any sense, yes, I think you'll be away from here by Christmas.'

Madame Lefèvre got into her car and opened the window. She said something to Alain and Hélène that I didn't understand, but there were smiles all round. As we waved goodbye, Debbie and I felt much happier than we were before our meeting that afternoon.

'It's not over yet but I think this calls for a celebration,' said Hélène, who walked into the kitchen and returned soon after with a bottle of rosé.

Chapter 14

Madame Lefèvre was right. A few weeks later, Charles agreed to pay us a few months' salary on condition that we left Mas des Collines as soon as the money arrived in our bank account. Debbie and I had spent many an hour, before we left our apartment for the final time, looking for somewhere to stay temporarily as well as a place to store our furniture. And then, one crisp and sunny morning, a week before Christmas, a man in a large removal lorry, who was due to have arrived an hour earlier, beeped his horn just outside the front gate. With the road being quite narrow outside and the gates not very wide, the driver had to make a few manoeuvres before parking in the middle of the courtyard.

'Right in the middle of the sticks, aren't you?' said a tall, burly man with an Australian accent as he jumped out of his lorry. 'Hi mate, my name's Michael but most people in these parts call me Skippy.' He laughed. 'Sorry I'm a bit late,' he continued, looking at his watch. 'Been flat out like a lizard drinking. Won't be minute. Left my phone in the cab.'

As he turned round, I mouthed to Debbie, 'Flat out like...' She shrugged her shoulders.

'Would you like a coffee?' Debbie asked as soon as he got back. She was smiling and very relieved that this day, as well as the driver, had finally arrived.

'That'd be great, love,' he replied. 'White, three sugars please.'

'I'm just going to get the great Dane to open the garage,' I said, before walking up the driveway. Magnus and Frida were having breakfast on the terrace at the end of the villa. On the table in front of them there were plates of cheese, ham, something pickled and a pot of coffee.

'I'm here to...' Without looking at me or answering, Magnus took a remote control out of his trouser pocket and placed it on the table next to me. He took a bite out of a piece of crispbread and said something to his wife in Danish. She laughed loudly.

'So, you're not leaving on the best of terms, then?' I heard Skippy say to

Debbie, who had just given him a brief rundown of our situation. 'Sounds like you're better off out of it. If it was me, I doubt your ex-boss would have any teeth left by now.' He laughed. 'Come on, let's get this loaded. Thanks for the coffee, Debbie,' he said, passing her his empty cup.

Two hours later, the curtain-sided truck was loaded and Skippy was fastening the final strap.

'Do you think we should say goodbye?' Debbie asked.

'Do I fuck!' I replied. 'Come on, let's get out of here.'

'We'll follow you,' I said to Skippy. 'You know the storage unit in Cannes, where we're going?'

'I do. Been there thousands of times,' he said as he started his engine.

As Skippy edged his way out of the gates, a car screeched to a halt inches away from the truck's front bumper. An argument then ensued between Skippy and the Frenchman, neither of which could understand what the other was saying. It did, however, result in the driver of the French car refusing to reverse. Not only that, in the space of only a couple of minutes, two more cars had pulled up behind the Frenchman and were hooting their horns.

So reluctantly, our new Australian friend gave in, though not before shouting, 'Fucking galah!' at the top of his voice as the French car passed, along with the others. 'Sorry about that, Debbie.' As Skippy tried to manoeuvre his lorry back onto the narrow lane, there was a huge bang. Skippy had reversed into the pillar that supported the left-hand gate, which was now dangling by the top hinge. He wound down his window and shouted to me, 'Shall I tell…'

'No, just put your foot down,' I shouted back. Not needing to ask twice, Skippy laughed and sped off.

Although Debbie was driving, I noticed in our rear-view mirror that Magnus was running down the drive. I smiled. I then watched as he ran back up the driveway, presumably to get his car. As we followed Skippy, I dialled his number.

'Pull over as soon as you can and then follow us,' I said. Realising that I

125

still had the remote controls for the garage and the gate on my lap, I opened my window and launched both into the Montauroux countryside.

Moments later and with Skippy following us, we drove off the lane and continued along a dirt track that I hoped that Magnus would not know. At the end of the track was a large roundabout that we would have to pass if we were heading to the autoroute. Twenty yards before the roundabout, Debbie stopped the car. I jumped out and peered over a hedge and waited. To our left was the road to Grasse and straight over was the dual carriageway that led to the autoroute. Which way was Magnus going to go? I didn't have to wait long for the answer. The Land Rover, belonging to Charles, came speeding along the carriageway with its headlights on full beam. It stopped at the give way sign and then raced off towards the autoroute.

'There he goes,' I said to Skippy, who had come to join me. 'Come on, let's get out of here.'

'I take it he doesn't know where you're going?' Skippy asked.

'Last person I'd tell,' I replied.

We got back in our respective vehicles and slowly meandered our way through the back roads to Cannes via Grasse.

As we pulled into the storage unit, Skippy got out of his truck and burst out laughing. 'God repays debts without money,' he said.

'That's true,' I agreed. 'Mind you, that gate's going to cost a fair bit to fix. Happy Christmas, Charles.'

We'd found a place to stay over Christmas in the seaside town of Cap D'Agde, forty miles west of Montpellier. There, we'd be able to recharge our batteries, get Charles and Belinda out of our systems and work out a plan for the new year. The photos that we had seen of the apartment, which was owned by a young English lady, looked inviting and the town seemed vibrant, full of small restaurants and cafés. In the winter the laws in France forbidding dogs on the beach were usually quite relaxed, so there would be plenty of space for Guss to run around.

After a three-and-a-half-hour drive, Debbie and I pulled up in a side street opposite some iron gates. It was two o'clock in the afternoon and we were due to be met by the owner's representative, Michael. By a quarter past two, there was no sign of him, or anybody else for that matter – there was no one about. The wind was howling, spots of rain were starting to fall on our windscreen and Debbie was beginning to get quite agitated.

'We'd better phone,' she said, snatching her bag from behind the passenger seat. 'Better bloody turn up.' Debbie dialled the number. Moments later, she hung up and shook her head. 'Been delayed apparently. Had to go to the doctors. Will be here at three.'

'And he didn't think to phone us?' I asked.

'He would have done but he's got an English mobile and he can't phone France.'

'Good grief. What shall we do?'

Debbie turned on the ignition. 'No point in hanging around here. Let's go and see what's around.'

We headed for the seafront. As we drove along, sprays of water from the choppy sea came over the walls and onto the road. Rusty metal signs on A-boards outside the cafés flapped in the wind. There were a few people walking with their dogs, while holding onto their hats at the same time. We noticed that there were very few shops open and most of the restaurants had signs in the window with *Fermeture Annuelle – Ouverture Février 2015* written in large black ink.

'Not open until February,' Debbie said, and then she sighed. 'The owner mentioned that it was really quiet and relaxing here this time of year. She didn't tell me it was a bloody cemetery.'

I laughed. 'Come on, let's go back.'

At ten past three a skinny man in his twenties came walking towards us. He was wearing a red body-warmer, jeans that came up to just below his waist and I noticed that the tops of his training shoes were coming away from the soles. As he walked, he inserted a nasal spray into his right nostril and sniffed quite heavily.

He repeated the procedure with his left nostril, turned towards the gate that was the entrance to the apartment block where we were due to be staying and then spat. Debbie was about to turn on the ignition and presumably drive off when the man noticed us. 'Hello,' he said as Debbie wound down her window. 'I'm Michael. Sorry I'm late. Been to the doctors. Got a bit of a…' Before he had chance to finish, Michael threw back his head and then sneezed into his hands, which he rubbed together and wiped down the side of his jeans.

'What do you reckon?' I said to Debbie, who was looking reluctant to move.

'We're here now,' she reasoned. 'Might as well have a look.'

As we got out of the car, Michael smiled and offered his hand.

Debbie smiled. 'Do you mind if I don't?' she said, looking warily at Michael's hand.

For a moment he seemed confused. He then laughed nervously and said, 'Oh, oh I see. Never really thought about it before. Follow me, please.'

We walked through the courtyard. Weeds grew up between the paving stones and we could see that some of the owners hadn't bothered clearing up after their dogs. Once inside, Debbie, Michael, Guss and I stood closely huddled together in a lift that took us to the seventh floor. Debbie turned her back to Michael, took a tissue out of her handbag and held it over her mouth. Michael let out a small sigh and raised his eyebrows.

'Here you go,' said Michael, opening the door to the apartment. Debbie walked past him, stared at the gas bottle in the kitchen, scowled at the painting of a female, Spanish Flamenco dancer in the lounge and looked disdainfully at the pink quilt cover in the bedroom.

'This isn't it,' Debbie said, scornfully.

'This isn't what?' replied Michael, who was standing next to the cooker and shoving his nasal spray up his nose again.

'This is not the apartment that I saw in the advert,' Debbie snapped. 'It's nothing like it!'

'Must be the other one then,' said Michael, swapping nostrils.

'What other one?' asked Debbie, who was in no mood to be messed around.

'She's got another one down the road. It's just been done up. It's really nice. It's…'

'Can we see it then?' interrupted Debbie. 'As that is the one we thought we were going to be staying in. You know, the one that was advertised?'

'I'm sorry, you can't,' replied Michael, who put his spray into his jacket pocket. 'That's better,' he said, breathing in deeply through his nose and looking very pleased with himself. 'It's rented out. Went almost straightaway. You should see it, it's love…'

'You've got to be kidding me,' Debbie said. 'Come on, Guss,' she said, attaching his lead to his collar.

'I take it you won't be staying then?' Michael asked.

'You're too fucking right we won't be staying!' Debbie replied angrily. 'You can keep this shit tip, your one-horse town and your stinking bloody cold. We're off. Jesus!'

'I don't think there's any need…'

'Oh, piss off!' interrupted Debbie as she walked through the front door. 'Three and a half hours. Three and a half bloody hours it's taken us to get here! Lucky we don't sue you.'

'I think it's blocked again,' said Michael as he took his spray out of his pocket and gently closed the front door behind us.

'Where to now?' I asked as I sat in the passenger seat of our car. Debbie looked up towards the apartment where we had just been and shook her head.

'I don't care,' she replied. 'As long as it's away from this godforsaken place.' We made our way to the end of the road.

'There's a sign there for the A8,' I said. 'Let's head back to familiar territory. We can stop half way. Drive for an hour to two, grab something to eat and find a cheap hotel.'

129

'Sounds like a plan,' Debbie replied, 'but I'll tell you one thing, Brent – I'm not driving all the way back.'

'I wouldn't expect you to.'

'You say that now, but I know what you're like.' Debbie smiled as we turned the corner. 'You won't be happy until we're back that way, but I'm not doing it. I think I've driven enough for one day.'

Four hours later we were almost in Saint Raphaël, less than an hour away from where we'd originally started that morning. Debbie and I weren't speaking to each other as I'd managed to find excuses for turning down every restaurant and hotel along the way. Not only that, I insisted on trying to justify all of my reasons for not wanting to stay at one establishment or other. Rather than helping the situation, it seemed to worsen Debbie's mood, who was by then tired, hungry and very fed up with driving.

'That's it,' said Debbie. 'The first place we see, we stop. I don't care how much it costs, I want something to eat and a good night's sleep.'

As we approached the centre of Saint Raphaël we joined what turned out to be a very long traffic jam. The Christmas market was in full swing and many of the roads had been cordoned off. In a vain attempt to cheer up the motorists, some street artists, standing on stilts and dressed in some very glamourous costumes, stood at the kerbside, waving. They were greeted by children waving back and drivers shouting profanities at them in equal measures.

'Why is it,' I asked, 'whenever there's a traffic jam, there's always a policeman standing at the front of it?' Debbie smiled. 'Look at him, we've been sitting here for nearly an hour now and what's he doing? Waving his arms around like a bloody windmill!'

'Is that how long we've been here, an hour?' said Debbie. She yawned.

'I'm afraid so. Look, there's a side street just there and it's empty. Maybe we could cut through this. What do you reckon?'

'As long as you're sure. No one else has taken it.'

'Of course I'm not sure. I don't know this town any better than you do.'

'OK,' said Debbie. 'Let's give it a go.' Debbie turned right. We went down the empty one-way street, turned right again and re-joined the back of the traffic jam where we had been an hour ago.

'Nice work, Einstein,' said Debbie, just before leaning forward and putting her head on the steering wheel. I thought it best to say nothing.

At about nine o'clock that evening and having been in the jam for a good two hours, we found ourselves opposite a very luxurious hotel. Debbie noticed a parking space outside one of the shops opposite and pulled in.

'You'd better go and ask,' said Debbie, who was gazing at her reflection in the rear-view mirror. 'I can't go in looking like this.'

'You can't go in? How do I look?' I replied, looking at my coffee-stained, white polo shirt and old jeans.

'Like an unmade bed, if I'm honest.' Debbie laughed. Reluctantly, I got out of the car, went round to Debbie's side of the car and waited for a gap in the busy traffic. I tapped on Debbie's window, which she wound down.

'What if people start offering me loose change?' I asked. Debbie laughed.

'Off you go and be quick about it. I'm starving,' she replied.

As I walked into the entrance of the grand lobby, I was passed by several people who were in evening dress. Ladies in elegant ballgowns swooped past without so much as giving me a second look. I noticed a few gentlemen wearing tuxedos who were making their way out of the building and carrying enormous cigars. Two large, crystal chandeliers shone brightly in the middle of the room and a full-length mirror adjacent to the toilets highlighted my immaculate dress sense. I placed my right hand over the stain on my shirt and made my way to the reception desk, where I was greeted by a young lady.

'*Oui, monsieur*,' she said.

'Do you have a room available for this evening?' I asked.

'Yes,' she replied, looking down at her schedule. 'How many persons?'

'Just two and a dog.'

'A small dog?'

'No, not really. Medium, I'd say.' The woman began to look at me suspiciously. Many times when I'd taken Guss out for a walk and had encountered some small children and their parents coming the other way, I'd often hear the youngsters shout, '*Loup!*', or 'Wolf!' Nonetheless, the receptionist didn't seem too bothered. I seemed to have done enough to get us a room for the night and that was all that counted at that moment.

'Do you have any room in the restaurant?' I asked.

'As you can see,' replied the receptionist, who was being handed a room key by one of the elegantly dressed ladies, 'we have several Christmas parties here this evening, but we may be able to squeeze you in – provided you have a jacket and tie, that is.'

Five minutes later, I was back at the car. Debbie wound down her window.

'So, what did they say?'

'We've got a room for the night.'

'Great,' replied Debbie, who then let out a huge sigh of relief. 'And what about something to eat?'

'They're full, I'm afraid, but there is a pizzeria down the road. Very good apparently.' Debbie didn't bother to reply. Instead, she took the keys out of the ignition, opened her door, got out and wearily made her way to the back of the car. She opened the door. Guss sat up, put his chin between the headrests and watched to see what we were going to do next.

'Oh, shit,' Debbie said.

'What's up?'

'When we left Montauroux, I didn't think it would matter in what order we packed the car. We were supposed to be staying in that bloody apartment for a month.'

'And that makes a difference because?'

'And that makes a difference because, my love, the two suitcases that we need for tonight are at the back and we've got all of these bags in front of them. Come on, give me a hand.'

In full view of the bemused hordes of Christmas shoppers in Saint Raphaël, Debbie and I began to unload the contents of our car onto the pavement – and it wasn't just carrier bags. Much to the amusement of the passers-by, our forty-two-inch plasma screen also had to come out of the car. Tins of dog food and a dog bowl were also on the pavement and the edges of the duvet which had been used to shield our goods from prying eyes were getting trampled on by all and sundry.

After what felt like an eternity, Debbie, Guss and I made our way across to the hotel. Soon we were making our way up to our room. As we stood in the lift on the ground floor, waiting for the doors to shut, a woman walked towards us. 'Which floor?' I asked. The woman looked at Debbie and I, looked down at Guss and then headed for the staircase.

'Charming,' Debbie said as she pressed the button for the fourth floor. 'Anyway, I'm not quite sure what you did that for.'

'Did what for?'

'Book a room with a sea view. It's pitch bloody black outside, you fool.' Debbie laughed.

'I didn't book a room with a sea view. What do you think I am? Mad?' I replied indignantly.

'I think you'll find you did. Thought it was a bit odd. So did the receptionist for that matter.'

'Oh, bloody hell,' I said. 'Do you want me to go and change it?' I asked as a ringing in the lift signalled our arrival at the fourth floor.

'No time, my love,' replied Debbie. 'Too much to do.'

'How do you mean?'

'Well, you go and find us something to eat, while I…' Debbie stood in thought for a few moments.

'While you?'

'While I get on the Internet and try and find us somewhere to live. Tomorrow is Christmas Eve and to all intents and purposes, right now, we're homeless.'

133

Chapter 15

I woke up the following morning at about three o'clock, in need of the bathroom. Debbie was not beside me, but I noticed that there was a lamp on in the small sitting room. 'What are you up to?' I asked.

'Just looking,' replied Debbie, who was in her dressing gown and sitting at a small writing desk with her computer in front of her.

'Been up long?' I asked.

'About an hour.'

'Found anything?'

'Maybe one in Antibes,' she replied. 'Come on, sit down. I'll show you.'

'Just need the loo. Won't be a sec.'

By the time I returned, Debbie had put some pictures up of a small house on her screen. 'What do you think?' she asked.

'Seems reasonable. That bedroom's different. Looks more like a cave. The walls aren't flat. Are you sure it doesn't belong to the Flintstones?'

Debbie smiled. 'I thought that might appeal to you. Rustic charm is how it's been described.'

'Not sure how charming it will be if you hit your head on one of those boulders in the middle of the night. That'd hurt.'

Debbie smiled again. 'Pass me my water, would you?'

I reached over to the coffee table. 'So, what's the deal?'

'The deal is,' replied Debbie, who was replacing the cap on her bottle, 'it's available between now and the beginning of May, after which the prices go up from eight hundred euros a month to eight hundred euros a week.'

'Bloody hell.'

'I know, but May's when the tourist season starts. Besides, we need to have found a job by then, otherwise we'll run out of money. Anyway, I've sent an email – just hope they haven't packed up for Christmas.'

'Was there anything else?'

'Not that I could see,' replied Debbie, who stood up and reached for the switch on the table lamp. 'I'm off to bed. Too tired to do anything more now.'

At eight o'clock that morning, my phone rang. 'Hello,' I said, wearily.

'Hello, this is Sally here,' replied a very frantic voice. 'You've asked about the house in Antibes and you want it today?'

'Yes,' I replied.

'That's really short notice but it is available. It needs a bit of a clean. I'm going there now. Can you be there for eleven o'clock? Try not to be late, only I'm picking my family up from the airport. They're coming for Christmas, from Leeds. I'll send you directions to the house now. It's down one of the backstreets which is pedestrianised, so you'll have to park up and walk. Sorry about that. It'll have to be cash. Is that OK? See you later. Byeeeeee!' she shouted in a shrill voice.

By nine o'clock we'd checked out of the hotel and were following signs to the A8.

'I hope it'll be all right,' I said as I typed the address into our GPS.

'To be honest with you, after the last few days we've had I don't really care as long as it's not a complete tip,' Debbie replied. 'I just want somewhere to relax for a while. I'm just glad to be away from Montauroux. Anyway, I'm sure it'll be fine.'

We drove towards the town centre in Antibes and parked in an underground car park next to the post office. The town was packed full of shoppers and there was a queue to one of the *boulangeries* that stretched back for a hundred yards or so. Far from being stressed about the wait, the French customers appeared to be used to this and were laughing and joking with each other. Debbie, Guss and I walked through a small maze of streets until we came across a terraced house with the front door wide open. Inside, there was a woman on her hands and knees, who was scrubbing the kitchen floor. I tapped on the doorframe.

'Oh, hello,' said a woman in her early thirties. 'I'm Sally,' she continued,

135

while standing up and removing her pink marigolds. 'Glad you made it,' she said, looking at her watch. She smiled. 'And early too. Did I tell you I have to leave for the airport soon? Why don't you have a look around? I'm nearly done here. Bedrooms downstairs. Hello lad, you're gorgeous,' she said, patting Guss on the head.

'Is the kitchen fully equipped?' asked Debbie, who was scanning what was to her the most important room in the house.

'Pretty much,' Sally replied. 'Although, there isn't an oven, but you can always get a portable one from the shop down the road. Follow the sign to Port Vauban – it's just before the archway. Don't think they're very dear.'

Beyond the kitchen was a small lounge with a television and a very comfortable-looking sofa. On that sofa were several cushions with brightly embroidered covers. To the right was a staircase that led down to the bedroom.

'This is even better than I thought,' I said to Debbie, who was just behind me.

'Definitely a boy's bedroom,' she replied as she looked quizzically at the granite walls. 'Not much light in here either. It's a bit dingy, if I'm honest.' Debbie was right. As we looked around, we could see that the only source of natural light was a tiny window that looked onto the street above. As we watched, we saw the ankles and feet of several passers-by as they made their way through the backstreets of Antibes.

'What do you reckon?' I asked.

'What I reckon,' Debbie replied, 'is that for now we don't have much choice. In fact, we have no choice at all. Anyway, it might be all right. And if it's not, we only have to stay for a month.' Debbie smiled. 'This place might really grow on me. Who knows? It's totally different from where we've ever been, and you know what? For once we're not completely isolated. We've got shops and restaurants. Actually, I think we're really going to like it here. Yes, I have a good feeling…'

'Are you OK down there?' interrupted a voice from the top of the stairs.

'Yes, we're fine thank you, Sally,' I replied.

'Look, I'm sorry to rush you, but I really do need to get going now. Can you tell me what you've decided?'

'We'll take it,' I said as I climbed the stairs. I took my wallet out of my trouser pocket.

'That's great,' replied Sally, who began to count the eight hundred euros that I'd just passed to her. 'Any problems, just call. You've got my number.' When she'd finished counting, she passed me two keys. 'One each,' she said, smiling. 'Couldn't be simpler.'

'Thank you,' replied Debbie, who had joined us.

'You're welcome,' replied Sally. 'Merry Christmas,' and with that she hurried down the street and disappeared in amongst the crowds.

'What's the plan, Stan?' I said to Debbie, who had just shut the front door.

'You go and see if you can find us an oven while I go shopping.'

'Don't you think we should get our stuff out of the car first?'

'No,' said Debbie. 'The French don't celebrate Christmas Day – they celebrate Christmas Eve. If we don't get a move on, the shops will be shut, and not only will we not have a turkey, we'll have nothing to cook the bloody thing in.' I laughed. Leaving Guss behind to guard our new home, Debbie headed off in search of food, while I began to ask the Christmas shoppers for directions to Port Vauban.

'Blimey, that was a struggle,' said Debbie, who arrived back at the house a couple of hours later. She placed two carrier bags that were full to the brim just inside the front door. Gasping for breath, she reached for a glass and poured herself some water from the tap. 'I see you've got an oven then,' she continued, looking at the shiny new appliance that I'd put on top of the work surface.

'That wasn't easy either,' I said, and then I smiled.

'Why so?'

'It was the only one in the shop – it was on display, so they didn't want to sell it.'

'Why ever not?' Debbie asked.

'Something to do with not wanting to leave a gap on the shelf. Makes the shop look empty, apparently,' I replied.

'Oh, for heaven's sake,' Debbie said, who was beginning to unpack the carrier bags.

'It was only when I explained our predicament and that the oven wasn't a gift, the shop's manager decided to let it go. There is a small scratch on it, by the way.'

'I'm not worried about that, so long as it can cook this beast,' Debbie said, producing a turkey large enough to feed a small army. I laughed. Debbie went over to the oven and opened the door. 'Just,' she said, placing the turkey inside. 'No room for the roast potatoes, though. They'll have to be done separately. Never mind. Oh, and you won't believe this…'

'I won't believe what?' I interrupted.

'Not a single fresh Brussel sprout in the town. I must have visited six or seven shops. Not a one. Can you believe it? Sold out.'

'Either that or the French don't like Brussel sprouts. Can't blame them really. I remember my grandmother used to put them on in November.' Debbie laughed. 'Bloody hell, they were horrible. Stewed Brussel sprouts. Can't think of anything worse.'

'Ah, but look,' said Debbie, who produced a tin from one of the bags. 'Not completely foiled.' She smiled.

'Tinned Brussel sprouts,' I said. 'Good grief. I hope they taste better than they look in that photo. Looks more like a warning to try and put people off instead of a *Come and get me*. Have you taken leave of your senses?'

'You can't have Christmas lunch without a Brussel sprout,' replied Debbie. 'Those are the rules. Anyway, have you managed to get any of the bags out of the car?'

'Done it.'

'Wow.'

'Yeah, but we do need to move the car. That car park is quite expensive. Apparently, it's free down by the sea this time of year.'

'Good idea, but not today or tomorrow, hey?' replied Debbie. 'Let's just enjoy Christmas, starting from now,' she continued, opening a kitchen drawer and passing me a corkscrew.

Christmas morning began with smoked salmon, scrambled eggs and a Kir Royal for breakfast.

'Not bad for two people who this time yesterday were homeless. Here's to Sally,' Debbie said, raising her glass and smiling.

Christmas lunch with our small oven was a complete success, except for the Brussel sprouts which were consigned to the bin after one mouthful.

'I thought that by adding some butter and black pepper, they'd be all right. Never mind, we'll know for next year. You never know – might still be here.'

'Two Christmases in the same house?' I replied. 'That would be some kind of a record for us.' Debbie laughed.

By the twenty-eighth of December, we'd settled into our new home. With no sign of a tumble dryer or an outside terrace, we'd put up a small washing line in the bedroom, which ran from the small window to the right side of the bed. It also crossed the stairs at about head height. Forgetting it was there, I walked into it on a few occasions in the middle of the night, nearly garrotting myself in the process.

On the morning of the twenty-ninth, at about five o'clock, I woke up in need of the bathroom and began to get out of bed. 'Bloody hell fire!' I shouted.

'What's up?' asked Debbie, who was barely awake.

'What's up is the floor,' I replied. 'It's bloody soaking.' I reached for my phone and shone the torch.

'Shall I put the light on?' asked Debbie, who was coming to.

'No, not until I see how it is. Not sure if the water's got as high as the plugs.' As I walked around the bedroom, I felt that the water was ankle-high, and it seemed to be coming through the middle of the wall at the far end of the bedroom. The base of the bed was sodden and water had got into the wardrobes. I pulled out our empty suitcases and put them on a chair. 'I'll be back in a minute,' I said to Debbie.

'Where are you off to?' she said, sitting up and trying to focus through the dim light.

'To turn the water off,' I replied as I picked up my training shoes and headed towards the stairs. 'The water meter's just outside the front door. Sorry, you're going to have to get dressed in the dark or take your clothes upstairs.'

'Fucking hell.'

By ten o'clock, Sally was at the front door.

'They were supposed to have fixed it,' she said quite angrily. 'Bloody French plumber. There was a burst pipe behind the wall in the bedroom about a month before you arrived. They fixed it, or so they said. It's been drying out since then. I've only just got rid of the smell of damp. Now look at it. I blame the owner. Cheap bloody labour is what it is. Doesn't want to pay the money and now look.'

'So, what are we going to do?' asked Debbie, who turned the tap on in the kitchen, only for nothing to come out. Quite forcefully, she put her cup down on the draining board.

'Well, you can't stay here,' Sally replied. 'It's a health hazard. And besides, I need to get the workers back – bloody cowboys.'

'Have you got any other properties?' I asked.

'I have, but they're all full,' Sally replied. Debbie let out a sigh.

'Look, I've some friends who've got their own property rental business. I'll give them a call. Give me until lunchtime, could you? I've just got to get some keys from someone.' And off she went.

140

'Is it us?' asked Debbie as she closed the front door. 'I can't believe this happens to other people. I mean, we haven't been here five minutes and I was just beginning to get to know the backstreets and the shops. Suppose we'd better start packing again. How are the cases?'

'Nearly dry.'

'That's something, I suppose.'

'Anyway, it might be a blessing in disguise.'

'How do you mean? asked Debbie, who was taking her knives out of the kitchen drawer.

'Well,' I began, 'there's only one exit – the front door. The window in the bedroom is too small for anyone to get through.'

'Your point?'

'If there'd been a fire upstairs and we were in the bedroom, we would have had it.'

True to her word, at lunchtime Sally phoned.

'Good news,' she said. 'They've got a top floor apartment just down the road, right next to the covered market. It's on two floors and there's a terrace which is a bit of a suntrap. It's only a few minutes from where you are now. They want to know if you can be there in half an hour. I'll send you the address. Is that OK?'

'Sure,' I replied.

'I love that market,' said Debbie, who was warming to the idea. 'Fresh fruit and vegetables every day and a fishmonger. If that's where I think it is, it would be ideal. Not sure where we're going to park though. I don't think there's any spaces round there.'

We were greeted at the front door of the property by two well-dressed ladies and a small black Shih Tzu that Guss found quite fascinating. He had been well-groomed and had a huge fan for a tail, which also acted as a mop. They introduced themselves as Lorna and Sarah. They led us up the three flights of

141

steep stairs and through the front door of the top apartment, which was immaculately clean and free of clutter. There was an ornamental fireplace in the lounge-cum-kitchenette with a note attached to the glass saying that it should not be lit. Some shutters opened onto the busy street below and we could see the market just to our left. There was a small set of stairs going up to the terrace, from which we could see the sea as well as the Picasso museum. For a few moments Debbie and I didn't say anything, not so much because we didn't have anything to say but more because we were trying to get our breaths back after climbing the stairs.

'We'll leave you for a few minutes to have a think about it, if you like,' said Sarah. 'We'll wait downstairs.'

'What do you think?' I asked Debbie once I was sure that the two ladies were out of earshot.

'I like it enough,' said Debbie, 'but what about those stairs? How are we going to manage with the shopping? It was hard enough getting ourselves up here, let alone with a few heavy carrier bags. And there's nowhere to park.'

'Come on, I'm sure we'll manage, and get fit at the same time. We'll be fit as fleas by the time we find a new job.'

'We'll take it,' I said to Lorna and Sarah, who were standing just inside the entrance door of the building.

'That's great,' replied Lorna. 'You do know that it's only available until the beginning of May?' she said.

'That's a long time in our world,' I replied, reaching for my wallet, at the same time as noticing looks of concern on the faces of the ladies, following what I had just said.

'Don't worry,' I said. 'I was referring to the fact that we'd only been in the apartment down the road for less than a week and now look.' I smiled.

Hoping that our new landlords had been reassured, I made my way back upstairs, where Debbie was rummaging through the kitchen drawers. I went up to the terrace. Just as I arrived, my usually quite placid dog let out a large bark.

142

He had his front paws on the wall and was wagging his tail. The seagull that he had just scared away didn't seem quite so amused and was flapping its way back to the sea shore. Soon after, I was lugging suitcases and carrier bags up the steep stairs and was looking forward to staying in our second apartment in Antibes in less than a week.

Chapter 16

Having spent a month or so getting to know Antibes and the surrounding areas, it was time, once again, to start looking for a job. It was the beginning of February and we only had two months left before we had to vacate the apartment.

'This is interesting,' said Debbie, who was in the lounge and looking at her computer. 'We've just been sent an email about a job in the Cap D'Antibes. The ad says it's for the summer but possibly permanent if they find the right couple.' I laughed. 'What's so funny?'

'You know what that means?' I replied. 'They want a couple who will run themselves into the ground over the summer. The couple will do it in the hope that they'll get a nice relaxing winter and be paid for it too. At the end of August, the employer will thank the couple for all of their hard work and say that they hope to see them the same time the following year. Seen it all before. There's no permanent job there – a long, hard summer, yes, but no job.'

'You don't trust anybody these days, do you?' replied Debbie, who looked up from her computer. 'Do you think we should at least apply?'

'Nothing to lose,' I said. 'Anyway, where is the Cap D'Antibes, exactly?'

'About a mile away. It's where the super-rich are, apparently. Being bought up by the Russians. I'm certainly not working for them. Clap their hands or snap their fingers when they want something and if they get bored they start throwing food around. Worse on the yachts. They think nothing of waking up the hostess at two in the morning because they've drunk too much vodka and now fancy an omelette.'

'Who told you that?'

'Sophie at the agency. One hostess did manage to get her own back in the end, though.' Debbie laughed.

'How did she do that?' I replied, sitting down on the sofa and reaching for my coffee cup.

'Well,' Debbie said, 'the yacht had been chartered by four huge blokes. No manners, any of them. No tips either, which given the amount of work the crew had to do, didn't go down well.'

'I can understand that,' I replied. 'Sounds familiar.'

'Anyway, just before the Russians were due to get into their helicopter and fly to Milan, the hostess offered them all a cup of strong, black coffee with a vodka chaser, which they all gratefully accepted.'

'Seems quite generous, given their behaviour.'

'Well it would have been,' replied Debbie. 'Except that the hostess laced their coffees with the strongest laxative known to man, and that was that. The crew waved the Russians off cheerily as they set off on an hour-and-a-half journey in a helicopter with no toilet facilities.' I laughed. 'Never a good idea to upset the people who are in charge of making your food. Speaking of which, what do you fancy for lunch? I'm starving.'

A few days later, Debbie and I were sitting in front of our computer and being interviewed on Skype by Madame Amari, a charming Syrian lady in her mid-sixties. She called us from the hotel that she owned in Damascus and she seemed to be very kind.

'I go out for dinner quite a lot when I come down,' she explained, 'so you won't have to cook all of the time, Debbie, though I do like your menus. I can't wait to taste your food. The only thing is, Brent, if you're not driving me when I go out for dinner, I do like you to wait up as I'm very security conscious and we do set the alarm at night. It's a shame but there is a lot of crime on the Cap.'

'Really?' I replied. 'That's surprising.'

'The thing is,' Madame Amari replied, 'there is a lot of wealth in the area and because we are not in the centre of town, the police don't patrol the area much. They think, perhaps, that we have enough money to look after our own security. Either that or the police don't like rich people, especially foreign ones.' She laughed. 'So, the thing is, Brent, part of your responsibility is to make sure that we're all tucked up safe and sound at night. Not literally, of course.

That might be asking a bit much.' She blushed. 'I have to go but you seem like reasonable people, so why don't you go and have a look at the property. I have a mad gardener called Bashar who will show you round. He can be a bit awkward but as he's only there first thing in the morning and last thing in the evening, you can try to avoid him. I know I do,' she laughed.

'Why is he only there then?' I asked.

'Well,' she replied, 'firstly, he has his own full-time job, so he does this for a bit of extra cash and, secondly, my garden isn't that big and doesn't need much maintenance. So, it suits us both. The trouble is, he thinks he owns the property, but don't take any notice.' She laughed again. 'If all goes well, you can start at the beginning of May as you have requested. It's a bit early as I'm not due until June but I have a feeling that if I don't secure you before now, you may fly away. I love that picture of your dog. Perhaps he can make sure we're all safe too, unless he bites us all. He doesn't bite, does he?'

'No,' replied Debbie. 'He's very gentle. Soft as butter.'

'That's good,' replied Madame Amari. 'Let me know how you get on.' She waved and smiled just before the screen went blank.

'Sounds promising,' Debbie said. 'And just down the road too.'

'Gardener sounds as though he could be a bit tricky,' I replied. 'Had my fair share of those. I know she laughed it off but...'

'Look, we've got nothing to lose,' Debbie interrupted. 'At least let's go and see the place. In the meantime, we'll keep looking. We've got some time on our hands yet. Right, I'm off to the market,' Debbie added, while doing up the laces on her pink training shoes. 'You coming?'

'Why not? It'll give me chance to try this out,' I said, picking up a harness that I'd bought for Guss. He'd never been good on a lead. He was used to roaming free in the countryside when we went out on walks. In the towns, he was horrendous. He seemed to forget that I was on the other end of the rope that was attached to his collar. I'd be minding my own business, gazing into a shop window, when he would suddenly lurch forward. As he discovered a new smell, a tempting bush or even a cat, he'd drag me with him, much to the amusement of the passers-by.

Enough was enough, and he was soon dressed in a smart, new black harness with 'Julius K9' emblazoned on the side. As we walked through the market, one of the traders who had got to know Guss by sight said, 'Good morning Julius.' As we often did, Debbie went in search of ripe cherry tomatoes, salads and all things seasonal, while Guss and I headed off to the small bakery. There, I bought a croissant, which the lady assistant fed to Guss. I continued to the beach, where Guss had a run and chased the occasional seagull or kite. At around midday we met up at a bar, where we enjoyed a glass of wine and a few olives.

'How's the harness working?' Debbie asked.

'Brilliant,' I replied. 'Guss now thinks he's a flipping husky and I'm a sled.' Debbie laughed. 'It's actually made him worse. The more I pull him back, the harder he pulls.'

'Not the total success the advert said then?'

'No.' I replied. 'Going in the bin as soon as we get back.'

A couple of weeks later I was sitting in the lounge looking at my computer when Debbie came in from the bedroom. 'You're up early,' she said, looking at the clock on the kitchen wall. It was six-thirty. 'Are you OK?' She yawned.

'Sort of,' I replied.

'What do you mean, sort of?' she asked, looking worried.

'The thing is,' I replied, 'I'm bleeding.'

'You're what?' she said, now fully awake and sitting down on the sofa next to me. She put her hand on mine. 'Where are you bleeding?'

'It's not so much where, as when,' I explained. 'When I go to the loo, there's blood. Not every time but more often than not.'

'You mean when you sit down to go?' Debbie asked.

'Exactly that,' I replied.

'How long has this been going on?'

'About a week or two,' I replied.

'Why didn't you say anything before?' Debbie said.

'I didn't want to worry you. Thought it would have cleared up by now.'

'It's probably an age thing. You're in your fifties now. Probably spent too much time sitting on warm radiators when we were in the UK.' Debbie smiled. 'Come on champ, I wouldn't worry about it. You haven't got any pain anywhere, have you?'

'Only a bit in the side but I think that's from lugging heavy carrier bags upstairs.'

'Well then, it's probably nothing. In future, ask me to give you a hand. Won't look good, us starting a new job with you having a hernia, will it? Either way, you'd better get it checked out. I'll make an appointment with the doctor. And whatever you do, don't google…' Debbie stopped mid-sentence and looked at me. 'Oh, God, you already have, haven't you? So, how long have you got to live?'

'Well, as you say,' I replied, 'it could be several things. Anything from haemorrhoids to the big one.'

'Bloody dangerous, sometimes, the Internet.' Debbie sighed. 'Please don't keep looking up your symptoms – it'll drive you mad. Now, where's my phone?'

As Debbie phoned the doctor, I got Guss into the car and headed off to the Valmasque national park in Mougins. We walked along the footpaths that were shaded by tall trees and strolled along the river that was next to the golf course. Guss jumped in to cool himself off and, at the same time, took a drink. That morning we passed a lady who I recognised from our previous visits to the park. She was walking her scruffy-looking terrier and I noticed that the woman was wearing a crash helmet.

'Looks like you've forgotten your bike.' I said, and then I smiled.

For a moment she looked confused and then replied, 'Oh, I see, this.' She pointed her finger towards her head. 'I was here yesterday when a golf ball whistled past my head.'

'No one shouted "fore?"' I asked.

'Wouldn't have heard it if they did. Normally, I have my headphones on. Not taking any chances today. Must get on,' and away she went. It was often the case that Guss and I would come across a golf ball that we'd throw back over the stream but thus far we hadn't had any near misses. As we walked through the forest, I noticed that the twinge in my side was getting slightly worse and I was getting out of breath quite quickly. Maybe Debbie was right. I needed to pay more attention to the stairs going up to our apartment.

'How did you get on?' Debbie asked, the day after I'd been to the doctors.

'OK,' I replied. 'She seemed quite reassuring but has made me an appointment with a gastroenterology specialist in Grasse. "Better not take any chances," she said.'

'She didn't examine you?'

'No, she didn't, which frankly is a bit of a relief,' I replied, slumping down onto the sofa.

'So, when's the appointment?' Debbie asked.

'Tomorrow morning.'

'Good grief, that was quick.'

'Do you really think I need to go? There's plenty I could be doing here.'

'Yes, I do,' Debbie replied, who was looking through one of her recipe books. 'As I said before, it's probably nothing but it'll put your mind at rest – and mine, for that matter. Spanish chicken for tomorrow night OK?'

'Lovely.'

'Right, I'm off to the shops, then,' Debbie said as she picked up her purse from the sideboard. 'And stay off the bloody Internet while I'm gone. Better still, I need a couple of red peppers and this chorizo chopping up,' she said, passing them to me from the fridge. 'And make sure you take the paper off the chorizo first. I also need a couple of red onions finely chopped. That should keep you out of trouble for a while. And, if you get time, can you cook Guss's lunch? Chicken's in the fridge and you know where the pasta is. Bye,' she said, and quickly disappeared through the front door.

On Tuesday morning, I made the forty-minute journey to Grasse. I sat in the waiting room and began to wonder whether I really needed to be there at all. I didn't feel particularly unwell. I hadn't bled that morning and I didn't want to waste the doctor's time. I felt fairly certain that there were other people more in need of his services than mine. I looked at my watch. My appointment was scheduled for ten o'clock – it was now ten thirty.

I got up from my seat and began to make my way over to reception, where I thought to make my excuses and leave, when one of the consultation room doors flew open and a very tall, thin man said, 'Monsieur Tyler.'

'*Oui*,' I replied, walking towards him.

Smiling warmly, he offered his hand. 'Hello, I am Doctor Boussoukaya,' he said, 'but you can call me Samy, if you like. It's a bit easier.' He laughed, before offering me a seat in his consulting room.

For about half an hour, he asked questions and wrote down my replies. At the end of the conversation he concluded, 'Well, Monsieur Tyler, you need to have a colonoscopy. I will be doing it myself.'

'Isn't that a bit invasive?' I asked. 'Surely there must be another way?'

'I know you'd rather hear me say that there is another way but it's the only way we can be sure. You will also need some scans. You will need a CT Scan and an MRI scan.'

'What's the difference?' I asked.

'Well,' he explained. 'A CT scan uses X-rays, whereas and MRI scan uses magnetic fields and radio frequencies. They both look at your body but in different ways,' he said, getting up and going to his printer, where several pieces of paper were being run off.

'Do they take long?' I asked.

'No,' he replied. 'The CT scan takes about three minutes and the MRI about fifteen, but you will need blood tests just before.

The good thing about the MRI scan is that you can take a CD with you, if you like. It might be interrupted by an occasion clunk from the scanner but other than that it's quite peaceful. Now,' he continued, 'here is a prescription for the medication that you will need to take before your colonoscopy, which I have booked for Friday.' I raised my eyebrows. Bloody hell, that was quick, I thought. 'You need to be here by seven-thirty in the morning and go to the reception marked *Service ambulatoire*. I'll see you Friday.' He passed me the papers, smiled again and said, '*Au revoir.*'

Still wondering whether what had just happened had been a complete waste of time, I made my way back to Antibes where I began to explain everything to Debbie.

'Well, they do say that the French have one of the best health systems in the world,' reasoned Debbie. 'I imagine they're just being thorough, that's all. And he didn't bother to examine you?' she said, with an air of surprise.

'No, he didn't. And there was me thinking that it was a French national pastime.'

'You thought what was a French national pastime?'

'Sticking their fingers up other people's bottoms.'

The following morning, while I went to the pharmacy to collect the medication for my colonoscopy, Debbie studied the list of food that I could and could not eat beforehand. For two days I was on a low fibre diet. I wasn't allowed any fruit, vegetables or red meat, but chicken, fish and pasta were on the menu. On Thursday evening, I began taking my medication, which went through me like a Porsche. It seemed that every time I went to sit down on the sofa, I was straight back up again and heading for the bathroom. The same happened when I went to bed. I thought that at least if I was asleep I'd be able to avoid the toilet until the morning. I couldn't have been more wrong. At about six o'clock in the morning, half an hour before we were due to leave, my stomach finally settled down.

We drove through the pretty streets of Grasse, passing several perfume factories along the way. By the time we got to the hospital I was exhausted and was actually looking forward to some sleep. I was likely to be at the hospital for a good couple of hours, so Debbie and Guss headed off for a good, long walk. Once I'd registered at reception and signed a couple of forms, I was shown into a private room where I changed into a pair of blue, disposable pyjamas. I was also given a pair of slippers and hat, similar to one of those usually worn by restaurant kitchen staff. I briefly looked in the mirror and promised never to do so again until I was back in my own clothes. What did I expect? I was never going to look anything other than ridiculous, so I lay on the bed and waited. Soon, a porter came in to wheel me towards the theatre. He parked me just outside, and not long after that a pretty, young nurse came to ask me if I had any allergies. She also asked me my name and my date of birth.

She then produced a needle, asked me to clench my fist and said, '*Je pique*,' which translates to 'This is going to sting.' She wasn't wrong. Just at that moment, Samy, who was wearing scrubs and a multi-coloured hat, came through a set of swing doors.

He smiled, walked towards me, picked up the notes that were attached to a clipboard at the bottom of my bed and said reassuringly, 'You'll be fine. It'll be over before you know it.' I was then wheeled into the theatre and was asked to turn on my side. 'Can you count down from ten?' Samy asked, smiling. I think I managed to get to eight. The next thing I remember was coming round in the recovery ward. To my right was a bed in which was a woman who was still under anaesthetic. To my left was a man who was in the same condition as the woman and in front of me was a desk where several nurses were milling around. After an hour or so, and having been detached from the machine that measured my heartbeat, I was wheeled back to my private room, where I got changed. I was then shown a small waiting room, where I was offered a baguette, some jam, a glass of orange juice and some coffee. That was all very nice but my mind was distracted by my aching arm, which still had the needle in it.

'Doctor Boussoukaya will be with you very shortly,' said a nurse who came to remove the needle. As she pressed some cotton wool onto my skin, which she asked me to hold, I could see Debbie through the glass window that looked onto reception. She had just arrived. She put two thumbs up and nodded her head. I reciprocated and then went to join her.

'No point in you hanging around here,' I said. 'Why don't you go and wait for me at the café across the road. Might be a while yet.'

'Are you sure?' replied Debbie. 'You're not still feeling the effects of the anaesthetic?'

'No, not at all. Must have been very light.'

'OK, I'll see you in a bit,' Debbie said, before opening the door.

'Well,' began Samy, who came to greet me, 'it all went very well but I can't give you any further information until after your scans. Then come back and see me. Try not to worry. We'll find out what the problem is very quickly. Bye, bye.'

'All good then?' asked Debbie, who was sitting at a small table just outside the café. She put her book down.

'Yes, all fine.'

'You fancy a coffee?'

'What time is it?' I asked.

'A quarter past twelve,' replied Debbie.

'*Monsieur, monsieur,*' I shouted towards the waiter, who was standing behind the bar and looking up at the television. He looked at me and smiled.

'Two glasses of rosé, please – large!'

'Are you sure about this?' Debbie asked. 'You've just come round from an anaesthetic. 'Sure you'll be OK?'

'I'll be fine. Anyway, when we get back I'm going to bed. Nothing like the liquid cosh to help you sleep.' Debbie laughed.

Chapter 17

'Eleven o'clock, Sunday morning,' Debbie announced as I walked into the lounge, having had a good three hours' sleep.

'What is?' I asked, yawning.

'Our visit to the villa in the Cap D'Antibes.'

'Oh, that,' I replied, going into the kitchen and opening the fridge door. 'Wow, it's full,' I replied, 'which is great because I'm starving!'

'I did some shopping when you were asleep but please don't stand there with the door open – you'll let all the cold out.'

'How else am I supposed to find out what's in here, if I don't look inside?'

'Ask me, that's how. Would you like me to make you something?'

'Yeah, I think I'd like some lobster Thermidor.'

'Then you can think again.'

By Sunday morning, I was back to normal. I had been fed and watered and I felt well rested. The three of us jumped in the car and headed towards the Cap D'Antibes. As we drove along the waterfront we saw a group of men playing *pétanque* by the side of the road. They always seemed to attract quite a large audience made up of locals, intrigued tourists and people walking their dogs. An impressive fountain just in front of the sea was in full flow and the restaurateurs were beginning to get ready for lunchtime service. We drove slowly passed the Eden-Roc hotel, often frequented by film stars when visiting the south of France. We didn't see anyone famous but noticed, at the hotel's entrance, some men dressed in sharp, black suits.

'Bet you won't stay there for fifty quid a night with a complimentary breakfast,' I said. Debbie laughed.

'Probably not. Doubt we'd get as far as reception,' she replied, looking suspiciously at one of the men who was wearing dark sunglasses and talking into his lapel.

The villa where we were due to arrive at eleven o'clock was half way down a one-way street. Nobody had bothered to tell us that it was one-way and it seemed no one had informed our GPS system either. We drove one way and then another, but whichever way we drove we somehow always managed to arrive at the wrong end of the street. The security men outside the hotel were beginning to recognise our car and glared at us as we passed them for a third time.

'Oh, stuff it,' said Debbie as we were about to repeat the procedure. At the top of the road she put her foot down. I closed my eyes. There was a screech of tyres and moments later we were parked outside Villa Bellevue. We got out of the car.

As I surveyed our surroundings, I laughed. 'What is it?' asked Debbie.

'That's so French,' I replied. 'Look,' I continued, pointing to a small French car. 'They've put bollards up to stop people from parking on the road and what do the French do? They just park on top of them.'

'I see what you mean,' said Debbie, who then laughed. Along the street there were rows of cars, underneath which were flattened, plastic bollards. Sure, the bollards were attached to the road, but it didn't stop the French from parking on them. Not only did the drivers not take any notice of these parking restrictions, it seemed that the police weren't bothered either. There were one or two signs posted on the outside walls of the villas that threatened vehicles with being towed away but, these too, were ignored.

We rang on the doorbell and moments later the large, black gate slid to one side. An elderly, small, wiry man, who I assumed to be of North African descent, smiled, until he noticed Guss and then his face changed completely.

He frowned, screwed his eyes up and started wagging his finger at us. '*Pas de chien*,' he said.

'We have spoken to Madame and she is happy for us to bring our dog,' I replied.

'You wait there,' he said, not allowing us onto the property. As the gates closed, I watched the man, who we knew to be the gardener, reach into his trouser pocket. He produced a phone with a cracked screen and began to dial. As we waited outside, he soon started shouting, presumably at our potentially new employer.

'Good start,' said Debbie, who was watching another bollard being flattened.

'Shall we go?' I asked. 'Can't see us putting up with that idiot all summer.'

'We're here now,' replied Debbie. 'Anyway, it's not him we'd be working for.'

'Clearly, he thinks it is.'

Debbie was just about to reply when the gate opened again. Looking very red in the face and still quite angry, the frustrated gardener beckoned us in.

'Madame says OK, but no caca on my plants, you understand, mister. No caca on my plants,' he said, wagging his finger. Guss went up to greet the man but was shooed away, so he did the next best thing. He peed on the gardener's geraniums.

'*Merde!*' shouted the man, before disappearing round the side of the villa and returning with a garden hose. As he stood there, spraying much more water than was actually needed to clean up after Guss, the three of us went for a walk around the garden.

'He did that to prove a point,' I said to Debbie.

'I know,' she replied. 'He obviously doesn't like dogs and Madame wasn't joking when she said he thinks he owns the place.' As we walked, we were never far away from a pair of eyes that were staring at us.

'I reckon someone must have arrived in Antibes with a job lot of these,' I said to Debbie as I looked at a long row of flowers towards the end of the lawn. 'Agapanthus and Jack Russells. The town's full of them. That's all you ever see here.' Debbie laughed.

In the middle of the lawn was a swimming pool. Around the edge were two five-foot blue plastic statues. One was a polar bear and the other a dolphin.

'Different,' I said to Debbie, who raised her eyebrows.

There was a small gypsy's caravan, which was only big enough to take one person at a time. There was also a separate building that housed a pizza oven. As we walked inside, there was a horrendous stench. At the back and just under the oven was a pile of logs that were covered in what looked like rat droppings. As I looked closer, in between the logs were some squirrels' tails that were surrounded by flies. I looked up to my left and saw a window that was open. It seemed that at some point over the winter the squirrels had climbed in and had jumped down onto the metal worksurfaces but couldn't climb back up again. I could only imagine what carnage must have taken place in there.

'I think I'm going to be sick,' said Debbie, who was keen to get back outside.

'Look at this,' I said as we headed towards the door. 'What on earth is a seat from Chelsea football stadium doing in a pizza hut in the south of France?' I pointed at the seat, which had a number on the back of it.

'No idea,' replied Debbie, 'but have you seen these deckchairs? They've got portraits of cats on them. And what are *they*?' she asked, pointing at two red and yellow striped tents, each measuring six feet tall by two feet wide, that were at the end of the garden.

'Changing rooms, I imagine. I wonder if the inside of the house is just as mad?'

As we walked around the rest of the garden, Debbie and I watched as several squirrels ran along the top of the perimeter fences. Occasionally, Guss would jump up at them, bark and wag his tail.

'You know the difference between a rat and a squirrel?' Debbie asked.

'Go on.'

'Marketing.' I laughed.

Instructing Guss to remain outside, Debbie and I walked into the villa through a side door that had a keypad on the outside. The door led into a kitchen that hadn't been renovated since the nineteen-seventies. The work surfaces were yellow and stained and we could see that some of the cupboards were only just being held on by their hinges. The numbers on the dials of the oven, which was also old, had all worn off. The deep-red tiles on the floor were cracked and our shoes squeaked as we walked over them.

'Doesn't look like this has been cleaned for ages,' Debbie said. As she carefully opened one door after another, she announced, 'This is going to take some sorting out if I'm going to work in here,' she said. 'I couldn't work like this. I'd never find anything. And look at this fridge-freezer.'

'What about it?' I asked.

'The fridge is all right, but the freezer is tiny. Just about big enough for two bags of ice.'

We walked into the lounge, where there were four square pillars that held up the ceiling. A broad grin spread over Debbie's face. She noticed that half way up one of the pillars was a fish's head. Just behind it, on the other side of the pillar, was the fish's tail. There was a large painting of a woman in a long coat who was flying above some houses, at the same time holding a bunch of gladioli.

'That's odd,' said Debbie, who was looking at the sofa. 'Not seen one like that before.'

'That's because it's outside furniture,' I replied.

'What?' said Debbie, who was looking extremely confused.

'It's hard plastic with some outdoor cushions. They're designed so that they can be left outside in all weathers. Not supposed to be inside at all.'

'Oh, I see,' Debbie said. 'She seemed so normal.'

'None of them is normal,' I replied. 'They're all bloody mad.' Debbie smiled.

There was a marble chess set on a cast iron table in the middle of the floor. As I picked up the red queen, her head came away from her body. The same happened with the king and one of the knights.

'That's not been put up right,' I said as I studied a metalwork piece of art above the television.

'How do you mean?'

'It's a shoal of fish.'

'And?' Debbie asked.

'And their eyes are supposed to be at the top. They are at the bottom. So, according to that, they're swimming upside down. Neat trick if you can do it.' Debbie put her hand over her mouth.

'I can't open this door,' said Debbie, who had wandered back towards the kitchen.

'Hang on, I'll just try this,' I said, pressing a button which was on the wall just to the right. As I pressed it, I heard a sound and a lift came down from the floor above. The door opened automatically. After a few seconds it closed.

'Impressive,' I said. 'Let's go and have a look at the bedrooms.'

'Sure,' replied Debbie, 'but I'm not going up in that contraption. If it's anything like the rest of this place I could be stuck in there for a week.'

At the far end of the lounge there was a staircase that led to a landing and three bedrooms. As we got to the top, we noticed two chairs and a *chaise longue* that were covered in plastic sheets.

'Told you there's no all-year-round job here. Lying bastards,' I said.

'What makes you say that?' asked Debbie.

'This place gets moth-balled over the winter. Doesn't get used.'

'Doesn't get cleaned either by the looks of it,' said Debbie, who had just run her finger along a wooden cabinet.

'I thought the gardener's daughter was supposed to come in once a week,' I replied.

'If she does, she doesn't do anything when she gets here. This place hasn't been touched for months.' We went into the first bedroom, which smelled very musty. Debbie opened the windows and shutters to let in some air. Again, all the furniture and the bed were covered by plastic sheets.

'Madame Amari said that the middle bedroom is hers, so I think this is probably it,' said Debbie, who reached for the door handle. As she opened the door she let out a scream. 'Oh my God,' she said, patting herself on the chest.

'Nearly frightened the bloody life out me. Look at this.' As I peered into the darkness, I could just make out at the far end of the room the figure of a man sitting in a chair. As my eyes began to focus, I could see that he was made of wire mesh. Not only that, he was life-size. 'Bloody hell, Brent, what's he doing in here?'

'Maybe Madame likes a bit of company at night. Naughty girl,' I said, laughing.

'I hope there aren't any more surprises like that one,' Debbie replied as she opened the shutters.

'Wouldn't bank on it.'

'Look at this view, Brent. This is amazing.' As we stood on Madame's balcony, we were looking straight onto the Mediterranean Sea. The sun was shining and there wasn't a cloud in the sky. A few boats were bobbing up and down in the gentle breeze. 'I don't normally get jealous,' Debbie said, 'but on this occasion I could make an exception.'

There was a walk-in wardrobe with at least fifty pairs of shoes. Very expensive dresses were hanging from the rails and small, plastic carrier bags with designer names emblazoned on the outside were dotted around the floor. We went to inspect the third bedroom, which was very similar to the first.

'Where's our accommodation?' I asked.

'Not so much accommodation as a room,' Debbie replied.

'Eh? I thought you said there was a studio here.'

'There is,' said Debbie, 'but it gets used by guests in the summer, apparently. No, sorry, but we're in a room just above the kitchen.'

'You, me and the hound in one room?'

'I'm afraid so.' I let out a sigh. 'Now's as good a time as any,' Debbie said. 'Let's go and have a look.'

Moments later we were in the room. Water was dripping from the air-conditioning unit onto the floor. Paint was peeling from the walls and a single lightbulb dangled from the middle of the ceiling. There was a bed with a mattress that had a huge dip in the middle, two wooden bedside cabinets and a wardrobe with no doors. The bathroom was tiny, the shower head was covered in limescale and the toilet had not been flushed.

'I hope we manage to find another job,' I said. 'We haven't started here and I'm already dreading it.'

Chapter 18

One evening in early March 2015, Debbie, Guss and I were making our way to the Arnault Tzanck Clinic in Mougins, about a forty-minute drive from Antibes, for the first of my two scans. Once there, I handed the results of the blood test that I had taken the previous day to the nurse and sat in the waiting room. I also gave her a box that I had collected from the chemist containing a liquid that was due to be fed into my arm intravenously while I was being scanned. Soon after, I was sitting in a chair having a needle inserted into my arm once again.

'Please undo your trousers,' the nurse said. 'You don't need to take them all the way off, just down to your knees,' she explained. 'I need you to lie down here and place your arms above your head. When we inject the liquid, it may feel a bit warm but that's normal. Do you have any questions, Monsieur Tyler?'

'Not that I can think of.'

The nurse smiled and began to walk out of the room. Just before she got to the door she turned and said, 'You must listen to the instructions. Nothing difficult, but you will be asked to hold your breath every now and again. I'll see you again soon.'

As my body was being moved forward into the small arch, I closed my eyes and within a very short space of time, the scan was over. Certainly, the nurse had been right about the warmth, but the procedure had been painless.

'How did it go?' asked Debbie, who was walking Guss around the grounds of the clinic.

'No problem,' I replied. 'Blood tests are fine, and the scan hasn't shown anything, so all good so far.'

'That's a relief. I must admit, I was a bit worried. Just the MRI to go on Wednesday and that's that.'

'Bit of a bugger that it's Guss's birthday.'

'I'm sure he won't mind,' said Debbie, who then smiled. 'Look, it's probably a good omen. Anyway, we can celebrate afterwards.

Me to drive, you to drive?' Debbie asked as she took the car keys out of her jeans pocket.

'You, if that's OK. I've got a litre of water to drink to get that jollop out of my system.'

'They didn't say anything about being able to drown it with beer?'

'Apparently not,' I replied, before getting into the passenger seat. 'A litre,' I said, picking up the bottle. 'Seems an awful lot. I don't normally drink that amount in a week.'

'Just do as you're told for a change,' said Debbie, who was waiting for the car park's barrier to be raised. 'The doctor knows best.'

'We'll see about that.'

Three days later we were back at the clinic and I was sitting in a small cubicle with another box that I had collected from the chemist. This box was considerably larger than the previous one – about eighteen inches long. I'd already taken a peek inside. There were two enormous syringes. Quite what they were going to do with them, I had no idea. A few moments later a male nurse arrived and passed me some blue, disposable pyjamas and some paper underpants. He picked up the box and took out the syringes.

'You need to insert the contents of these two syringes,' he explained.

'Really?' I asked. 'Where do I need to insert them?'

'It is your bowel that is being examined, is it not, Monsieur Tyler?'

The penny dropped. 'You're having a fucking laugh,' I replied.

'Does it look like I am having a fucking laugh?' replied the nurse sternly. 'Oh, and Monsieur Tyler, please mind your language. This is a hospital. If you have any problems, please let me know, although I am sure you can manage. I will see you later.' Clearly, he wasn't interested in helping, so I removed the syringes from the boxes and then attempted to do as I was instructed. Within seconds, I burst out laughing. My arm could not reach the end of the plunger. I remember thinking, *What does the nurse think I am? An orangutan? Is he expecting to find me*

163

scampering around the cubicle on the back of my knuckles when he gets back? I didn't know. When the tears of laughter stopped rolling down my cheeks I started again, this time mindful of the fact that if I slipped, I could quite easily disembowel myself.

After fifteen minutes or so, I was led into a room with a much larger scanner than the first. 'I understand that I can listen to a CD while I'm in there?' I asked.

'You can,' replied the young nurse. 'We have some of our own, or you can…'

'Here you go,' I said, proudly handing over my copy of Bruce Springsteen's Wrecking Ball. I lay on the bed, closed my eyes and waited. Very soon after, the welcome sound of 'We Take Care of our Own' came through the speakers. All was going well until about six or seven minutes into the scan.

'Aaaaaaaaaargh!' I shouted.

'Monsieur Tyler,' said a very concerned voice from the control booth behind. 'Are you in pain?'

'Yes, I'm in pain,' I replied. 'Or at least my ears are. You've just stuck bloody U2 on!' I laughed.

'Sorry,' said the nurse as 'In the Name of Love' was turned off quite abruptly.

'That's OK,' I said. 'Just please not them, or Sting. I haven't quite lost the will to live yet.'

Five days later, I was back at the clinic in Grasse for the results.

'Monsieur Tyler,' said a very smiley Doctor Boussoukaya, 'please sit down.'

'You have my results?'

'I do,' he replied. 'Monsieur Tyler,' he continued, 'I am sorry to tell you that you have cancer.'

At that point it became like one of those movies where everything

164

becomes blurred as if someone had smeared Vaseline onto the lens of the camera. The doctor's mouth was moving but I could hear no sounds. I had just been told that I had cancer, but how could that be? My mother, who was a nurse, had always said that cancer was hereditary. There was no history of it in our family, not that I had heard of anyway, so how could I have cancer? Surely, there had been a mistake. I didn't feel unwell. I'd passed a bit of blood and had a bit of pain in the side, but...

'Monsieur Tyler,' Doctor Boussoukaya said, waving his hands in front of my face. 'Monsieur Tyler. Have you heard anything that I have just said?'

'I just heard the word "cancer," that's all.'

'I'm sorry, that's quite natural. It must have come as quite a shock.'

'I'll say.'

'Monsieur Tyler, you have cancer, but we can cure you,' he said, smiling. 'You have cancer of the bowel and you will need to go to Marseille to be treated.'

'Marseille?' I replied. 'That's a bit of a long way to go. Can't you do it here?'

'I'm afraid not,' Samy said. 'This is beyond our level of expertise. They have a team of specialists who will make sure that you are given the best advice and treatment available. It is.' He picked up the phone, 'one of the best cancer hospitals in the world. Don't worry, you're going to be OK. Doctor De Chaisemartin,' he said to the person on the other end of the phone. Samy continued to speak rapidly in French. Not understanding what he was saying, I gazed out of the window, at the same time trying to make some sense of the madness of the situation. I was finding the whole thing very difficult to absorb. Surely, someone was going to pinch me in a minute and I'd wake up. 'Monsieur Tyler,' Samy said, at the end of his conversation, 'you have an appointment at the Institut Paoli-Calmettes on Monday at ten o'clock.'

'That's only three days away,' I said.

'I know, but the sooner we get you there, the sooner we can make you better,' Samy replied reassuringly. He then got up and went over to his printer, where a small forest of paper was being churned out. 'You will need to give these to Doctor De Chaisemartin,' he said, putting the sheets of paper into a folder that also contained some images of my scans. 'She is a brilliant surgeon. You are lucky to have her.'

'I'm going to need surgery? Are you sure?' I replied, once again feeling shocked.

'I imagine so,' he said, passing me the folder, 'but Doctor De Chaisemartin will explain everything to you. Try not to worry, Monsieur Tyler, you are going to be all right,' Samy continued, seeing the worried look on my face. 'Goodbye.'

I walked down the stairs and headed to the car park, where I noticed Debbie wandering around with Guss. As I approached her, I shook my head and closed my eyes. I explained what had just happened and we both burst into tears.

'Bloody hell, Brent,' Debbie said, just before taking a tissue out of her coat pocket and blowing her nose. 'I didn't see that one coming.'

'Me neither,' I replied. 'What a shock. I'm still not sure I can quite believe it.'

'Look,' said Debbie. 'He said you're going to be OK. He did say that, didn't he?'

'Several times.'

'Well then, we've got nothing to worry about. Might be tricky with a new job and all that but we'll manage. Always have done, always will. Come on, I need a drink. A glass of rosé across the road?'

'No, a bucket.' Debbie laughed.

For an hour or so, the three of us sat at a table outside the café just over the road from the hospital. Debbie and I tried to translate the printed pieces of paper but there were a lot of medical terms that we wouldn't have understood in English, let alone French.

'Probably best,' said Debbie.

'How do you mean?' I asked.

'Trying to take this amount of information in, all in one go, is impossible. Not to mention it's likely to fry your brain at the same time.' She smiled. 'Come on champ. One step at a time is my advice. Ask questions as you go along. Right, have we paid the bill?' Debbie asked as she picked up the car keys from the table.

'No, I'll do it,' I said, getting up and walking towards the café's entrance.

'We've got a couple of emails!' shouted Debbie, who was sitting at her computer, only a few minutes after we got back to our apartment.

'Go on,' I said as I returned from the bedroom.

'Firstly, Madame Amari's accountant has written to ask for our bank details. He's also confirmed our start date at the beginning of May.'

'Hold me back,' I said, slumping down on the sofa.

'This'll cheer you up then,' Debbie said.

'What will?' I asked.

Daniel and Samantha are coming to Antibes, two weeks today.'

Although we had had the occasional Skype meeting with them, we hadn't seen Daniel and his wife, Samantha, in person since they returned to England a few years previously. They had found a guardian's job; however, they said that they were still missing France, but not the boss that we had all worked for in the past.

'Coming to see us, or just a coincidence?' I asked.

'Coincidence, I think. Last-minute decision apparently, but that doesn't matter. Will be good to see them. They've booked an apartment for a week in the Rue de Marc or the Rude Remark, as Daniel has already christened it.' I laughed. 'They'd love to meet up. They've also asked if you can pick them up from Nice airport.'

'They're not hiring a car?'

'Don't need one. They're staying right in the town centre, just around the corner from the Carrefour supermarket. Anyway, you know what they're like. They much prefer to be hopping on a train or a bus. I don't think Daniel's a big fan of cars. Not sure Sam is for that matter. I'm so excited. We must have them over for lunch,' said Debbie, who got up from her chair and walked over to the shelf containing her cookery books.

'Do you want me to go to Marseille with you on Monday?' Debbie asked.

'No, you're OK,' I replied. 'You'd better stay here with Guss. I have no idea how long I'm going to be there. Come to think of it, I have no idea how long it's going to take to get there,' I said, picking up my laptop and sitting on the sofa. 'Anyway, it's all motorway, so probably best I go on my own.'

On the Monday morning at nine o'clock, I said goodbye to Debbie, who was washing up after making a breakfast big enough to keep me going all day. Soon after, I was heading down the A8 on my way to Marseille. Two hours later, I drove into the public underground car park at the Institut Paoli-Calmettes. I parked, got out of the car and said hello to an elegantly dressed woman who I assumed to be one of the institute's patients. As she got into her car, which was next to mine, I noticed that her face was ashen and her hands were shaking. She turned on the engine and then struggled to manoeuvre the Toyota Landcruiser round a tight corner. She reversed over a bollard, which she completely flattened, and then sped towards the exit. I could only imagine what news she might have just received but I hoped that she would be OK.

I made my way into the building marked IPC2 and up the stairs to the waiting area, where there were screens displaying photos of the consultants and which rooms they were in. Pleased to have made it with ten minutes to spare, I sat and waited, and I waited, and I waited. My appointment was scheduled for eleven o'clock and it was by then ten past twelve. I watched as several people went in and out of Doctor De Chaisemartin's consulting room, but my name had not been called. Surely, I had got the right day, I thought to myself as I looked through my folder. Yes, there it was in black and white – March 21, eleven o'clock. As the next patient left the room, I knocked on the door. 'Doctor De Chaisemartin?'

'*Oui*,' was the response.

168

'I am Monsieur Tyler,' I began. 'My appointment was…'

'Scheduled for over an hour ago,' interrupted the very pretty and elegantly-dressed doctor, who was looking scornfully at her watch.

'I was here,' I replied. 'I thought you'd forgotten about me.'

'No, Monsieur Tyler, I did not forget about you. You have not registered downstairs.'

'I didn't know I had to,' I replied, quite sternly.

'Well, now you do,' said the doctor, who forced a smile. 'And be quick please. I am very busy.' While the doctor called out the name of the next patient, I made my way to the hospital's reception and returned half an hour later.

'What I think we need to do, is operate as soon as possible and then chemotherapy afterwards,' Doctor De Chaisemartin said, looking at the images of my scan, which she had up on her screen. 'But it's not just my decision,' she explained. 'There is a group of us…'

'Chemotherapy, really?'

'Yes, Monsieur Tyler – chemotherapy, is highly likely. Do you have any other questions?'

'Do you have any idea how long I have had the cancer?'

'The tumour could have been there for up to eighteen months. Difficult to say but it does need to be removed. I need you to come and see me again in a week's time. Goodbye Monsieur Tyler.'

Chapter 19

'Are you always late?' asked Doctor De Chaisemartin, who was tapping her fingers on her desk and staring at me.

'There was a lot of traffic,' I began.

'Then you should have left earlier,' the doctor interrupted.

'It was rush hour.'

'Exactly my point. Anyway, we've decided to operate first,' she said, looking at the diary on her computer screen.

'When?'

'In five days.'

'And who is going to be doing the operation?' I asked.

'Me, of course. Who did you think would be doing it?' Suddenly and unexpectedly, I felt that a huge weight had been lifted off my mind. In less than a week's time, I would be free of cancer. 'You will need to follow this regime exactly,' explained the doctor, who handed me several prescriptions. 'I will see you in five days' time, although you need to be here the afternoon before. Goodbye.'

'Bloody hell,' said Debbie as I walked into our apartment carrying two large paper bags. 'You've got enough there to start your own pharmacy.'

'I know,' I replied. 'Just hope I can work out what to do with it all. If I don't, that doctor's going to go ape shit!'

'She sounds quite fierce,' said Debbie.

'No, she's not,' I replied. 'I think she's really nice. Probably doesn't have a lot of time to spare and gets a bit frustrated when fools like me go round wasting it.' Debbie smiled.

'Anything I should know?' Debbie asked as she began to unpack the contents of the carrier bags.

'Only that I might have to have a colostomy bag for a few months.'

'Sounds attractive,' replied Debbie, who was neatly stacking up the boxes on the coffee table. 'Why's that then?'

'To protect the surgery, apparently. Gives my insides the chance to heal properly.'

'Bloody hell. How many boxes of painkillers do you need?' Debbie counted them. There were twelve. 'And what's this jollop?' she asked, undoing the lid of a bottle.

'Betadine. It's an antiseptic. I have to shower in it the day before the operation.'

'If we had a spare room, you'd be sleeping in it,' replied Debbie, who was none too impressed with the smell. 'Not exactly Armani Code, is it?' I smiled. 'Do you know what? I've been looking at my cookery books all day and I still haven't decided what to cook for Sam and Daniel when they arrive on Saturday.' She sat down on the sofa in frustration.

'Well you have had a lot on your mind,' I replied.

'I've also had all day. Never mind. You can eat what you like today?'

'Pretty much.'

'Good, because I'm doing lemon chicken, with saffron rice and haricots verts. Sound OK?'

'Oh, I think I can manage.'

On Saturday morning I drove to Nice airport to collect Sam and Daniel. As we drove down the A8 autoroute I asked, 'What's the weather like back home?'

'Like a fairy tale,' Daniel replied.

'Really?' I said.

'Yeah, fucking Grimm.' I laughed. 'It's been pissing down non-stop for the past week. Hardly been out of the house except to do a bit of shopping.'

'Wouldn't recommend we come back then?'

'No, I bloody wouldn't. The place is a shit hole these days, Brent, and we're in one of the poshest areas of the country – Tunbridge Wells.

The pay's good but that's about it. You wouldn't recognise the country now.'

'Boss is all right, though?' I said.

'Brilliant, just brilliant,' replied Daniel, who closed his eyes and was enjoying the sunshine.

'That's great,' I said. 'What does he do?' I asked.

'He cuts hedges – very big ones,' replied Daniel.

'Oh, really?' I asked, looking a bit confused.

'No, he does not,' snapped Sam from the back seat. 'He's a hedge fund manager, and a very successful one too.'

'Oh, that's what he does,' Daniel said.

'You know fine well what he does,' said Sam. 'We worked out he earns about six grand a day.'

'That's one hell of a hedge,' said Daniel. 'You'd need a fucking big ladder to get to the top of that one, which is why we hardly ever see him.'

'He's right about that,' said Sam. 'We've been working for him for just over a year now and we've only seen him twice.'

'Sounds ideal. And the lady of the house?' I asked.

'Oh, she's all right,' Sam said. 'A bit nuts, like the rest of them. Told me off last week for putting her smalls out on the washing line. Doesn't want the neighbours to see them. I wouldn't mind but they haven't got any neighbours...'

'Must be the size of that hedge.'

'Oh, shut up, Daniel.'

Within an hour, we were back in Antibes. I watched Sam and Daniel wheel their suitcases towards Rue De Marc and went in search of a parking space. I'd agreed to come and meet them at their apartment at about eight o'clock. From there, we'd walk through the labyrinth of backstreets, finishing up at our apartment in Rue De La Tourraque.

'This is lovely,' said Sam, who was giving Debbie a huge hug. 'Eight hundred euros a month,' she continued, admiring the lounge.

172

'You haven't seen the best bit yet,' said Debbie, who was clearly very happy to see our friends. 'Come on, I'll show you.' As Debbie led our guests up to the terrace, I went to investigate the aromas that were coming from the kitchen. On the hob, there was a large, flat pan that was covered in tin foil. Gently, I lifted the foil. Bastards, I thought. They're having paella and I can't have any of it. I'd been consigned to maggot soup, or something that looked like it. To the right of the hob were two white plates that were covered with cling film. Underneath was some *charcuterie*. Debbie had made a real effort to put together an array of local, cold, cooked meats. Shopping and discovering nice food was something that she very much enjoyed.

'Fabulous place you've got here, Brent,' said Daniel, as the four of us stood chatting in the lounge. 'Though, those stairs coming up are a bit of a bastard. I'm sure you're about half the size since I last saw you.' I smiled. 'You'd think they would've put in a lift.'

'Brent, you do the drinks if you wouldn't mind,' said Debbie. 'I've got a few things to do and I'll be right with you.' As I poured the rosé and chatted to our friends, I watched as Debbie ferried cutlery, plates and napkins upstairs. She also took bottles of water, a wine cooler and the *charcuterie*. A few minutes later, she came to join us. She sat down, sighed and raised her glass. 'Sorry, first time I've sat down all day,' she said. 'Cheers, everybody.'

We'd only been talking for a very short when we heard a crash which we thought had come from the terrace above. 'I'll be right back,' said Debbie, who ran up the stairs. 'Bastards, fucking bastards!' shouted Debbie. Sam, Daniel, Guss and I rushed to investigate. As we got to the top, we found Debbie holding a piece of clingfilm in one hand and a cracked plate in the other. 'Bloody seagulls,' said Debbie. 'Little sods,' she said, laughing. 'I went to all of this effort and now look. Bastards have eaten all the meat. Guss, if you see any seagulls,' she continued, looking at him quite sternly, 'you bite their bums.'

'That looks amazing,' said Sam, who was admiring the paella that Debbie had just uncovered. Three large, butterflied prawns that had been grilled in garlic and parsley butter sat on top of a bed of rice. Mussels, clams, scallops and calamari were in abundance, while a few quartered lemons and a sprinkling of parsley completed the dish.

'I'm sorry you're not allowed any of this,' said Daniel, who had just finished his first mouthful.

'That's OK. I'm just glad that you're here,' I replied. And I was glad that they were there – very glad. Hopefully, Sam and Daniel would be able to give Debbie a bit of moral support over the coming days if she needed it. Although she said very little, it can't have been easy for Debbie. She'd never been one for sharing her innermost feelings when things were tough – not even to me, so she was very unlikely to open up to our friends. Even so, they were only just down the road, if needed.

The four of us spent the rest of the evening reminiscing over old times in Castres in which Xander Smythe, our previous employer, soon became the main topic of conversation.

'He's up to about five hundred now,' Sam said, before reaching for her glass of rosé.

'Five hundred what?' asked Debbie.

'Ways to remove Smythe from the planet.' I laughed. 'He writes them all down,' Sam explained. 'I hope we never get raided by the police. They'll lock him up and throw away the key.'

'Not when they find out what a bastard he is,' replied Daniel. 'They'll thank me for my services to mankind. I'll probably get knighted. Sir Daniel Winters, Le Grand Fromage of Ilkley Moor. Would you pass me the bread please, Debbie?'

Debbie and I spent the next morning preparing for our trip to Marseille. In reality, I did very little. I watched as Debbie packed my clothes very neatly into a suitcase, sorted out toiletries and ticked items off the list of things that I had to bring. It wasn't that I didn't want to help. It's just that Debbie is far more

174

organised than me and I knew from previous experience it was best not to get in her way. At about two o'clock, I took Guss to Sam and Daniel's apartment, where he was due to stay until Debbie returned later that evening.

'Are you sure you don't want Sam and Daniel to come?' I asked when I got back. 'They did offer – it's not too late.'

'I know, that was very sweet of them,' Debbie replied. 'I'm not sure I'd be much company, if I'm honest. Not sure if I want any either for that matter. That and we have no idea how long it's going to take to get you settled in. Anyway, who wants to spend part of their holiday at a hospital in Marseille? No, I'll be fine.'

'You will call them, though, if you need to?'

'Of course I will. Come on. Let's go.'

Two and a half hours later, we arrived at the Institut Paoli-Calmettes. Once we'd registered, we found my room, in which there were two beds. There was one man already there, who had unpacked his suitcase and had put a small radio by the side of his bed. A French radio station was playing a track by U2. I raised my eyebrows.

'Bastard,' I mouthed to Debbie. She smiled. Within an hour, Debbie had finished organising my locker which was to the side of my bed and we were almost ready to say our goodbyes.

'Come on,' I said. 'I'll walk you to the car.' Debbie's eyes began to well up. 'We've got Skype. We can talk tonight and then afterwards tomorrow. Anyway, you will call me to let me know you've got back safely?' Debbie nodded but was unable to speak. I walked Debbie down to the car park and kissed her goodbye. I went back up to the road and waited. As our car passed me, Debbie tried to wave but her face just crumpled, which caused mine to do the same. Within a few moments, she had joined the Marseille traffic, and I was making my way back upstairs.

That evening I was visited by all sorts of people. I had a blood test, I had my blood pressure taken, and I was offered some sedatives and given something to eat, which I cast to one side. Half an hour later I was approached by a male nurse who offered me a small electric razor. I tried to explain to him that I already had a razor of my own, but he was quite insistent.

'It is not for your face, monsieur,' he explained, and then he began to point to all the regions that I needed to shave, most of which were below my waist. He recommended that I did this in the shower and thrust a bottle of betadine into my hand. 'Your hair too,' he said. 'You need to wash your hair with this, also.'

Bloody hell, I said to myself as I got out of the shower. *I've seen oven-ready turkeys with more hair than me*. I smiled and then I began to think about Debbie and Guss. A tear rolled down my cheek.

Later that evening I spoke to Debbie. 'I didn't stay,' she said. 'I felt a bit guilty because when I got there, Sam and Daniel had laid the table for three people.'

'Oh, shame. So, what stopped you?'

'Partly what you said to Daniel.'

'Meaning?' I replied.

'That you insisted that he walk me home if I were to spend the evening with them.'

'Sorry, but who knows who walks those streets at night?'

'It's OK. It wasn't just that. I'm not really in the mood for eating. I think it's going to be a few glasses of the liquid cosh for me and that's that.'

I laughed. 'Wish I could join you.'

'You will, soon enough, my love. Anyway, how are you getting on?'

'Oh, you know – never a dull moment. I seem to be more popular than the Pope.'

'You're not too worried?'

'No. I'm thinking it's a bit like having my appendix out. Besides, by this time tomorrow I'll be cancer free and that's what counts. I'd best go. Looks like I'm going to be stabbed again,' I said, noticing a nurse coming towards me with a grey cardboard tray that contained a syringe. 'Love you.'

'Love you too. We'll talk tomorrow. Good luck,' said Debbie, before blowing me a kiss.

The rest of the evening was quite peaceful except that I'd somehow managed to tangle the cord to which the emergency button was attached around the metal headboard next to my pillow. Consequently, every time I turned over, a red light would start flashing on the opposite side of the room, soon after which a nurse would appear.

At about two o'clock the following morning, a very disgruntled nurse came in to get to the root of the problem. She made me sit up, untangled the cord, muttered something quite uncomplimentary in French and disappeared into the night.

Following my shower at seven o'clock that morning, a porter arrived with a wheelchair. He checked to see that I was appropriately dressed. I was wearing a very fetching navy-blue set of pyjamas with hat and slippers to match. I'd also been kitted out with a pair of deep vein thrombosis socks that it took two nurses to get onto my calves, which are big enough to grace a baby elephant.

I was wheeled along one corridor and then another until we got to a lift with a *No Entry to the Public* sign on it.

'Wait there,' instructed the porter, who pointed to a small bench. As I sat down, I couldn't help but wonder why I couldn't have walked there myself in the first place. Soon after, a nurse arrived, asked me for my name and date of birth and then began to inject a needle into my hand.

'Follow me,' she said once she had finished. She led me into an operating theatre that had a huge light just above the bed. 'Lie down here,' she said. I thought I had done exactly what had been asked of me when she said, 'Face, face, you need to move your face.' So, I sat up. The four or five nurses that were in the surrounding area started laughing. '*Fesses, fesses*,' she said, slapping her backside. 'You need to move your *fesses!* How was I to know that the French word for buttocks was *fesses* and pronounced exactly the same as face? My education hadn't stretched that far. 'OK, we'll begin,' said the nurse.

And that's the last thing I remembered until some time later, when I saw a masked face looking down at me.

'Monsieur Tyler, Monsieur Tyler,' said a voice that I recognised to be that of Doctor De Chaisemartin. 'Do you know where you are?'

I tried to focus. 'Hell?' I asked. I could hear a few sniggers in the background.

'He's fine,' concluded the brilliant doctor. I went back to sleep.

The next thing I remember is waking up again in my room. The chap in the next bed was snoring away and the sun was streaming through the window to my left. Slowly, I began to push myself backwards with my arms so that I could sit up. I was attached to a drip stand to my right with two tubes that were connected to my hand, which ached. There were a further two tubes that were attached to my stomach. I also remember a nurse telling me, prior to my operation, that I would have a button close at hand so that if I felt any pain I could self-administer a shot of morphine. This I was able to do once every fifteen minutes. I took advantage.

Shortly after, I was finding everything and everybody hilariously funny and grinning like a Cheshire cat. I was in a world of my own and very much enjoying it. I skyped Debbie later that evening but didn't remember a word of our conversation. I, apparently, sounded as if I was drunk and kept breaking into a rendition of The Banana Splits song. 'Tra la la la la la la,' was apparently all I kept saying. I also kept lolloping in and out of shot, which caused Debbie to give up on me fairly quickly. She was just glad that they had but barriers up at the side of my bed – not that I would have felt much pain had I fallen out.

The next morning a nurse came and removed the tubes from my stomach and, while she did so, the snoring man from the next bed came to say goodbye. He wished me luck and gave me a copy of the local newspaper, which I struggled to focus on. I was then advised by the nurse to use the morphine more sparingly. She showed me how to remove and attach a colostomy bag to the plastic plinth that had been sewn into my stomach. She said that she would also show Debbie how to change the plaster that surrounded it when she arrived, all being well, at the weekend.

As the nurse wheeled away the privacy screen that she had put around the bed, I saw that I had a new companion. In the bed next to me was an elderly gentleman who, even though unconscious, was suffering from extreme flatulence. Every minute or two he exploded, which, at first, I found quite funny – until the morphine began to wear off, and then I didn't. I turned the television on and put up the volume to drown out the noise, but it made no difference. He was louder, or at least his bottom was, so I gave up. At seven o'clock that evening a nurse came in with my supper and I thought to ask her if, maybe, she could find me or him another room. She put a tray down in front of me and I began to raise my hand to ask her a question. She hadn't seen me. Instead, she walked over to the gentleman, who was then awake. He beckoned to the nurse to come closer and whispered something her ear. Minutes later she was back and was wheeling said gentleman out of the room. Thank God for that, I thought. Maybe the poor old man had been embarrassed. I put the television back on and started to tuck into my Brie-filled baguette. I put on The Simpsons and let out a sigh of relief. I'd just watched the opening titles with the family sitting on the sofa, when the sound of breaking wind started again. Had they brought the old man back? Was he in the next room and the walls were made of paper? And then it dawned on me. It wasn't him at all. It had been me all the time. He'd asked to be moved. Oh, the shame of it! I stared at my stomach accusingly. Debbie and I were due to start a new job in a couple of weeks – 'Hello Madame Amari, I'm Brent,' followed by me breaking wind was not likely to be the best introduction anyone's ever had to a new employer. And I certainly couldn't tell her about the cancer. That would be game over before we'd even got there. What were we going to do?

'Don't worry,' said the nurse, who then laughed. 'It's quite normal just after your operation. It will settle down soon enough.'

'Do these things come with silencers?' I asked. 'I mean, if the old guy could hear it and asked to be moved, what is everyone else going to think?'

'Oh, I very much doubt he heard you at all,' explained the nurse. 'He's virtually deaf. He was due to be moved anyway. His operation is tomorrow. Try not worry,' she said reassuringly, before chuckling away to herself and leaving the room.

'Monsieur Tyler, what are you still doing in bed?' asked Doctor De Chaisemartin as I was sitting up in bed and looking at my computer at about eleven o'clock the next morning. 'You need to get some exercise. You won't get much in bed.'

'You don't know the nurses very well then, do you?' I said.

'How are you feeling?' she asked, looking quite exasperated.

'I feel OK.'

'That's good,' replied the doctor, who then pulled back my bedsheet and began to prod around my stomach. 'I've made you an appointment with an oncologist in Mougins for your chemotherapy.'

'Oh, really? When's that then?'

Doctor De Chaisemartin took her phone out of her back pocket and scrolled through some screens. 'May the thirteenth,' she said. 'Eleven o'clock.'

'May the thirteenth?' I replied. 'Sorry, can't do it.'

'What do you mean you can't do it?' said the doctor, who was frowning.

'It's my wife's birthday and...'

And then all hell broke loose. 'Monsieur Tyler!' she bellowed. 'Monsieur Tyler!' she shouted again, this time even louder. Frankly, a bomb could have gone off in the next room and I wouldn't have heard it.

'Ah, shit,' I said, cupping my hands over my ears.

'This is chemotherapy. Do you know how important that is?'

'No, but clearly you do.'

'It might just save your life, which is a bit more important than a birthday, wouldn't you think? I recommend you keep the appointment. You will have all the details before you leave.'

'Which is when?'

'Friday, if there are no problems. Unless, of course, I can find a good reason to keep you here over the weekend, which right now seems quite tempting.' She smiled. 'Now, I suggest you start taking some exercise along the corridor. And please don't keep interrupting the nurses while you're at it. I'm sure they have enough to do.'

'Spoilsport.' Doctor De Chaisemartin began to make her way out of the room. She muttered some words of exasperation in French and closed the door behind her.

Chapter 20

I was much relieved to be back in our Apartment in Antibes on the Friday evening, although the return journey from Marseille seemed a bit strange for me. I hadn't realised how quiet the hospital had been and the sounds of the outside world took some getting used to – for the first few days everything appeared to be amplified. In my absence, Debbie had organised a Skype interview with a young man whose family had a large property in Maussane-les-Alpilles, about a hundred and fifty miles north east of Antibes. Nestled in the heart of the Bouches-Du-Rhône, the château where we would be working, if all went well, was in a very rural location. The area would be nothing like the hustle and bustle of Antibes to which we had become accustomed, but Debbie reasoned that a more relaxed way of life might be exactly what we needed to help with my recuperation.

'We'd really be dropping Madame Amari in it,' I said, 'if we took that job now. They want someone to start at the beginning of June, latest. I know she's not due to get there until then but even so, it's not going to give Madame Amari much chance to find replacements. Most people who do our job are already booked.'

'I know,' replied Debbie, 'but for once it needs to be about us. Anyway, we haven't been offered the job yet. We should at least have a look.'

On the Saturday morning we had a Skype interview with Hamish and his wife Hannah. They both appeared to be very personable and it transpired that the château was owned by Hannah's parents, who were extremely wealthy property developers based in Edinburgh. During our conversation, Hamish explained that the outgoing guardian, Christophe, was an alcoholic whose wife had left him six months previously along with their two-year-old son. Since then, Christophe's problem with alcohol had worsened and Hamish was then having to get taxis from the airport as he had no idea in what condition Christophe was likely to arrive.

'One day, he didn't turn up at all,' Hamish said. 'Hannah and I were

182

standing outside Avignon airport for a good fifteen minutes and there was no sign of him, so we phoned. It was Monday morning, and he thought it was still Sunday.' They both laughed. 'So, we landed up getting a taxi. Even then, when we got back to the château and went to his apartment, all I could hear was snoring. Not much of a welcome, was it? I don't expect the red-carpet treatment, but I would like my guardians to be awake when we get there – for the first five minutes, at least.' Then he laughed again. By the end of our conversation, which seemed to have gone very well, we agreed for Hamish to organise a visit for us to Maussane-les-Alpilles. He would contact Christophe, who would hopefully be there for our arrival. More importantly, he explained, Hamish would like us to meet the French gardener who I would be assisting three days a week. The other two and a half days I would be working on my own. Debbie's initial tasks would be to organise the kitchen that had had no attention paid to it for years and to make sure that all the rooms were properly aired and to report any areas of real concern such as damp, faulty appliances and errant workmen.

'I've employed a couple of masons,' Hamish explained, 'but I can't be sure if they turn up and there's no point in asking Christophe. I doubt he can remember what he was doing five minutes ago if I'm honest with you. Every time I come down to the château, very little work seems to have been done except on their invoices, which I can only describe as ambitious. The thing is, there is really a lot to be done as we would like to restore the place to its former glory before next summer, which is a bit of an ask but we would like to start renting the château out. You'll see a coffee table book when you go into the main salon, Debbie. It has all of the most beautiful properties in the area listed inside. Ours is one of them but you wouldn't recognise it now.'

'That's a shame,' replied Debbie. 'What happened?'

'Previous owners,' explained Hannah. 'Ran out of money. Nothing done to it for years, and these places need a lot of money to maintain. In the end, they were forced to sell it. Daddy bought it for a song.' She smiled. 'And now, he's given it to me.'

'Us,' interjected Hamish, whose wife ignored him.

'We need a couple that can hit the ground running,' said Hamish. *Here we go*, I thought. 'We've got to get a lot more skilled workmen in, ones that we can trust. The trouble is, getting anyone to turn up there at all is like herding cats, and we can't do it from here. So, look, we'll be back to you soon and once you've visited we can, perhaps, start making a plan. Sorry guys, but I've to go now. Got a client on the hook. Catch up soon.' Hamish and Hannah smiled and waved, and the screen went blank.

As Debbie was about to take the roast chicken out of the oven at lunchtime on Sunday, an email came through from Hamish apologising for the short notice, but he'd arranged for us to meet Christophe and Patrice, the gardener, on Monday at eleven. He sent a code to get in through the gates in case nobody answered when we arrived. Apparently, it had happened to Hamish on more than one occasion, so we shouldn't be surprised. Once we had finished our visit, Hamish suggested that we have lunch in the town, which he would pay for.

'Blimey, he's keen,' I said to Debbie, who had by then put all of the food out on the table. 'When are the other twelve people coming?' I asked jokingly as I looked at the carrots, peas, roast potatoes, broccoli, green beans and sausage meat stuffing that had been brought to the table.

'I know,' Debbie replied, smiling as she poured some gravy into jug from a saucepan that she had just taken from the stove. 'Needs to be used up,' she said. 'Anyway, we can always take a packed lunch with us tomorrow. If we eat at the restaurant instead, I'm sure Guss will appreciate this food,' she added, looking at our dog, who was fast asleep in the corner. Before we sat down to eat, I sent an email to Hamish confirming our appointment the following day.

'There's remote and there's remote,' I said to Debbie as we approached the entrance to Château La Croix at ten to eleven. We had just driven along a few miles of country lanes that were surrounded by fields of vines and olive groves.

We hadn't seen a car for ages but had seen a few tractors. We'd passed through the town on the way, but it certainly wasn't within walking distance. 'Gates? What gates?' I asked as we drove between two stone pillars. Certainly, the gates were there but they were also flung wide open. 'Glad to see they're on top of security,' I said as we wound our way along the drive that was flanked by some very impressive, lush lawns.

'*Sangliers*,' I said to Debbie. 'Wild boar.'

'What about them?' she asked.

'Electric fences everywhere. Look,' I said, pointing towards them. 'That'll please Guss.'

'And me,' replied Debbie. 'Nothing I like more than Guss shouting at *sangliers* at three in the morning.' She smiled. 'No better way to start your day. Look, we're here now,' she said as we pulled up next to an old blue Renault saloon car that had several dents in its bodywork. The three of us got out of the car and began to wander around. We poked our heads into the barn where there was a tractor, to the side of which were several rusty attachments. There were two rusty bicycles with flat tyres, a chainsaw, a leaf blower, some shears and odd pieces of pipe, as well as random bits and pieces for the watering system. On the beams just above our heads were old, wooden doors, sheets of plasterboard and several lengths of wood.

We left the barn and walked through a side entrance. Electrical wires dangled out of some recently plastered walls and we had to watch our footsteps as some floorboards were missing. We called out, 'Hello' and '*bonjour*,' but there was no response. Were we on our own? Had Hamish got the wrong day? We simply didn't know. Sure, we'd arrived at jobs where our presence wasn't welcome by the outgoing guardian, but we'd never arrived at a place that was completely deserted.

'I think that's it over there,' said Debbie. 'The guardian's apartment.' As we walked across the courtyard, Guss spotted a very thin, medium-sized, elderly white dog. Guss wagged his tail. As we got closer, the dog put its tail between its legs, began to shake and then urinated. 'Poor thing,' said Debbie, who put Guss on his lead. 'He's terrified. Sorry Guss, not this time. Why don't you go and see if he's there? I'll walk Guss around a bit.'

I walked towards the apartment. Just outside there was a small, unkept garden. On the porch was a child's plastic tricycle, a bucket and spade and a bowl of dog food that was attracting flies. The front door was open.

I tapped gently on one of the windows and called out, '*Bonjour.*' There was no response. I looked towards Debbie and shrugged my shoulders. She looked at me quite sternly and motioned for me to go inside. Gingerly, I did as I was instructed. Surely I was trespassing? Besides, he could be dangerous. He was another person who had just lost everything. How deranged was he, exactly? For a few seconds I stood at the entrance, looking inside at the kitchen-cum-living room. It wasn't particularly messy. Yes, there was clothing dotted about the place and the sink was full of dishes, but I concluded it wasn't much different from many a bachelor pad that I had seen or lived in myself. I was about to take a step forward when one of the loudest sneezes I have ever heard came from a room that I took to be the bedroom. I nearly wet myself. The sneeze was followed by a groan and the groan was followed by snoring. I turned round and left the apartment as quickly as I could.

As I did so, I pointed with my thumb and mouthed to Debbie, 'He's in there.'

'Are you OK?' Debbie said. 'You're shaking.'

'I'm not surprised,' I said. 'He could have been in there, waiting with an axe for all I know.'

'You've been watching too many films,' Debbie replied. 'Come on, my brave little soldier.'

'Oh, sod off!' Debbie laughed.

'Where to now, Einstein?' I asked.

'Might as well go and have a look around inside the château,' Debbie replied. 'Wait to see if Sleeping Beauty wakes up. Come on.'

One thing that Hamish was right about was that the château had had nothing spent on it in a very long time. Although the formal gardens had been well cared for, the décor inside the building told a different story. We'd seen this scenario many times since moving to France. Landed gentry who now lived in just one room in a sizeable property to keep running costs down were more common than we had first thought. In the end the owners would be forced to sell, which we imagined to be difficult when the estate had been passed down through several generations. Guss and I followed Debbie, who was making notes about each room. We went up to the first floor and into one of the bedrooms. It smelled very musty, so Debbie opened the shutters. We looked down onto a courtyard in which there was a long, stone table complete with a red and white tablecloth. Sitting at the table were two workmen enjoying their lunch. Noticing us, one of them, who had just torn off a piece of baguette, looked up and shouted, '*Bonjour.*'

'*Bonjour,*' I replied. '*Bon appetit.*'

'*Merci,*' he said, waving his piece of baguette in our direction, at which point the other workman did the same.

'What time is it?' I asked Debbie.

'Eleven-thirty,' she replied, looking at her watch.

'That's a bit early for lunch, even by French standards,' I said.

'No wonder Hamish wants someone here sooner rather than later,' Debbie replied. 'But do you know what's more worrying?'

'What's that?'

'They didn't bother to ask who we were. We could be anybody,' Debbie said, looking through the wallpaper-lined chest of draws to the right of the four-poster bed.

'Maybe they knew we were coming,' I reasoned.

'Wouldn't bank on it. Come on, let's go and talk to them,' Debbie said as she closed her notepad and put her pen in her coat pocket. 'Doesn't look like there's much going on round here.'

We went downstairs and chatted to the two workmen. We asked about both the guardian, who they rarely saw, and also the gardener, who usually came to the château three times a week, though the days that he worked tended to vary.

'Patrice is a very good gardener and has many contracts in the village,' one of them explained, 'so he has to juggle things around. He's normally here by now,' he said, looking at his watch. 'He starts early. So, you're going to be the new guardians?' the man asked, just before dunking a piece of baguette into his coffee.

'We're not sure,' replied Debbie, who was clearly not at all impressed with the situation. At that point we noticed a man approaching us through the archway that led towards the drive. He was dressed in jeans, Wellington boots and a blue pullover. He acknowledged the two workmen, pulled up a seat and began to talk to them. Debbie and I struggled to make out what he was saying but assumed it was to do with the work on the property.

After about ten minutes, he turned to me and said in French, 'You're taking my job then?'

'I don't think so. What do you do?' I replied.

'I'm Christophe, the guardian. You didn't know that?' He laughed.

'As you haven't introduced yourself, how would I?' I said, before glancing at Debbie.

'So, you have had a look around already?'

'Yes,' replied Debbie.

'Good, then I don't need to show you,' he said, at the same time as taking out a silver hip flask from his trouser pocket. He unscrewed the lid and took a swig. The two workmen looked at each other and shook their heads.

'And what about Patrice?' I asked.

'Patrice?' replied Christophe, who laughed again. 'Not today. He will be servicing Madame Bovary,' he said. He winked at the workmen, who smiled.

'Servicing?' Debbie asked.

'Yes,' said Christophe, 'Servicing. She is a widow and Patrice services both her and her garden. At least he will do until his wife finds out and then there will be real trouble. She has a big temper. I should know, she's my sister.'

I raised my eyebrows. 'You haven't told her?'

'You must be joking. Patrice is a good friend. I can phone him if you like to see if he'll come and meet you, but I doubt I'll have much success.'

'The thing is,' I explained, 'he was supposed to be here to show me the gardens and how it all works.'

'He won't do that,' said Christophe. 'He doesn't want any help in the garden. He's already told that to Hamish, but Hamish doesn't listen. He said that if Hamish employs another gardener he will end the contract. He doesn't need the work.'

Christophe's phone rang. For a few minutes Debbie and I sat in silence while Christophe talked. Suddenly we could hear shouting. Christophe got up and began to pace around.

'Hamish is not happy that Patrice is not here. I tried to explain that he is busy with Madame Bovary but that just made him mad.'

'He knows about Madame Bovary?' I asked.

'Everybody knows about Madame Bovary, except one,' replied Christophe, who then laughed. He reached again for his hip flask, which he had put on the table. 'I'm going for my lunch now. Feel free to continue having a look around.' He belched and staggered towards the archway.

Debbie and I got up, said our goodbyes to the workmen, got Guss into the car and made our way down the drive. 'What do you reckon?' I said. Before Debbie had chance to answer, the phone rang. 'It's him.'

'It's who?' Debbie asked.

'Hamish.'

'Bloody hell, that was quick.'

'Christophe must have phoned him. Hello Hamish.' I put the phone on loud speaker.

'What do you think?' he asked.

'I think it's a very impressive château,' I said. 'It has a lot of potential.'

'So, you'll take the job?'

'I think so,' I said, 'but Debbie and I haven't had chance to discuss it yet.'

'Not much to discuss, I would have thought,' replied Hamish cheerily.

'Any negatives, I'm sure we can iron them out.'

'I just have one concern,' I said. 'We didn't get to meet the gardener.'

'I'm sorry about that,' replied Hamish, 'He's really busy and he doesn't have a phone.' Debbie smiled and shook her head. 'He was really looking forward to meeting you and I'm sure you'd make a great team. Got to run. I'll call you later and we can discuss contracts and start dates.' The line went dead.

'Lying bastard,' said Debbie.

'So, what do you think?' I asked.

'Sounds a bit of a hornet's nest to me. It's a tough one. Also, Hamish has just lied to us. Patrice doesn't have a phone?'

'Maybe he just didn't want to give the number to Hamish. You've seen how manic he can be.'

'He's not only manic, he's also desperate,' I said, reaching into the glove compartment for a boiled sweet. 'Want one?'

'No thanks.'

'He's offered us the job before we got out of the drive. That's just weird.' During our journey back, Hamish phoned a further two times to ask if we'd come to a decision. In the end, Debbie just said, 'Forget it. The man's clearly nuts.' I phoned Hamish, who became very angry, so angry that I put the phone down on him. That, however, didn't stop him from contacting us. Five minutes later we received a text demanding that we write in no more than three hundred words the reasons that we had decided to turn the job down. We didn't reply.

Chapter 21

With no other job prospects on the horizon, Debbie and I loaded our car one early Sunday morning in May and headed to the Cap D'Antibes, where we were due to start work the following morning. We were greeted by the very sceptical gardener, who had parked a large, rusty blue van in the middle of the drive. The back doors were open and inside there were piles of palm leaves stacked up alongside branches of bougainvillea. He motioned for us to park around the side of the villa and watched suspiciously as we unloaded the car. Guss took the opportunity to explore the garden, watering the agapanthus as he went.

I went to examine the pool's technical room, while Debbie spent some time in our bedroom trying to decide what clothes we would need for the summer. At midday the gardener got into his van and disappeared through the gates without saying a word to Debbie or me.

'Couldn't give a damn,' said Debbie, who was by then in the kitchen and inspecting the crockery. 'We don't work for him. Anyway, he's only supposed to be here first thing in the morning and early evenings. He's got his own job.'

'Greedy bastard.'

'They all are. Have you seen the state of these?' she said, pointing to a pile of plates that were next to the sink. 'Nothing matches. Looks like they've been bought from a jumble sale.' Debbie laughed. 'How on earth do they hold dinner parties round here? And they're filthy too, like the rest of the villa. It's going to take me ages to get this place up to scratch, which is a bit of a bugger because her son and daughter-in-law are due to come down from Switzerland next week. Hope I can do it.'

'Can't you tell Madame Amari what the place is like?'

'What can she do? Anyway, that's what I'm paid for.'

'It's also what the gardener's daughter has been paid for throughout the winter and she has done fuck all by the looks of things.'

'I know. It amazes me how people get away with it. I mean, the more we seem to do, the more people want. Yet other people get away with it for years. We're doing something wrong here, Brent.' I smiled.

We worked through the afternoon and then about six o'clock we went to sit outside at the dining table on the patio next to the lounge.

'Cheers,' I said, raising a glass of rosé. 'Here's to the season. Good luck everybody.' Debbie raised her glass and smiled.

'Do you think we're OK sitting here?' Debbie asked.

'How do you mean?'

'Well, out here on the patio. What if he comes back and sees us?'

'What if he does? We're not working. We're not even due to start until tomorrow. Anyway, we're not prisoners confined to one room. Forget it.'

'I suppose.'

At two o'clock the following morning, I shouted, 'Ouch, ouch, ouch!'

Debbie woke up. 'What's up?' She put the light on.

'Pain in my back.'

'Where?'

'Here, and across my ribs,' I said, putting my hands on my side. I got out of bed and for a short while the pain subsided, so I got back into bed. Then it started again. I tried sitting up. I tried one side and then the other. I even tried kneeling on all fours, but it made no difference. I was in agony.

'Right, that's it,' said Debbie. 'Get dressed.'

'Why? Where are we going?'

'Hospital – that's where we're going. Come on.'

'We've only just got here.'

'I don't care. Get dressed.' Reluctantly, I got into the car along with Debbie and Guss, and we made our way to La Fontonne hospital, where Debbie and I sat in the emergency waiting room. I described my symptoms and was soon taken for an X-Ray.

'We have found a bed for you,' said a nurse around thirty minutes later.

'For me?' I asked. 'There must be a mistake – I don't need a bed, just some antibiotics.'

'You are Monsieur Tyler?' she asked, looking at her notes.

'I am.'

'Then you need a bed. Monsieur Tyler, you have pneumonia.'

'Fucking great. Exactly what we need,' I said.

At seven o'clock that evening, Debbie came back to see me. 'How are you getting on?' she asked.

'Much better thanks,' I said. 'The pain's beginning to go. And you?'

'Been busy with the villa. I've also been trying to throw the gardener off the scent.'

'How do you mean?' I asked.

'Well, he won't have seen you, but he will have seen a tub of chlorine and your pool testing kit next to the pool. He'll also have seen your work boots outside the front door.'

'Cunning.'

'I know,' said Debbie, smiling. 'Have to leave some evidence of you lying around. Any idea how long you're going to be in here?'

'Hopefully, not long. I'm on the mend now.'

'Thank God for that. You're a walking disaster area, my boy. Right, I'd better go. I'll see you tomorrow.'

On the Friday, Debbie came to collect me from the hospital. Somehow, she'd managed to keep the charade going for the gardener. We'd got away with it.

While I was in hospital, Debbie had received an email from Madame Amari saying that her son, Jonny, and his wife, Pamela, would be driving to the villa from Switzerland on Saturday. She didn't know how long they would be staying. Jonny was, apparently, always very evasive when it came to his schedule. Having said that, Madame Amari felt that they were very unlikely to be staying any more than a week. She also mentioned that they might be joined by their teenage daughters, so Debbie should make up three of the four bedrooms that were in the villa.

'Any idea what time they're arriving?' I asked Debbie, who was busy ironing some bed linen in the lounge.

'Not got a clue,' she replied, 'but I think I'm ready.' We waited, and we waited. Debbie tried phoning Jonny's mobile but each time it went straight to answerphone. At nine o'clock that evening we assumed they weren't coming, so we sat outside with a glass of wine.

I'd just taken my first sip when I shouted, 'Ouch, bastard!' and started flailing my arms in the air. 'I've just been bitten by a mosquito – the little shit.'

'Where?' Debbie asked.

'On the chin.'

'Which one?'

'Oh, very funny. Have we got any spray?'

'In the back kitchen.'

As I walked into the kitchen, I could see some lights shining through a gap in the gates from the outside. I heard a car door slam and then someone rang on the buzzer.

'Shit, they're here!' I shouted to Debbie.

'Oh, bollocks,' she replied. As I picked up the clicker to open the gate, I heard the clanking of glasses and a bottle as Debbie began to clear the table outside. I opened the front door and Guss, whose tailing was wagging at a rate of knots, rushed past me to greet our visitors. Once the gates were opened, a white 4x4 BMW pulled into the drive. I followed Guss and waited. After a few moments, the back door of the car began to rise and the driver got out of the car. The passenger, who I assumed to be Pamela, was on the phone and stayed in the car.

A tall, thin man in his mid-fifties with a mop of grey hair introduced himself. 'Hello, I'm Jonny,' he said in a voice reminiscent of Arnold

Schwarzenegger. He didn't really look at me but, instead, began to examine the bonnet of his car under the lights that shone from the outside walls of the villa onto the driveway.

'Fucking bugs. They get everywhere. I'll have to clean them off after dinner,' he said. *Dinner, what dinner?* I thought to myself. Debbie certainly hadn't been asked to prepare anything. Maybe they were going out. 'Open the garage doors please, Brent. That fucking tree is lethal. I hate it,' he said, looking up at a very tall pine tree. 'The sap from that will ruin the paintwork on my car. I've asked my mother many times to cut it down. Oh, shit. The garage is full of junk,' he said, peering into the double doors. 'That gardener is the messiest bastard I've ever known. Can you get him on the phone? He can come round here now and sort this out. I'm not leaving my car out here tonight.' I did as I was told but the gardener's phone was switched off.

As I looked into the garage, in which there was a sit-down mower, plastic petrol cans, discarded shoes and other work clothes, a woman passed me and said, 'Pamela.' As I turned round, I saw her disappear into the house.

'I'll have to park on the lawn tonight,' Jonny said, and he went back to the car. I wandered into the kitchen, where Debbie was talking to Pamela.

'But you're supposed to be the cook. So, why is there no food?' Pamela said, looking at Debbie quite sternly.

'Housekeeper-cook, actually,' replied Debbie, who was ready to defend herself. 'I cook when I'm asked to and as nobody has asked me to, I haven't cooked.'

'Well, I'm asking you now,' snapped Pamela.

'Then you're asking too late,' said Debbie, who had become very flushed. 'There's nowhere open to buy any food, except restaurants. Besides, I haven't been given any petty cash.'

With that, Pamela scowled, opened her black clutch bag, took out five one-hundred-euro notes and thrust them towards Debbie. 'Here,' she said. She then looked at me. 'Bags,' she said.

'Which bags?' I replied.

'The bags that are in the car. Where are they?'

'In the car, I imagine.'

'In the car? In the car?' Pamela said, with her face contorted. 'Did you not see the back door open when we arrived?'

'I did.'

'Well, that was your signal to unload the car.' I was about to retaliate when I saw Debbie shaking her head and motioning me to go outside. For a few seconds I glared at Pamela, while weighing up my options. We'd made it through week one, I thought, but if I said what was on my mind, there was very unlikely to be a week two, so I took Debbie's advice and left. I brought five or six cases into the villa and took them into Jonny and Pamela's bedroom, where Debbie was asked to unpack while our visitors sat outside. The car had been moved onto the lawn, in which there were now two very long trenches about three inches deep where the BMW's tyres had sunk into the grass. I noticed that the lights of the car had been left on, so I went to tell Jonny, who was sitting down with a large scotch and puffing away on an enormous cigar.

Not at all bothered by my presence, he turned to his wife and said, 'Pamela, you've left the lights on. Leave my fucking car alone.'

'Sorry, Jonny, I dropped my phone in there and...' Without waiting for her to finish her sentence, Jonny got up and walked around the side of the house towards the lawn.

'Couldn't give a shit, that one,' I said to Debbie as we went up to our room at just after eleven.

'That one being?' Debbie asked.

'Jonny. Look at what he's done to the lawn,' I said, pointing out our window.

'Oh, my God,' Debbie said, before putting her hand over her mouth. 'The gardener's going to go mad.'

At eight o'clock the following morning, I went to the grocery shop just down the road that I figured had to be one of the most expensive in the world. Everything was beautifully laid out and there wasn't a single blemish on any of the fruit or vegetables. I picked up a punnet each of strawberries, raspberries and blueberries, as well as a couple of baguettes, some fruit juices, a few yoghurt pots and half a watermelon. I took out twenty euros in readiness to pay. A very pretty woman in her twenties who was wearing a skirt that was only just bigger than the average belt tapped away on the till.

When she finished, she smiled and said, 'That's thirty-five euros and twenty cents, please.'

I somehow stopped myself from blurting out, 'Fuck me, you're having a laugh,' and instead, took my wallet out of my trouser pocket. Dick Turpin usually wore a mask, I thought to myself – clearly not on this occasion. I'd just been fleeced. Outside, I studied the receipt that the young woman had put into my shopping bag. Everything was at least double the price of the shop ten minutes down the road. I was just glad it wasn't my money.

'The quality is much better, according to Pamela,' Debbie explained when I got back. 'She can tell the difference, she says.'

'Of course she can,' I replied sarcastically, while tearing into a baguette that I had bought for ourselves. 'A strawberry, is a strawberry, is a strawberry...'

'Not in her world,' interrupted Debbie. 'Give me a hand to lay the table, would you?'

'Seen anyone yet?' I asked as Debbie passed me some placemats and cutlery.

'Not a soul.' And we didn't see a soul until eleven o'clock. Jonny appeared dressed in some swimming trunks, a polo shirt and flip-flops. He wandered towards the kitchen. In his right hand he was holding a small, clear toiletry bag that was full of tablets. Debbie rushed to the fridge and took the fruit out to the table outside for the third time that morning.

Jonny scratched his head, yawned and said, 'Coffee.'

'Filter or Nescafé?' I asked.

197

'Nescafé's fine.'

'Sugar?'

'No.' Jonny left the kitchen. When I took his coffee outside, Jonny was standing on the small step machine next to the dining table and pacing up and down. He was also puffing away on a cigar. The food had not been touched. Moments later, Pamela arrived in her dressing gown. She sat down without acknowledging either me or Debbie, who were hovering around just to make sure that everything was OK. Pamela picked up a handful of blueberries, put them into a bowl, poured in some plain yoghurt, mixed the two together and began to eat.

With her mouth almost full she said, 'Tea. Lapsang souchong.'

'Milk?' I asked.

'Don't be ridiculous.' I brought Pamela her tea and soon after she announced that she was going shopping. Jonny, who by this time was sitting at the table and watching YouTube videos on his laptop, paid no attention. Pamela disappeared into her bedroom and returned five minutes later in a short, patterned dress and what I can only describe as Roman sandals that were laced up around the ankles. *I'm Spartacus*, I thought to myself.

Jangling a set of car keys in her right hand she said, 'See you later, Jonny.' Jonny grunted and turned up the volume on his laptop. Pamela walked back into the kitchen and left through the side door. Debbie and I let out a sigh of relief. Moments later we heard some tyres spinning. Then they stopped and then they started again. This happened several times before we heard a car door slam, some cursing that we assumed to be in Arabic and the sound of some footsteps that were rapidly approaching the villa.

'Bloody car,' Pamela moaned. 'I can't move it.'

Jonny reluctantly put his video on pause, slowly got out of his seat, asked Debbie and I to follow him and sauntered off towards the lawn.

'Oh, fuck, Pamela! What have you done to my car? Look at the state of it!' he said as he looked at his BMW that was now covered in mud. Not only that, the wheels had sunk further into the grass and the car was a matter of inches from sitting on its frame.

'It's not my fault,' Pamela protested. 'The grass is too wet. It's like a sponge,' she said as she pressed down on the lawn with her right foot.

'It is not a fucking sponge,' replied Jonny. 'You tried to drive too fast. Give me the keys, Pamela, I'd better do it. Debbie, Brent, you'd better give me a push.' While we stood at the back of the car, trying our hardest to move it, Pamela stood, watching from the side with her arms folded.

After a few minutes the car had not moved an inch. Jonny wound down his window. 'Pamela, you'd better help,' he said.

'I can't,' she replied. 'Look at me. I'm not dressed for it. Besides, I'm not strong enough.'

'Do you want to go shopping or not?'

As the three of us pushed, the wheels span once more, and Jonny shot off at high speed down the lawn and came to a halt about two feet from the cherry tree. Debbie and I cheered as we'd managed to get the car out of the muddy trench, while Pamela frowned as she looked down at her mud-spattered legs. She then marched off back into the villa while Jonny slowly drove the car back onto the drive. He got out and walked over to the side of the garage, where he turned on a tap that was connected to a garden hose. He began to wash the car, at the same time looking for any signs of damage. While he did that, Debbie and I returned to the breakfast table, where we began to clear away what had been used and began to load the dishwasher. We watched through the kitchen window as the BMW made its way through the front gates. Jonny soon joined us and started opening the kitchen cupboards.

'Can I help?' I asked.

'Coffee,' Jonny replied.

'I'll bring you one if you like,' Debbie said.

'Thank you.'

'Any damage?' I asked.

'Only to the lawn.' Jonny replied.

'Bashar's not going to be pleased,' I said.

'Fuck Bashar,' said Jonny, before heading back outside. I smiled.

As I took Jonny's coffee, I noticed a couple of seaplanes that were getting close to the surface of the sea and then taking off again. Intrigued, I said to Jonny, 'What are they up to?'

'Collecting water,' he replied. 'It's for the Esterel forest. Gets very hot this time of year. They spray it so we don't get fires.'

'Has there ever been a fire?' I asked.

'Just the one,' Jonny said. 'About ten years ago, which was a bit unfortunate for one diver.'

'One diver?' I asked. 'What's a diver got to do with a forest fire?'

'Usually nothing,' Jonny replied. 'But on this occasion, he'd finished his dive and was just coming up to the surface when one of the planes swooped down to get some water. Unfortunately, it picked him up as well as the water and dropped him straight into the fire.'

'Really?'

'Yes, really.'

'Did he survive?'

'Wouldn't have thought so.'

Chapter 22

'I've left the boot open, Brent,' Pamela announced as she returned from her shopping trip. She forced a smile and marched past me towards the front door of the villa, which she swung open. I put down my secateurs, removed my gardening gloves and went to the back of the BMW. I took a tissue out of my pocket and wiped away a small drop of blood from my arm that I'd scratched while dead-heading the roses. *Heaven help me*, I thought, *if I drip anything over Pamela's designer bags*. I leaned over and picked up three small paper bags that were very light. On my way into the villa, I passed Jonny, who, once again, came to inspect the bodywork of his car. When I got back, he was gingerly rubbing away at a small blemish on the bonnet.

Jonny groaned, 'I paid a lot for a garage to coat the hood with an anti-bug spray and look. There's more than ever – bastards. I reckon they're attracted to it.' While I continued to tackle the rose bushes, Jonny spent the next half an hour or so painstakingly removing the debris from his car. Occasionally he'd stop and utter some expletive or other before returning to his task.

I smiled as I looked at our eight-year-old, black Honda CRV whose paintwork was faded and scratched but had managed to survive the rigours of driving in France. It had been up and down pot-holed country lanes, had both wing mirrors taken out by some careless French lorry drivers and survived a heavy branch falling on its roof, thanks to a careless idiot with a chainsaw who hadn't bothered to warn us of what he was doing. More accurately, it was his mate who was standing in the middle of a lane when we were in Montauroux who was at fault. He was the lookout but instead of asking us to wait, he waved us through. The wave was followed by a large bang. The bang was followed by me shouting and the lookout apologising profusely. I tried to explain that he could have easily killed a motorcyclist or a pedestrian, but he just grinned sheepishly and that was that. Our car wasn't at all flash although I had managed to get it stuck in the middle of the Paradis Porsche procession in Saint Tropez the previous October.

There was only so much waiting that I was prepared to do in a side street while a procession of white Porsche 911s passed me, so I pulled out. Horrified spectators put their video cameras down and a *gendarme* blew his whistle before flailing his arms around, but I wasn't stopping. Debbie put her head in her hands and tried to make herself look invisible, while Guss stuck his head out of the open back window to see what the fuss was all about. A Porsche behind me flashed its lights and hooted its horn but I figured that we had the right to be on the road as much as anyone else, so I stayed in the procession until I saw a sign to the A8, where we parted company. Crowds who had lined the streets jeered and shook their fists. There were a few more beeps of horns and eventually Debbie sat up and declared me a total embarrassment. Nonetheless, I was then, and still am now, very proud of our car. It was the one thing that had been consistent since we'd been in France and, more importantly, it had never let us down.

My reminiscing was interrupted by Jonny saying, 'I'm off to the airport soon to pick up my daughters. How long do you think it will take, Brent?'

'About three quarters of an hour,' I replied. 'Probably a fair bit quicker in yours.' I smiled.

'I doubt it, I never speed. I'd better make it an hour.' Jonny then left to go inside. I'd never really thought about it before, but it was often the case that I'd been stuck behind a car with Swiss number plates while driving along the coast road. However powerful the car, it would dawdle along at twenty miles an hour either oblivious or not caring about the line of traffic behind it. As the driver rarely pulled over to let others pass, this would quite often create a dangerous situation. I'd watch in my rear-view mirror as a car two or three behind me would leap out and go for it. The driver would hoot his horn and flash his lights, which was very much the same action taken by the driver of the car coming the other way who was trying to avoid a head-on collision.

As I walked into the kitchen one morning at coffee time, I could hear raised voices. 'You really do need to tell me a little sooner,' snapped Debbie, who was locking horns with Pamela..

'It's only two more people,' replied Pamela.

'That may be,' said Debbie,' but I've only bought enough fish for two. The thing is, Pamela, I shop on a daily basis. The reason I do that is, firstly, so that the food is fresh and, secondly, the fridge doesn't get very cold, so the food will go off otherwise. Now I have to go out again. Surely you must have known some time ago that your daughters were coming today?'

'You must be able to freeze some things?' Pamela replied

'I could,' said Debbie, 'if Jonny hadn't filled up the freezer with ice cream.' Pamela, whose face had turned bright pink, spun on her heels and left the kitchen, slamming the door as she went.

'That went well then,' I said.

'There was no need for it, though,' said Debbie. 'These people just don't think about anybody except themselves.' She wrote down a few things on a piece of paper. 'Can you go to the shops for me, please? I've got too much to do here. They want lunch and there's a good chance they'll be in for dinner too. Thank you.' Debbie passed me the list, picked up her cleaning bucket that was full of sprays and dusters and headed towards the bedrooms.

I returned an hour later and went straight to the kitchen, where Debbie was preparing some starters. 'Pretty,' I said, looking at the verrines that were on the work surface. 'What's in them?'

'Well,' Debbie replied. 'The bottom layer is avocado, the next is crème fraîche and chives, and the top is smoked salmon.'

'What have they done to deserve that?' I asked. 'Don't suppose there's a...'

'Yes, there is,' Debbie said, passing me a verrine. 'A bit late now but could you check it for seasoning?'

'Perfect,' I replied, after taking a mouthful.

'Just need to add a couple of chives on the top for decoration and they're done. Would you set the table for me, please? I'm behind as it is.'

As I reached to take out two water jugs from one of the top cupboards, two girls in their late teens came through the side door and brushed past Debbie and me without saying a word. Dragging their suitcases behind them, they hurried through the door that led to the lounge and towards the lower bedrooms. Realising that Jonny was unlikely to be far behind them, Debbie and I glanced at each other but said nothing.

'Ashtray,' said Jonny, who moments later was opening and shutting all the cupboard doors in the kitchen. Debbie casually picked up an ashtray from the draining board next to the sink and passed it to him.

'Thank you,' he said, before walking into the lounge. As he did so, I kicked away the doorstop that had held the lounge door open and watched it slowly close.

Just before it shut completely, I heard one of the girls shout, 'Mummy, Mummy, I'm starving. Can we eat now?'

'Fat fucking chance,' I heard Debbie mutter as she continued to pin bone a cod steak that should have already been filleted by the fishmonger.

'How long to go?' asked Pamela, who stuck her head round the corner soon after.

'About twenty minutes,' replied Debbie without looking up.

'Not sooner?'

'Only if you want your fish raw and full of bones.' Pamela went back into the lounge. I smiled as I put some glasses and knives and forks onto a tray.

Debbie was usually quite mild-mannered when it came to most things, but the kitchen was her domain and wasn't about to be messed around by anybody – including owners. Timing was everything and stupidity was not tolerated. We were working at a villa a few years back where Debbie was cooking by herself for twenty people, when a young woman sauntered into the kitchen and asked, 'Would you happen to know where I can find a charger for my iPod?'

I had never heard such language leave the lips of my wife.

'Are you going to apologise?' I asked when the party was over and we were doing the washing up.

'Am I buggery,' replied Debbie. 'Gormless bitch.'

After lunch, Jonny informed us that he was taking Pamela and his daughters to a hairdresser's in Juan-les-Pins. They shouldn't be more than a couple of hours, but I was to drop the girls back there later that evening as there was an open-air concert for which they had already bought tickets. He wasn't sure whether he and Pamela would be eating in or not but advised Debbie to have something ready just in case.

At around five o'clock, Jonny returned with Pamela. He took a tumbler out of the cupboard that he took into the lounge and poured himself a large scotch.

I was outside checking the chlorine and pH levels in the pool when I heard Jonny call out, 'Brent!' I stopped what I was doing and walked into the lounge via the patio doors. 'My daughters are still having their hair done,' he explained. 'I couldn't be bothered to wait. They'll call when they're ready. You can pick them up from outside the casino – is that OK?'

'Sure, no problem.' At six o'clock, Jonny told me that his daughters were just having their hair dried, so I should leave as soon as possible. I grabbed my car keys and began what was normally a fifteen-minute journey to Juan-les-Pins. As I approached the town I also hit gridlock. As usual, at the front of the jam was a *gendarme* waving his arms and blowing a whistle. I was stuck only minutes from my destination, but I hadn't moved. Jonny was phoning every five minutes, which just added to the stress. I turned the corner where I could see to my left a stage and two large men in black t-shirts putting an enormous speaker onto a stand. Someone was doing a sound check through a microphone and a drummer, who had already set up, was banging away. Rows of seating had been put up in what, up until that point, was the car park and *gendarmes* were cordoning off the arena with waist-high metal barriers. As I looked in my rear-view mirror, I noticed someone put a barrier just behind my car, thereby closing the road completely to traffic.

I was relieved to the see the casino in front of me. I looked hard, but I could see no sign of the girls. Jonny phoned. 'Where are you, Brent?'

'Outside the casino.'

'Can you see the girls?'

'No.'

'Hang on. I'll call them.' I listened intently as Jonny dialled from another phone. 'They can't see you either. Are you sure you're there?'

'Yes. Ask them to wave.'

'They are waving. And you still can't see them?'

'No. Can you ask them to do star jumps?'

'Don't be stupid. They're not exactly easy to miss. What can you see?'

'The casino and a big sign offering a ten-euro free bet when you join. Texas Hold'em on Friday nights…'

'What are you doing there?' Jonny asked.

'You told me to meet them outside the casino, so that's where I am.'

'Not the gambling casino,' Jonny shouted. 'The grocery shop, Casino! There is a hairdresser's next to it. Do you know where that is?'

'No.'

'Don't you know Juan-les-Pins?'

'No.'

'Wait, I'll get them to come to you.'

As I inched along the road in the traffic, two teenage girls approached the car. I tried not laugh. Their hair was still in large curlers and they were not looking at all happy. With faces like thunder, they got into the back of the car, simultaneously slamming one door each. Up until that point, I didn't realise that it was possible to glare at someone via a rear-view mirror but, somehow, they succeeded. Not only did they succeed, they managed to keep it up for the entire journey back to Antibes. It seemed to me, in a very short space of time, I'd become public enemy number one and, for once, Debbie didn't appear to be faring much better.

'Pizza. Tonight we would like pizza, Brent,' Jonny said just after lunch the following day. *What's that got to do with me?* I thought. Did he want me to order them? Was I to pick them up? Tapping away on his phone, Jonny continued, 'You'd better get the fire started at about four o'clock. It takes about three hours to get the oven up to temperature. Have you ever used a wood pizza oven, Brent?'

'No.'

'Well, then you need to learn fast. My mother loves pizzas and so do her friends. See you later.'

Hurriedly, I rushed back to the kitchen where Debbie was washing up. I sat down at the small table in the corner of the room and started to bash away on my computer.

'You OK?' asked Debbie, who could see I was looking a bit flustered.

'Pizza, tonight. They want pizza tonight.'

'And that's got what to do with you exactly?' Debbie asked as she took her hands out of the sink and reached for a tea towel.

'That's what I thought,' I replied. 'They want me to make it in the pizza oven.'

'Bunch of bloody clowns. They really have got no idea.'

'How do you mean?' I said, not realising how big the task was that I'd just been given.

'Meaning, my love,' Debbie replied, who was by then looking through the kitchen cupboards, 'we're going to need some double zero flour and to the best of my knowledge…Nope, we haven't got any. Assuming that I have time to make the dough, which is debatable, it'll take a couple of hours to rise. Also, I've never made it before, so this has got a very good chance of going Pete Tong. Fuckers, Brent. They could have given us a bit of notice. Did they give you any idea of what toppings they would like?' I shook my head. 'Well, the girls are both vegetarian…'

'I'll stop off at the butchers.'

207

'I'll write out a list of ingredients and then you'd better go,' Debbie said. 'It seems a way off, but we haven't got much time.' As Debbie scribbled as fast as she could, I ran upstairs to fetch my wallet and phone. Soon after, I was heading to the town centre.

'Well done,' Debbie said as I returned an hour later. I put all the shopping on the kitchen work surface and made my way to the pizza hut. Shortly after, I was back.

'Shit, shit, bollocks, bastards and shit,' I said.

'What's up?' said Debbie, who then smiled.

'Firelighters, we've got no fucking firelighters. Three empty packets but no firelighters. Bastards.'

'You didn't think to check before you left?' Debbie asked, reading the back of the packet of flour.

'Clearly not. I thought they were full. Who keeps empty packets of firelighters lying around?' I replied, before grabbing the car keys off the kitchen table and heading out the door again.

Once back, I had a decision to make. Either I should read more about wood pizza ovens and how to use them or I should just go and light the thing. Figuring that reading about it was probably going to waste time that I didn't have, I bundled a load of logs into the oven. The logs were followed by a packet of firelighters and the firelighters were followed by a match. I crossed my fingers. Fifteen minutes later, the pizza hut was filled with smoke and there was no sign of a flame.

'They're not seasoned,' said Debbie, who had come to investigate. 'The wood's not seasoned,' she repeated, picking up a log from the pile outside.

'I don't see how adding any salt and pepper is going help,' I said. 'What's that got to do…?'

'Are you completely mad?' replied Debbie. 'This wood is not dry enough. It needs a season to dry out, otherwise it's very difficult to burn. I'll give you bloody salt and pepper!' She laughed. 'Have you tried the wood behind the hut?'

'Didn't know there was any.'

'You astonish me sometimes,' said Debbie, who then sighed. 'These will do you,' she said, examining a log. 'Right, I'm going to see how the dough's getting on. Just make sure you leave enough room to get the paddle into the oven.'

By seven-thirty that evening I had created a raging inferno. The pizza hut had become a sauna and I was soaked through with sweat from the heat. Debbie came back and forth from the kitchen carrying small, plastic containers, which she put in the pizza hut's small fridge. Each container was full to the brim with chopped vegetables. There was one with chorizo – a particular favourite of Jonny's. While I was waiting, I studied a takeaway menu that I had picked up from an Italian restaurant next to the beach.

'Trial run,' Debbie announced as she rolled out the first piece of dough onto the metal work surface to the side of the oven. 'What do you fancy?' she asked.

'You really think that's necessary?'

'I do,' Debbie said, who was ladling some tomato sauce onto a dough base. 'You've never done this before. Nor have I, for that matter. Hope this is going to be as simple as it looks.'

'Piece of cake,' I said, smiling.

'Well?'

'Ham, mushroom and mozzarella.' As Debbie prepared the pizza, I sprinkled the metal pizza paddle with flour. When she'd finished I slid the paddle underneath and gingerly walked towards door of the oven, which Debbie opened. The aperture wasn't very large but there was enough room for one pizza at a time, maybe two with a bit of practice. I pushed the paddle forward and then pulled back in an attempt to make the pizza slide off. It slid half way.

'Harder,' said Debbie. As instructed, I gave the handle a proper tug. The back of the pizza flipped up in the air, shot forward and sealed the front edge of

209

the pizza perfectly. Unbeknown to me at the time, I'd just made my first calzone.

'Shit,' said Debbie. 'You need to be more careful next time.'

'You told me to give it a tug.'

'I know, just not that hard. Anyway, try putting a bit more flour on the paddle next time.' The second pizza shot off the paddle like a ship being launched down the ramp on its maiden voyage and landed up in amongst the embers at the back of the oven. Such was the speed that it took off – it was also concertinaed.

'We're ready now,' said Jonny, who put his head through the side window. Apart from a few burnt edges, by the third go we'd got the hang of it. As Debbie much preferred to be in the kitchen, I was tasked with serving Jonny and his family. Unfortunately, I hadn't had chance to get changed. My hair was soaking wet, as was my t-shirt, which was also covered in flour. Jonny's daughters, who were dressed in designer summer dresses and completely made up, continued to scowl at me.

I hadn't been made aware of it beforehand, but not only was I responsible for bringing Jonny and his family their food, I was also responsible for pouring the wine, mixing gin and tonics and replenishing the water jugs. After an hour or so, Debbie declared, 'Last pizza,' as she sprinkled some Emmental onto a base. 'Hope they don't want any more.' I smiled and opened a top cupboard, just to Debbie's left.

'Good thinking Batman,' she replied when she saw three packets of pizza bases that I had bought earlier.

'Couldn't be too sure,' I said, and closed the cupboard door. I took the last of the eight pizzas out to the family. Jonny ordered ice cream for him and watermelon for the girls. Once they'd finished, I went back into the pizza hut, sat down and took the lid off a very cold beer.

'What time would you like lunch?' Debbie asked Jonny after breakfast the next morning. 'No lunch,' he replied. 'We're leaving. I'm taking my daughters to the airport and then Pamela and I are driving back to Switzerland.

Tell Brent we'll need some help with the bags.'

Soon after, Debbie marched into the kitchen holding a tray. She had the biggest smile on her face that I'd seen in a long time. 'They're leaving. They're leaving,' she said, hardly able to contain her excitement.

'When?' I asked.

'Today,' she replied, putting the tray down next to the sink. Debbie punched the air.

'Woo hoo!' I shouted.

'Shh, they'll hear you.'

'Sorry. Nice of them to tell you before,' I said as I began the washing up.

'Couldn't care less,' Debbie replied. 'They're off and that's all that counts. Anyway, his mother has already told us he never tells anyone what he's up to – even her. Why would he bother telling us? Let's go out to lunch today to celebrate. What say you?'

'You're on.'

Chapter 23

We'd got to the know the staff at the Brasserie de L'Ilette quite well since Debbie and I had been in Antibes. The brasserie, where we'd occasionally stop off for a drink on the way home from shopping, had become a firm favourite of ours. When we had time, which was rarely during the summer, we'd go there for lunch. They'd recently employed a new chef who made everything from scratch and, unusually for many of the restaurants in this part of France, the food was perfectly seasoned. We used to sit at the front of the restaurant whenever possible, where we'd enjoy a fabulous view of the sea.

'That's new,' said Debbie. She smiled as she looked at the glass-domed dessert cabinet.

'Looks like a flying saucer to me,' I replied.

'Great display though,' Debbie said. 'Might even be tempted myself.'

'You and a dessert? Not likely, is it?'

'We'll see. Anyway, chemo tomorrow. How are you feeling?' Debbie asked as the waiter came to take our order. *'Gambas, s'il vous plaît.'*

'Monsieur, pour vous?'

'Le burger, s'il vous plaît – medium.'

'Peasant,' Debbie said to me as the waiter disappeared towards the kitchen.

'I know.' I laughed. 'But it is home-made.'

'Anyway, the chemo.'

'Well, I don't really know, to be honest. Doctor De Chaisemartin says it affects people in different ways – some badly, some not at all, so until I've had it I can't really tell. All I know is that they like to get it started as soon as possible after the operation to give it the best chance and they couldn't do it while I had pneumonia. Going to have to play it by ear. Come on, let's enjoy our lunch,' I said before picking up my glass of rosé. 'Here's to a good season and all that sail in it.'

'I'll drink to that,' Debbie replied and raised her glass. 'Whatever that

212

smell is coming from the kitchen, it's amazing. Hope it's mine.'

'How did it go?' asked Debbie as I returned from my appointment with the oncologist in Mougins at lunchtime the following day.

'Not what I expected at all.'

'What's up?' said Debbie, who was looking quite worried.

'Another bloody operation is what's up,' I replied, and then I slumped down onto the sofa.

'What? Why's that? Something they didn't tell you?'

'Maybe, or maybe I didn't understand or didn't ask. Either way, the oncologist has made an appointment for me to see a cardiovascular surgeon on Friday and straight after that, an anaesthetist. Apparently, I need to have a catheter fitted in my chest, next to my shoulder.'

'Why?'

'Because that's how the chemo gets administered. Bloody hell.'

'You're sounding a tad pissed off,' Debbie said, who reached into the fridge and passed me a beer.

'Pissed off? Doesn't begin to cover it. I've had enough of needles – and hospitals for that matter. Not only that, I have to have a blood test each time before I go. Sorry, I just didn't see this one coming.'

When I went to see the surgeon, he dangled a piece of metal wire in front of me that had a circular attachment on either end. He spoke no English and I found him quite difficult to understand but I managed to work out that he was going to insert the metal object into my chest. Once I'd seen him, I went to see the anaesthetist, who asked me about allergies, previous illnesses and my family's medical history.

A week later I had been operated on and was ready for the first of my twelve, fortnightly courses of chemotherapy. I walked into reception at the Arnault Tzanck hospital in Mougins and waited for my name to be called.

213

Within moments a young nurse came through some swing doors which she held open for me. She guided me to one of five armchairs and asked me to remove my t-shirt. She put an identification band on my right wrist and left for a few minutes. When she came back, she brought with her a drip stand that had two plastic pouches hanging from the top. In each bag was some clear liquid. The first contained FOLFOX, which was the chemotherapy, and the second was a rinsing agent. As I turned to my right, I saw that the nurse had a small but quite thick needle in her hand.

She felt around for my catheter and then said, '*Je pique.*'

'Fuck that hurt!' I shouted, which caused all of the activity in the room to come to a complete standstill. Momentarily, I saw stars in front of my eyes and began to feel quite sick.

'I am sorry,' the nurse apologised. 'Were you not prescribed an EMLA patch?'

'What's one of those when it's at home?' I asked.

'It's a patch that contains an anaesthetic,' she explained. 'You stick it over your catheter an hour before your chemotherapy and then you won't feel anything when I put the needle in. Did your oncologist not tell you?'

'No, he didn't. Bastard.' For some reason that I couldn't put my finger on at the time, I really didn't warm to the oncologist that I had seen in Mougins. I hadn't even had my first course of chemotherapy, but my mind was already beginning to think about going back to Marseille. While I waited for the FOLFOX to drip into my body, I had a look around the room. Nurses and doctors hurried about and a very sweet, elderly lady periodically visited each patient offering coffee and biscuits. I hadn't brought a book with me, so I thumbed through one of the few French women's magazines that were on a table to my left. After ten minutes, I gave up and lay back in the chair and thought to drift off.

'*Fini*,' said the nurse at the end of the two-hour session. She then attached a plastic bottle, about the size of a baby's bottle, to the end of the drip tube. She produced a black bag that had a belt, similar to that of a market trader, and placed the bottle inside.

'Stand up please, Monsieur Tyler,' she said. As I did so, the nurse put the belt around my waist and adjusted the strap. She then taped the tube which had the bag at one end and the needle at the other to my chest. 'You must keep this on for seven days,' she explained. 'After that, you need to see a local nurse who will remove it for you. I am just going to get your prescription, then you can go. You can put your shirt back on now.' As the nurse left my side and went to the office, I looked down. I now had two bags – one colostomy and one chemotherapy. Surely I wasn't going to get away with this at work? Someone would notice and that would be game over. I had suddenly become extremely self-conscious.

'No one will notice,' said Debbie, who was staring inquisitively at my new fashion accessory, once I'd got back to Antibes. 'We just need to buy you some baggy shirts, that's all.' I shook my head.

The next morning, I went down to the swimming pool to check the chlorine and pH levels. I took the plastic testing kit out of its box and lowered it into the water to take a sample. My hand came out of the water as fast as it had gone in.

'Ah, shit!' I shouted. I began to shake my wrist. The tingling at the end of my fingers, which was a possible side effect of chemotherapy, had affected me. I'd never felt a sensation like it. This wasn't going to be easy. It was the summer – the sun was beating down and I needed to remain hydrated. To my cost, I occasionally reached for a cold soft drink in the fridge, but I'd almost immediately drop it. I felt sick. It didn't matter what food I ate, it tasted metallic and I'd sometimes get a pain going across my chest. Not only that, two days after the first session of chemotherapy, I experienced what I called *wipeout*. I'd had the chemotherapy on the Tuesday and on the Thursday I was unable to get out of bed. I soon realised that this event was going to repeat itself a further eleven times. How we were going to keep this from Madame Amari I didn't know but we just knew that we had to.

I went back to Mougins two weeks later for my second bout of treatment. As I sat in my chair, I noticed my oncologist come in and out of the room several times. Surely he must have seen me? Even if he hadn't, he knew that I was there – he'd have a list of the day's patients, so why didn't he bother to acknowledge me? He could have at least asked how I was. Part of his job, surely? Anyway, how many English patients did he have? Not many, I thought. By the time I left the hospital two hours later, my mind was made up. I was going back to Marseille.

Later that afternoon I phoned the Institut Paoli-Calmettes and spoke to the receptionist responsible for booking the chemotherapy sessions. She agreed to give me the earliest possible appointment each day so, all being well, I would be back in Antibes after my sessions around lunchtime. Debbie and I decided that she would give me a list of shopping before I left so if any questions were asked about my whereabouts, we were covered.

'Someone new arriving tomorrow,' said Debbie a few days later. 'Natasha – Madame Amari's helper.'

'I didn't know she needed a helper,' I replied.

'Nor did I until just now. I had a phone call from her assistant in the London office,' said Debbie, who was dusting the television in the lounge. 'She doesn't like people to know but she has early stages of Parkinson's disease and needs some help getting dressed and getting about. Mentally she's fine – it's just affecting her mobility, which is a shame because, apparently, she's always been very active. Anyway, according to Sylvie at the London office, Natasha is a larger than life character in more ways than one so we'd better stock up the fridge – and the fruit bowl. She has a particular penchant for apricots.' Debbie laughed.

'I see. Sounds like this is going to be interesting. And she's sleeping where?' I asked.

'In the same room as Madame,' Debbie explained. 'So, we have to take one of the single beds out of the studio and take it up there.'

'Are you sure it will be big enough?'

'It's going to have to be.'

I was about to go back out to the garden when I turned and said to Debbie, 'This Natasha, does she speak any English?'

'Indeed she does,' replied Debbie. 'That's one of the main reasons she was chosen – so she could communicate with us. Went to Harvard, apparently. She's very bright.'

'And French. Does she speak any French?' I asked.

'Not as far as I'm aware,' Debbie said. 'This will be her first visit to France. Having said that, it wouldn't surprise me at all if she was completely fluent.' I laughed.

At eleven o'clock the next day a taxi pulled into the driveway. One of the back doors flung open and out jumped a woman in her mid-forties. She grinned broadly. I figured she weighed about two hundred and eighty pounds. She was wearing black jogging bottoms and a brown and purple hooped rugby shirt. She made her way to the back of the car. Clearly not the type of person who liked to be kept waiting around, she tapped twice quite heavily on the boot. The taxi driver wound down his window, scowled and asked Natasha to wait. She smiled at me and shrugged her shoulders. As the boot began to slowly open, Natasha pushed it up with all her strength. I could hear the hydraulics groan under the pressure. This was something which was not lost on the taxi driver, who came to investigate. Natasha grabbed a large suitcase, which she swung by its handle and put down on the gravel. There were a few other bags that came out at pace, forcing me and the driver to keep well out of the way. She pressed some notes into the driver's hand and asked me which way to go. I reached for the clicker in my pocket, which I pointed at the gates. The driver got back into his car. The gates began to slowly open.

'I'll take the big one,' I said, looking at the suitcases.

'Are you sure?' Natasha replied. 'It's quite heavy.'

'Positive,' I said, and then I smiled.

Bloody hell, I thought as I tried to lift the case with one hand. I managed to get it about an inch off the ground. So, I used both hands and dragged the case along the gravel, stopping every few seconds to catch my breath. By the time I got to the kitchen, Natasha had introduced herself to Debbie and also the fruit bowl. I watched in amazement as she popped one apricot after another into her mouth. Somehow, she still managed to speak. She placed a piece of kitchen roll onto one of the worksurfaces, where she deposited the apricot stones. Having polished off five, she asked Debbie where the bedrooms were.

'Brent will show you,' Debbie, who was rolling out some pastry, replied. 'I'm a bit busy right now.' Deciding that there was no way at all that I would be able to negotiate the stairs, I put the suitcase into the lift and followed it in. Looking at the six-foot-tall woman that was Natasha I also decided that there wouldn't be enough room for all of us, so I pointed towards the stairs and smiled. I pulled the grill across, which caused the outer door to close, and pressed the button to my right. By the time I got to the top, Natasha was standing outside. I wheeled her impossibly heavy suitcase into the master bedroom. Natasha threw it onto the bed with ease and began to undo the straps. Thinking that my services were unlikely to be needed upstairs, I went to join Debbie in the kitchen.

On my way there I heard one or two things clatter to the ground, followed by Natasha shouting, 'Shit.'

'That lady is half woman, half ox,' I said to Debbie. She smiled.

'She seems pleasant enough,' Debbie replied. 'Wouldn't like to be doing her job, though. She really is going to be on call twenty-four seven. Can you imagine? Hope she's paid well. Fax.'

'Fax. What about a fax?'

'That's another one coming through in the office. Been coming pretty much all day. Madame's itinerary. The London office must have phoned about five times already. You can tell she's on her way. Get it for me, would you? I'm all stuck up with stick,' she said, looking at her hands, which were covered in pastry.

Debbie was right. Madame Amari's pending arrival was like a roll of thunder in the background that was getting steadily closer. I went to get the fax, which was addressed to Natasha and me. We were to go to Juan-les-Pins, where we were to collect a car from Hertz. We were told to pay for it using Madame's credit card that had been given to Natasha before she left Syria.

'Just one question,' I said to Debbie. 'If I have to go to Marseille, how am I going to be driving Madame Amari about?'

'You're not,' replied Debbie.

'I'm not what? I'm not going to Marseille or I'm not driving Madame Amari?'

'You're not driving Madame Amari. That's Natasha's job. Well, most of the time, anyway. You might be asked to drive occasionally but that's it.'

'Really? Who told you that?'

'Sylvie at the office. I spoke to her this morning. Natasha's a professional chauffeur. She's also Madame's bodyguard.' I raised my eyebrows. 'She used to be in the army, so I wouldn't mess around with her if I were you.'

'Wasn't intending to,' I said. 'Blimey, who knew?' The door opened, and Natasha came into the room.

She smiled and then said, 'Is it OK if I have a bottle of water?'

'Of course,' said Debbie. Natasha picked up a bottle from the sideboard, removed the lid and then poured some water into her mouth without her lips touching the bottle. I'd attempted this several times in the past but only ever succeeded in soaking myself.

'Where are the apricot stones?' Natasha asked.

'I put them in the bin,' Debbie replied. 'Was that not right?'

'It's not important,' said Natasha, 'but in Syria we usually grind them up and cook with them. Thanks for the water,' she said, before leaving the kitchen to go back upstairs.

'Interesting,' said Debbie. 'I'm sure I read somewhere that apricot kernels contain cyanide.'

219

'Told you. They're all bloody mad round here.' The fax machine continued to chunter away for much of the day and several times during the night. If there was a change to the itinerary, rather than just send the one page that was affected, the London office would resend the full fifteen pages.

'No chance of making any mistakes that way,' Sylvie explained. Although Debbie and I found Sylvie's system to be both bizarre and wasteful, it did rather please the man at the stationery shop just down the road, who was doing record business in the sale of black ink cartridges.

With Madame Amari due to arrive the following afternoon, Debbie, Natasha and I sat down for dinner outside that evening. It would give us a chance to get to know Natasha and also to find out a bit more about Madame Amari, who we had, so far, not met in person. Debbie was due to have made a Moroccan lamb dish but by four o'clock all of the apricots had gone.

'Two sodding kilos in a day,' I heard Debbie mumble to herself earlier on. 'Bloody woman's not human.'

'She has a hotel, you know,' Natasha explained. 'Lives in a suite on the top floor. I've never been in it.'

'Why's that?' I asked.

'I'm outdoor staff,' Natasha replied. 'Madame Amari categorises her staff as indoor or outdoor and the two don't mix. Receptionists, nurses and cleaners – inside. Chauffeurs, gardeners and the hotel dog – outside. Everything and everybody has their place.'

'Nurses?' asked Debbie.

'Yes,' replied Natasha, who picked up her lamb shank, completely ignoring her knife and fork. 'Twenty-four-hour care,' she continued before taking a bite. 'Delicious, Debbie,' she said. She belched before Debbie had chance to thank her. 'Doesn't really need it, if I'm honest, but she likes to have people round her all day, every day.'

'Is she bringing a nurse here?' I asked.

'You're looking at her,' replied Natasha.

'Are you qualified?' I said.

'Nope, but I'm sure we'll manage between us. Anyway,' Natasha said, while licking her fingers, 'she's a tough old stick. Just a shame to see how much she's changed. She used to be so active – walked everywhere. No one could keep up.' She laughed. 'One minute she was in the lobby, the next in the kitchen and then in the garden. We had to get her a walkie-talkie in the end.'

'And now?' I asked.

'She still gets around all right, with the aid of a cane, which she hates. But don't be fooled – she can still move faster than most people. Sometimes she'll ask you to walk around the garden with her. She loves her gardens and she'll use you instead of her cane, which is fine, but she really pushes down hard when she's holding on. You just need to be a bit careful with your back. Other than that, she's lovely – a very kind woman. She knows the names of all her staff and most of their families.

'How many staff has she got?' Debbie asked.

'About a hundred.'

'And she knows all of their names,' I said. 'That's impressive.'

At around ten o'clock, we were all about to get up from the table, when Natasha put her right index finger in front of her lips and motioned with her left hand for Debbie and I to be quiet. She slowly and silently got out of her chair and made her way back into the house. Debbie and I watched as she walked through the living room and out of glass doors on the other side. She turned left. Suddenly, the silence was broken by someone letting out a scream – the scream was soon followed by a dull thud. Natasha appeared at the glass doors and beckoned me to follow her.

'I've only been here five minutes and I've already caught my first burglar,' Natasha said, who was looking very pleased with herself. She then took her phone out of the pocket in her jogging bottoms, turned on the torch and shone it onto the body of a man who was out cold on the gravel next to the garage.

'Nice work,' I said.

'Thank you,' replied Natasha.

'Though, that's not a burglar. That's Bashar, the gardener.'

'Holy shit!'

Chapter 24

News of Madame Amari's arrival had reached her preferred tradesmen, who were also Syrian, and they had made room in their very busy schedules to come and welcome this highly respected lady. Just after lunch the next day, the doorbell rang. Two very smart Mercedes people-carriers had pulled into the drive, one of which contained Madame Amari. Debbie, the electrician, the plumber, the mason, Natasha and I formed a small semi-circle and waited. One of the chauffeurs opened a side door. He stretched out his hand and began to help Madame Amari out of the vehicle. She was wearing a designer, blue, short-sleeved dress that came down to just below the knees. Her brown, shoulder-length hair was immaculate and, upon seeing her small entourage, she smiled. She was about to say something when Guss, who had a small, slightly deflated orange ball in his mouth, belted around the corner. He ran straight over to Madame Amari and dropped the ball at her feet in the hope that she would kick it for him. Natasha shouted 'Psst,' to try and shoo Guss away, but Madame Amari waved her away instead. With her cane in one hand and holding onto the chauffeur with the other, she shimmied one way and then the next. Guss, who was anticipating her every move, mirrored her. After one or two attempts of trying unsuccessfully to kick the ball past Guss, she acknowledged us.

'That's the best welcome I've had in a very long time,' she said, laughing. 'You and I are going to get along very well, Guss,' she said, bending down and stroking him on the head. 'It is Guss, isn't it?' she asked.

'It is,' I replied.

'He seems very friendly, though it won't do any harm for people to know we've got a German Shepherd here. Looks much more ferocious than he is. Mind you, after what happened last night, I'm not sure we need him.' Again, Madame Amari burst out laughing. Natasha looked quite sheepish. 'Don't worry, Natasha,' she said, reassuringly. 'It's his own fault. Snooping around in the dark like that.

He really should have known better. Bloody fool. Anyway, I've spoken to Bashar today and he's OK. He's got a bit of a sore head but that's it. We won't be seeing him for a few days, which I'm quite pleased about. That man can talk for Syria.'

As Madame Amari talked to the rest of the party and was being updated on the work that had taken place at the villa since she was last there, I went to help the chauffeurs with the cases.

'She's taking her afternoon nap,' said Natasha as she walked into the kitchen later that afternoon. She looked disappointedly at the fruit bowl, which was almost empty, and reached into one of the upper cupboards and took out a mug. 'Fruit tea. Do we have any fruit tea?' she asked. Debbie smiled, walked over to where Natasha was standing and opened a drawer that was full of every tea imaginable.

I was sitting at the kitchen table and as Natasha went to the sink to fill up the kettle I asked, 'So, what was Bashar doing here late last night? Did Madame ask him?'

'She did,' Natasha replied as she flipped the switch on the kettle and then opened the fridge door. Taking out a piece of Guss's ham, which we had bought so that we could get a worming tablet into him, and popping it into her mouth, she continued, 'The owner of the other property where he works arrived last night. She's very demanding, apparently. Rarely speaks to her staff – not nicely anyway. Clicks her fingers or claps her hands when she wants something, which is most of the time.'

'That's nice,' I said. 'Not Russian, by any chance?'

'How did you guess?' Natasha laughed. 'So, she arrived and went to sit outside in the cool breeze. She put on all the lights in the garden and didn't bother to light any mosquito candles. She got bitten to buggery. Stupid cow. She said to Bashar that it was his fault because he hadn't sprayed enough mosquito deterrent on the bushes, even though he'd only done it the day before, so she wanted it done again, there and then.'

'At ten o'clock?' Debbie asked.

224

'Yep, at ten o'clock. The problem was that Bashar had also sprayed Madame Amari's hedges yesterday, and he'd left the cannister here. She didn't care that Bashar got a whack for his troubles and still made him do it. She was actually more concerned that money had been coming out of her petty cash for the mosquito spray and that Bashar had been using it on Madame's bushes.'

'Bloody hell,' I said. 'That's a bit a much. Not often I feel sorry for Bashar.'

'How the other half live,' replied Natasha. 'Mean to her staff. Mean with money, which is probably why she's got much more than us. Just then we heard the familiar sound of the lift as it started to come down. 'She wasn't long,' said Natasha, looking at her watch. She reached for the kitchen door, which she opened. 'See you later.' The door closed behind her.

'We'd better get another worming tablet,' I said to Debbie, who was spraying the work surfaces with disinfectant.

'Another one? Why is that exactly?'

'One for Natasha. We could slip one into her food and save Madame Amari a small fortune.' Debbie laughed.

Moments later, Natasha was back. 'She wants you to walk her round the garden, Brent. Bashar's not here and you've done some gardening, right? I wouldn't know one plant from another. Come on.'

Madame Amari took me by the arm and held on tightly. She left her cane on her chair next to the dining room table and we began our walk. Natasha walked a few paces behind in case she was needed. According to Sylvie at the office, Madame Amari had fallen a few times in Syria, when no one was in close attendance. She was also very independent and rather than wait for some help, she'd launch herself in one direction or another, sometimes to her cost.

'That was supposed to have been a swan,' said Madame Amari, who then laughed as she looked at a piece of topiary that was by then more wire mesh than plant. 'And that was a butterfly when I first bought it.' She pointed at a plant in a similar condition to the first. 'The thing is, I don't think Bashar knows how to shape them. I've never seen him with a pair of shears.'

'Not exactly Edward Scissorhands, then?'

'No, I don't think so.' Madame Amari smiled. 'But he is good with other things,' she said, admiring the bougainvillea that was in full bloom. Stunning mauve flowers covered one side of the house. 'A few years ago it was nearly dead, but Bashar brought it back. He said he used fish guts.'

'That must have smelled nice,' I replied.

'No, not really, but it did attract almost every cat in Antibes. We started to get complaints. Not because of the amount of cats, but because they used to fight in the middle of the night. The noise was horrendous.'

'So, what did you do?'

'We planted a lot of lavender bushes. That's why we've got so many. Bashar says that cats hate lavender. I'm not sure if that's how he really got rid of them, but I'll take his word for it. Do you think you could shape these for me?' Madame Amari asked, pointing to three straggly, ball-shaped plants that were at the edge of the swimming pool.

'Sure,' I replied.

'That's Bashar's idea of a kitchen garden,' said Madame Amari, who then smiled as she looked down at the single tomato plant that was growing next to a lemon tree. 'I'm not really sure why he does it. Same every year.' We shuffled our way towards the perimeter hedge.

'This is dying,' she said, looking at the hedge that was covered in patches of brown 'Not enough water?'

'I'd say this is the problem,' I replied, reaching for one of the very pretty flowers that were in amongst it. 'Morning glory. It's a type of bindweed. Looks amazing but strangles everything in its path.'

'That's why Bashar pulls it out then?' Madame Amari said as she looked through the hedge and onto the road. 'Everyone can see in here as they walk past. This is supposed to be private.' She sighed. 'We'd better get Bashar to buy some of that green matting when he gets back. I don't want everyone staring at my guests.'

'Pulling it out won't help,' I said.

'Oh, no?'

'That'll probably just make it grow stronger. You need to paint glyphosate onto the leaves so it gets down to roots. Nasty stuff though. Need to be careful.'

'I doubt if Bashar's got the patience for that. Can you get some?'

'I'll see what I can do.'

As we continued our walk, Madame Amari told me that she was the patron of a classical music festival that was held annually in Damascus.

'Do you like opera, Brent?' she asked.

'Not really,' I replied. 'My mother took me when I was young. Both times a bit of a failure, if I'm honest.'

'That's a shame,' said Madame Amari as she stood admiring a rose bush that was in full bloom. 'What happened?'

'The first time I went, I discovered that the word *aria* is the Italian word for a song that will not end in your lifetime, so I went and hid in the toilets until the performance was over.'

Madame Amari smiled. 'I know what you mean,' she said as she bent down and breathed in deeply through her nose. 'Beautiful,' she said. 'Just beautiful. And the second time?'

'We went to see Pavarotti.'

'Oh, really?' Madame Amari replied. 'Where was that?'

'Glyndebourne. Not too far away from where we lived in Sussex.'

'And that wasn't good because?'

'That wasn't good because he didn't like it when I tried to join in.' Madame Amari burst out laughing. 'That was the last time my mother took me to the opera.'

'I can understand that,' she replied, before we walked back into the villa.

Each year Madame Amari would invite some musicians to her villa and this summer was no exception. There was an Italian conductor who was arriving by train later that afternoon and I had been tasked with collecting him and two women from the station in Antibes in our car. While I did that, Madame Amari was due to visit the hairdresser's.

Madame Amari went go to the salon once a week during the time she was at the villa – more if she got bored. She would suddenly announce, often quite late in the afternoon, 'Hairdresser's.' Natasha, who usually by then was lying on one of the sofas in the lounge, would pretend to be asleep, so I would have to take Madame. I'd take the car keys and help Madame Amari to her feet. Natasha would wink at me, I'd mouth the word *bitch*, and away we'd go. We'd stop outside the hairdresser's, which was on the main road, just opposite the seafront. I would help Madame Amari out of the car and, with very little space to pass, we'd cause a traffic jam. The French drivers would do one of the things that they did best – hoot their horns until the car was moved.

On this particular day, however, as I had been given a separate job to do, Natasha had to drive to the hairdresser's. They then visited a music shop, where Madame Amari bought an electric piano which was delivered later that afternoon.

At four o'clock, I waited at the train station for the guests to arrive from Cannes. Madame Amari hadn't told me how old the conductor was, so I was expecting an elderly gentleman, accompanied by what I imagined to be two matronly type ladies. I couldn't have been more wrong, or delighted for that matter. Two women in their early thirties, with hourglass figures, wearing tight summer dresses, wiggled past me. Just behind them a thin, young man, wearing a black designer suit and a pink, open-necked shirt stood still with his phone to his ear. I introduced myself and a few minutes later we were heading back to the villa.

'I bet your eyes nearly popped out of your head,' said Debbie, who was turning out a frittata that she's just taken out of the oven. She laughed. 'Need to take a cold shower by any chance?'

'I only have eyes for you, my love,' I said, opening the fridge door.

'Creep. Pass me the butter, would you?'

That evening, as I lit the candles on the dining room table on the back terrace, I heard some music coming from the lounge. As I peered through the patio doors I could see the young man, Gianluca, sitting at the piano. Claudia and Francesca, his travelling companions, were sitting on the sofa next to Madame Amari and watching his every move. Debbie, who was carrying some dinner plates, came through from the kitchen. For a few seconds she stood motionless, entranced by the beautiful music that was filling the room. She then, slowly, edged her way outside and joined me. Carefully, she put the plates down and we both stood there until the recital had finished ten minutes later. The lounge erupted with applause. Gianluca took a bow and Debbie and I continued to get things ready for dinner.

Just before one o'clock the next day, Madame Amari took Gianluca to lunch. 'The girls not going with them?' I said to Debbie, who was wiping down the dining room table.

'No,' she replied. 'They're just friends of his from Naples. They're not musicians, and Madame wants to discuss the running order for next year's concert, apparently. And besides, they've been on the mojitos since half ten,' she said, looking at the girls, who were sunbathing by the pool. 'Doubt they'd be of much help.'

I was finishing the washing up in the kitchen when Claudia came in and started to look in the fridge. Debbie had just completed her shopping list and had picked up the car keys. 'I'll see you later, and behave yourself,' she whispered in my ear, noticing that Claudia was wearing a bikini that wasn't covering very much at all.

'I'll do my best. Don't rush back.' Debbie scowled and then smiled. I heard the main gates shut and soon after I heard a loud splash coming from the direction of the swimming pool. Guss rushed past me with his slightly deflated football in his mouth and went to join the girls. As I watched through the lounge window I saw Guss standing by the pool's edge. They threw the ball just above Guss's head and he knocked it back to them. This went on for about fifteen minutes until I decided it was time to get Guss and bring him into the cool. If there was a ball involved, Guss didn't know when to stop, and with temperatures in excess of thirty-five degrees Celsius outside, I needed to get him in.

'Here, Brent, catch!' shouted a very excited Francesca. I got ready to catch the ball but, instead, she undid her bikini top and threw it in my direction. She then jumped in the air with her hands above her head, completely revealing the top half of her body.

'Good catch,' Claudia shouted. She laughed. 'Try mine,' she said, and then she did exactly the same as Francesca. 'Come and join us. It's lovely in here.'

'I think you'll find that's more than my life's worth,' I replied. 'Besides, I haven't got any trunks.'

'Nor have I now,' said Francesca, who removed her bottoms and placed them on the edge of the pool and then laughed very loudly. 'Come on, Brent. It's the south of France. There are no rules.'

'I don't think you'll find that's the way Debbie would see it,' I said. 'Kind offer but, on this occasion, I'm going to have to decline,' I added, taking Guss by the collar.

'Spoilsport,' replied Claudia. 'But look. Can you do us one favour?'

'I'm listening.'

'Take a picture of us. You can use my phone. It's just there,' she said, pointing to the small table next to one of the sun loungers.

'We can send the picture to our boyfriends.'

'Won't that make them jealous?' I asked.

'That's the whole idea,' Francesca said. The girls laughed. I let go of Guss's collar and, with the girls standing at waist height in the pool with their arms in the air, I took the photo.

Chapter 25

Only a few days later, I was taking the girls back to the train station in Antibes. They were going back to Naples and had promised, if I was lucky, to send me that photo. I wasn't. Natasha took Gianluca to Nice airport, where he was due to catch a plane to Armenia. He was getting married there in two weeks and Madame Amari was due to attend the wedding just before flying back to Salzburg, where she would spend five days at a music festival. Unfortunately, a week before she was due to leave Antibes, fighting broke out in Armenia. Jonny cancelled Madame Amari's flight without telling her, so she rebooked it. As soon as she rebooked, he cancelled it, and so it went on. In the end, she gave in. Any thoughts that Debbie and I had had of spending a few days alone in the villa soon evaporated as the day before Madame Amari was due to go to Salzburg, Jonny turned up at the villa with Pamela and their two daughters.

The next morning, I set off at six o'clock to go to Marseille. It was still dark outside and I was struggling to keep awake. In anticipation of this, I'd bought two cold coffees from the supermarket the day before. I plunged a straw into the lid of one of them and made my way along the road with my window open. My dipped headlights shone onto Bashar, who was walking along the path towards me, so I put them on full beam. '*Merde, putain, con,*' I heard him say as he covered his eyes. 'Thank you, God,' I said as I looked towards the heavens. I smiled.

By the time I got to the outskirts of Marseille at just before eight o'clock, the traffic was building up. My appointment wasn't until nine-thirty, but I knew that if I didn't time things right I could be extremely late. The journey itself seemed quite straightforward until I got to the toll booths. With the steering wheel on the right-hand side and payment area on the left, this was going to be tricky. Either I'd have to get out of the car and go round the front of the car, or I'd have to dive across the passenger seat, reach through the open window and insert my credit card that way. Not wishing to incur the wrath of the French drivers, who were not patient at the best of times, I chose the second option. This was all very well but when we first arrived in France, I did pretty much the same thing except that it was at the barrier at the mobile home site where Debbie and I were working. I'd been out in the morning to buy a baguette and some fresh eggs, which I'd put on the passenger seat. As I leaned across to put the key fob in front of the sensor on the site's entrance barrier, there was a crack and my then large belly had crushed all of the eggs. The baguette didn't escape either. I hoped that I wouldn't repeat the same process with my relatively fragile colostomy bag. I had, however, made a mental note to myself to bring a spare set of clothing the next time.

At a quarter to nine I pulled into the underground car park at the Institut Paoli-Calmettes. I went into the same building where I'd previously seen Doctor De Chaisemartin, registered at reception, went upstairs and waited. In front of me was a lift that was busily making its way between the three floors. Along the walls were television screens that imparted all sorts of information about the Institut Paoli-Calmettes. Every now and then a 'What am I?' question would pop up, the answer to which was either a type of fruit or vegetable. My French was weak enough for me to be interested in trying to translate. I was just getting into the swing of things when an extremely attractive woman with shoulder-length, brown hair and dressed in a grey, woollen trouser suit opened a consulting room door. I estimated her to be in her early forties. 'Monsieur Tyler,' she said, and smiled warmly. My new oncologist invited me inside and asked me to sit down.

'*Est-ce-que vous parlez Anglais, madame?*'

'*Pas du tout,*' she replied. This could be interesting, I thought. Doctor Ries doesn't speak a word of English and although my French was good enough to speak to plumbers, electricians and so on, when it came to medical terms, I was still not confident. I hadn't understood much of the paperwork that I had been given and had long since given up trying to translate the text into English.

Somehow, I managed to explain to the doctor what had happened at

Mougins and rather than comment, she just raised her eyebrows. She asked to see the results of my last scan, which I took out of a plastic shopping bag. I passed a folder with curled up edges and a circular coffee stain on the front cover to Doctor Ries. She smiled and shook her head. It then dawned on me that while I was in the waiting room, I had been surrounded by several people, most of whom were carrying enough folders to grace the average court case. Yet, somehow, almost all I'd considered to bring with me was a badly-cared-for folder.

'Have you brought your blood test results with you, Monsieur Tyler?'

'They are not in the folder?' I asked.

'No.'

'Hang on a minute,' I said as I stood up. I checked my coat pockets. They weren't there. I checked the front pockets of my jeans. And then I checked the back pockets. 'Bingo!' I shouted with delight as I passed a folded-in-half, ripped envelope across the table. Doctor Ries burst out laughing. Not only that, she had tears rolling down her cheeks. For about half an hour she asked me questions and wrote down my answers. She promised to remove the product that had caused the end of my fingers to tingle from the medication and would lower the dosage of FOLFOX as much as she could. She then examined my stomach, after which she gave me some paperwork to take to another building where I was to have my chemotherapy. As I went to say goodbye she offered her hand. Instead, and feeling a lot happier with the way I was being treated, I leaned forward and kissed her on either cheek. She didn't seem to object but I figured this was not quite the etiquette. She opened the door and smiled warmly once more. I made my way across the road.

As I walked into the chemotherapy waiting room I took a sharp intake of breath. I wasn't sure what I was expecting but this certainly wasn't it. In front of me were row upon row of chairs and they were full. I estimated that there must have been at least forty or fifty people in total. Certainly, some of them must have been friends or relatives of patients but, even so, this was a much bigger operation than Mougins. Women, some wearing headscarves and others wearing wigs, looked at each other across the room and smiled knowingly. There were men and women of all ages, some very smartly dressed and others much more casually. It was true what we've all heard before, but this brought it home – cancer respects no one, regardless of age, colour or creed.

At about eleven o'clock a lady with a basket offered baguettes to the patients and any left over were then offered to the visitors. Soon after this, my name was called I was led into a room where there was one other person already attached to a drip. The nurse checked to see if I had an EMLA patch, which thankfully I had bought earlier. In fact, I bought several.

I was to make a further ten trips to Marseille for my chemotherapy. I never got used to how ill the chemotherapy made me feel but I felt that, in the long run, it was for the best. Without a doubt, I'd been lucky that the cancer had been caught early enough. Some weeks later, when I finally had the last session and a nurse removed the needle from my chest for the last time, it reminded me when I had the braces taken off my teeth when I was a teenager. I did the same to the bottle that was in the pouch as I did to them. I put it on the ground, jumped as high as I could in the air and shouted *olé* as I landed on it. The bottle shattered into hundreds of pieces and I couldn't have been happier. With the exception of having my colostomy bag removed and my colon put back together, all being well, it would be another six months before I heard the words '*Je pique*' again. I was due to have a scan every three months but no more heading to Marseille in the darkness, no more sitting in an armchair for a couple of hours, no more *wipeout* and no more feeling sick. The sense of freedom was palpable, and I could begin to get on with my life again. Fortunately, to this day, the cancer has not returned.

'I'm very sorry,' said Natasha one lunchtime as I was sitting in the kitchen and looking at my computer. 'I've opened this parcel. I thought it was for Madame and gave it to her. The thing is, she knows what it is. Her ex-husband had cancer of the colon, so she knows what colostomy bags are. She's seen them. I'm sorry.'

'Oh, shit,' I said. 'We were trying to keep it a secret. She might not have employed us had she known at the start.'

'Not to worry,' said Debbie, who was making some tea. 'We've only got a couple of weeks to go and we've got through it.'

Although Madame Amari was a bit disappointed that I hadn't told her beforehand, she perfectly understood my reasons for not doing so and a week before she left to go back to Syria, I went back to Marseille to be put back together again by Doctor De Chaisemartin. As Debbie still needed our car for the shopping, I decided to take the train.

Three days later and with instructions not to lift anything heavy for at least three months, I left the Institut Paoli-Calmettes. My train home was not due to leave for nearly an hour, so in celebration, I treated myself to a meal from the world's largest hamburger chain. Five minutes after finishing my celebration it went through me. I nearly missed my train and when I did get it, I spent most of the journey in the toilet. I didn't know it then, but I was going to have to learn how to readapt to my digestive system. My brain had to work out what was wind and what was not, and I could only hope that it got it right most of the time.

I took a taxi from the train station in Antibes back to the villa, where I found Debbie, who was setting the table outside for dinner. As I looked towards the pool, I saw a man that I didn't recognise in the pool with Madame Amari. 'Who's that?' I asked.

'That's Michel,' Debbie replied. 'He's a personal swimming instructor. He's helping her with her coordination. He can help me with mine if he likes,' she continued, looking at his rippling muscles. She laughed.

'Steady.'

'Oh, don't worry,' she replied. 'Josephine's coming tomorrow. She's a gym instructor. I expect you'll get the chance for your eyes to pop out of your head then. Can you get the knives and forks for me? I'll sweep the terrace.'

'You never sweep the terrace.'

'First time for everything.' She smiled. As I left, I just caught, out of the corner of my eye, the swimming instructor wave. Debbie waved back. Bastard.

I was tasked with buying an inflatable for Madame as Michel had decided that she needed to exercise her legs more. Being the height of summer there were very few left in the shops, but I did manage to find one with a picture of a cat and the logo *Little Kitty* emblazoned on it. Far from finding this at all embarrassing, Madame Amari found it very funny and fell in love with her new piece of apparatus. Unfortunately, Guss also found the inflatable quite amusing and on the third occasion, when I was bringing it out to the pool from the pizza hut, he sank his teeth straight into it. As much as I tried plugging the hole with my index finger, we really weren't going to get away with it. So, after threatening to put my dog into the nearest animal sanctuary, I headed off to Antibes in search of a new one.

The next morning, I wandered across the garden to find that Bashar had just finished digging a hole in the garden. It must have been six feet long by two feet wide and six inches deep. To one side were the divots that he had removed, which he was watering.

'You're not thinking of burying yourself in there by any chance, are you?' I asked.

'*Je ne comprends pas,*' he replied.

'Why the hole, Bashar?'

'*Mechoui,*' he replied, and then he smiled, with his gold incisor gleaming in the sunshine.

'What's a *mechoui?*' I asked.

'Barbecue,' he said, very enthusiastically. 'Whole roasted lamb, Halal. Madame's summer party.'

'Halal?' I said, beginning to feel my blood boiling at the very thought.

'Yes, Halal. I despatch the animal myself,' he said again, gleefully. I shook my head.

'Then you are a nasty bastard,' I said, resisting the urge to do to Bashar what Natasha had done to him before.

236

'I put a towel over its eyes and cut its throat. It doesn't feel anything.'

'Maybe, one day, someone will do the same to you. See how you like it.' I walked away.

At the end of August Madame Amari returned to Syria and Debbie and I were given two weeks to shut the villa down for the winter. All of the bed linen was washed and ironed. The beds were remade and were covered in plastic sheeting. The deckchairs, loungers and plastic statues were put into the pizza hut, which we locked. We also closed the windows. The shutters on the villa were closed for the last time and the changing room tents by the side of the pool were dismantled. Bashar drove his decrepit van into the middle of the drive and left it there for days. On our final day we received a phone call from Madame Amari thanking us once again for our help and she hoped to see us again the following year.

Chapter 26

On the recommendation of a good friend of ours, James, who we'd rented an apartment from in Théoule-sur-Mer some years previously, we found a place to stay in Cotignac, a small town not far from Brignoles in The Var. He'd put us in contact with a property agent called Poppy, who seemed very pleasant when I spoke to her on the phone. She explained that the photos of the property on her website were quite old now but should give us a good idea of what to expect when we got there. We thought that a house for eight hundred euros a month with bills included seemed reasonable enough as long as it had wi-fi and was within walking distance of the shops and bars. James had moved into a villa just outside the town about a year previously and said that he was really happy there.

One Friday afternoon we met Poppy in the centre of Cotignac.

'You'd best follow me,' she said. 'A bit tricky at first but you'll get used to it.' We got into our car and followed Poppy along some very narrow two-way streets, reversing every now and again to let a car that was coming from the other direction pass. She led us to a car park at the top of a hill and waited for us to join her. I opened the back door for Guss, who leapt out and immediately went chasing after a cat. 'Sorry, I should have said,' Poppy explained. 'There's plenty of those round here. And those,' she said, scraping something off the bottom of her right shoe with a long twig.

'Here we are,' Poppy said a few minutes later as we walked through a small wooden gate with broken slats. Weeds grew up through the cracks in the patio and there was a plunge pool full of green sludge. As Poppy opened the front door there was the smell of damp and the windows were very grubby. 'Sorry, I haven't had chance to give it a proper clean. The previous lot only left a few days ago and I've been really busy. If you'd given me a bit more notice...' The work surfaces in the kitchen were covered in dust and the bin in the corner was overflowing. The tiny sitting room was full of unmatched furniture and chairs and the curtains were old and worn. There was a choice of three bedrooms, each with its own individually stained mattress and a choice of limescale-ridden bathrooms.

'What do you think?' Poppy said to Debbie.

'Have you got anything else?'

'No, sorry, that's it. All the others are rented. It's not that bad, is it?'

Debbie didn't reply but with nothing else on offer, we paid Poppy the eight hundred euros and said that we hoped to meet up for a drink that evening.

'Not sure if Captain Chaos will be about later. No one ever really knows what he's up to. Not even sure if he does most of the time.' Poppy laughed.

'Who?' I asked.

'James,' she replied. 'That's what they call him round here. Captain Chaos.' She laughed. 'I'm not sure whether he follows it, or it follows him, but he's chaotic all right.'

'One month and that is it,' Debbie said once Poppy had left. 'One month, which is probably what it'll take to clean this place. It's disgusting.'

'It's not that...'

'Yes, it is that bad,' Debbie interrupted, knowing what I was about to say. She then pulled out all of the cleaning materials from under the kitchen sink and placed them on the kitchen table. While she did that, I went to unload the car and Guss went for a nose around the garden. Debbie's cleaning standards had never been in question, but since moving to France she had become meticulous. She missed nothing. I, on the other hand, hadn't improved much since being a student, which really must have driven her mad.

At seven o'clock Debbie said, 'That's that,' and suggested taking a stroll into the town and having a beer or two. We walked the small streets and gazed into the first bar. A television was showing a football match and watching it intensely were two large men, one dressed in a Sunderland shirt and the other in a Newcastle shirt. Thinking that the atmosphere was likely to become somewhat rowdy, we walked on. We found a small café in the heart of the town and sat outside.

We'd just finished our first *pichet* of rosé and were just debating whether to order another, when we saw James walking towards us.

'Hello, you two,' he said, and smiled broadly. 'Wasn't sure when you were arriving, so thought I'd pop up for a quick one. Not drinking so much these days – got a lot of work on.'

'Rosé, James?' I asked.

'Thanks, Brent. Then I must go up to the other bar and see Poppy. I think she said she'd be there tonight. So, what do you think of Cotignac, then?'

'We've only just got here,' Debbie replied.

'You're going to love it,' James said before lifting his glass. 'Cheers. Good to see you both. They call it the Saint Tropez of the Var…'

'They call what the Saint Tropez of the Var?' I asked.

'Cotignac,' James replied.

'Cotignac?' I said. 'How can they call Cotignac the Saint Tropez of the Var? It's in the middle of the bloody countryside.' I laughed. 'I haven't seen a bit of water since we've been here.'

'I know,' said James. 'It is a bit like that round here. Can be a bit odd at times.'

'That'll be why you fit in so well,' I replied. James laughed.

'Thanks for the comment in my visitor's book, by the way, Brent. I'll never forget that.' He smiled. James was referring to the time that we'd rented the apartment just below his in Théoule. He'd often arrive at our door in the evenings, quite unannounced, and usually having been in the local bar for a few hours before. In each hand he'd have a bottle of wine and he would stay until silly o'clock. Before we left, I wrote, 'Have had a wonderful stay. Would love to come back again but will need a serious amount of therapy before returning.'

'Look, why don't you come round tomorrow, say about eleven? Only, you will have to watch Guss's tail.'

'Watch his what?' I said.

'Yeah, Guss's tail,' James replied quite firmly. 'I've got my satellite dish in the garden and it's on the ground. If Guss knocks it, I could lose my TV completely. Maybe I need to build a box round it first. Let's forget tomorrow for now. Oh, look, there's Poppy. Better go. Thanks for the drink.' James got up and swiftly marched towards the bar that we had just avoided.

'Nice but bonkers,' I said to Debbie, who was sitting there quite amused.

'Doesn't change, does he?'

The next morning, I went to the bakery in search of a baguette and saw Poppy, who was sitting outside a café and gingerly stirring a coffee. Whether she was wearing dark glasses due to the sunshine or a hangover, it wasn't clear, but I went to say hello.

'Good morning, Poppy,' I said quite cheerily.

'Oh, don't,' she replied. 'Too loud. I think I've got one of the Klitschko brothers trying to bash his way out of my head.'

'Good night was it?' I asked.

'More like a good morning,' Poppy said as she put her spoon down and began to massage the side of her temples. 'I've been Captain Chaosed again – for about the third time this week. I hate him. Bastard.'

'He said he was just stopping for the one.'

'Captain Chaos never stops for the one.' Poppy laughed. 'Ouch, that hurt,' she said, clutching her head. 'One barrel, maybe. He's fucking lethal, that man. I wouldn't mind but he can't handle it.'

'Take it he didn't drive home.'

'You take it right. Taxi drivers are used to him round here. They usually manage to get him to his front door but that doesn't stop him from sleeping in the hedge. He's a fucking nightmare. How's the house by the way?'

'It's fine, thanks…'

'Sorry, Brent, I think I'm going to be si…' And with that, Poppy put her hand in front of her mouth, leapt out of her chair and ran off inside the café. After breakfast, I wandered down to the tourist office to ask if they could recommend any nice local walks where I could take Guss.

'Just opposite,' the lady said. 'Over the road. It's a nice walk through the woods. And there's a beautiful waterfall when you get to the end. Does your dog like to swim?'

'He loves it.' So Guss and I headed across the road. After about ten minutes, we climbed a small but steep bank and five minutes further on we found ourselves at the bottom of an amazing waterfall. There was a huge cascade, in front of which was a lake. I'd never seen anything like it. I threw Guss's tennis ball into the water, which Guss swam towards and retrieved. He was in heaven. After about half an hour we came back and stopped off for a coffee before returning to the house. Cotignac's quaint charm was beginning to grow on me although I still had the feeling Debbie couldn't wait to leave.

'Fancy a bit of exploring?' I said to Debbie one Sunday morning over breakfast.

'As long as it's not too far,' she replied. The only thing Debbie disliked more than long car journeys was pointless ones. 'An hour max,' she said, looking up from her Kindle and taking a bite out of her toast.

'We could head towards the Gorges Du Verdon,' I said, gazing at a map on my computer.

'How far is it?'

'About an hour and a half, but there are plenty of small villages along the way, which might be interesting.'

'OK, you wash, I'll dry,' said Debbie, picking up her plate.

We'd only been gone about half an hour when we arrived alongside a river in the pretty little village of Quinson, where we saw a sign offering boat hires for just fifteen euros for half an hour.

'Shall we stop?' I asked Debbie.

'Suits me.' We pulled into a small car park just opposite a bistro. 'Maybe we could stop there for lunch, although I'm always suspicious of those,' Debbie said, pointing to an old chest freezer that had a tatty *Wall's ice cream* sticker on its front.

We got out of the car, walked down some steps, let Guss off the lead and began our stroll by the side of the river. To our left were some mobile homes and a little further along we passed the wooden cabin belonging to the owner of the boat hire company. There was an A4 sheet of paper pinned up outside with his phone number on it.

'Fancy having a go on the way back?' I asked.

'Could do,' said Debbie. 'Be interesting to see how Guss gets on. He's never been on a boat.' We walked along the riverbank for about twenty minutes and then turned back.

'OK for dogs?' I asked.

'*Bien sûr*,' replied the man, who I had called on the phone only minutes earlier. In gentlemanly fashion, he helped Debbie onto the boat, which was bobbing up and down in the gentle breeze.

'Come on, Guss,' I said to my dog. He was none too sure about the situation so he did exactly what he always does at the vets when I try to persuade him to get on the table. He sat down. Thirty-five kilos of Guss is not easy to lift at the best of times, even more difficult when he's totally against the idea. The owner shrugged his shoulders.

'I'll take the end with the teeth,' I suggested. 'You grab the other end.' Soon after, we managed to bundle Guss onto the boat. The man gave Debbie and me a quick lesson on how to steer the boat.

'Whatever you do, don't try and go too fast. You'll go nowhere. *Au revoir*.' As he clambered out of the boat I said to Debbie, 'Would you like to drive?'

'No, you're all right,' she said, sitting down at the back and enjoying the gentle breeze and warm sunshine. 'You go ahead.' I slightly opened the throttle and we coasted gently down the river. As a raft of ducks passed quite close to the boat, Debbie quickly grabbed Guss by the collar before he had chance to jump over the side. I figured we were only doing about two or three miles an hour and as the bridge in the distance that we were due to go under seemed ages away I pushed the throttle forward to full. We stopped. The propeller turned into an electric whisk and as I turned round to look at Debbie, I could also see the boat owner flailing his arms.

'Useless piece of rubbish,' I said, before handing over the controls to Debbie, who did a far better job of driving the boat than I had. Half an hour later and having, unknowingly at the time, taken one of the best photos ever of Guss, we returned to the boat cabin. The boat owner, who I thought must have seen this all before, smiled.

'Probably thought I was a blithering idiot,' I said to Debbie as we walked back towards the car. She didn't reply. 'Fancy stopping here for lunch?' I asked, looking over the road at the small bistro.

'We should have a look at the menu, at least,' she replied. 'Seems reasonable,' she added as she looked into a glass cabinet on the wall outside. 'Lamb chops, twelve euros. I'm up for that.'

'Right, let's go.'

We were greeted by a charming young waitress, who led us to a table in the corner at the far end of the restaurant. 'It'll be better for your dog,' she explained as we sat down. 'He's quite big. I wouldn't want to be the person standing on him.' She laughed. 'He is friendly, isn't he?'

'Yes, he's fine,' I replied. And he stayed friendly until for no reason that I could see, he started to growl. The growl was followed by a bark, which usually meant one thing – he'd seen another dog. I looked round but couldn't see one. I then looked at Guss's eyes, which were staring upwards. What Guss had noticed was the very large head of a *sanglier*, complete with tusks, that was sticking out of the wall to our left.

'That's bloody enormous,' I said to Debbie, who was also then looking up. 'Never seen one that close. Guss has got some balls to go chasing after one of those things.'

'Is everything OK?' asked the waitress, who had brought us our menus. 'You need to move?' she continued, having noticed what was going on.

'No, we're fine,' I said. 'Guss, down.' Guss did as he was told, though for the next hour he focussed his eyes firmly on the *sanglier*. In his mind, Guss needed to be prepared in case it managed to jump out of the wall.

After a very pleasant and reasonably priced lunch we meandered our way along the country lanes back to Cotignac.

In the absence of any jobs to apply for via the usual routes, we'd put an advert on a local ex-pat website a few days previously.

'We've had a response,' said Debbie only a few minutes after having walked through the door of our house.

'Do tell,' I said as I poured a couple of glasses of wine, which I brought into the lounge. 'Cheers.'

'Well,' began Debbie. 'It's a woman called Sam who's based in Malaysia. She has a villa in a small village not far from Cannes and she'd like to see our CV. What do you reckon?'

'Nothing to lose. Why not?'

An hour after we'd sent it, we got a reply, requesting a Skype interview the following morning at eleven o'clock.

As our computer screen began to focus on the subject before us, it revealed an attractive woman in her mid-forties with a very striking, brown mane, which she tossed back.

She smiled and said in a West Country accent, 'Hello chaps. Thanks for taking the time to have a chat.' She went quite methodically through our CV, asking questions along the way, which Debbie answered. As the conversation progressed, it became clear that the lady from Malaysia wasn't really looking for guardians as we knew the job.

'The villa's not really big enough to need full-time guardians,' she explained. 'There is a garden but not extensive grounds and as the villa is mainly occupied in the summer, it doesn't need a full-time housekeeper either. Having said that, I do think it's better if someone's living it. Just as much can wrong, if not more, when things aren't being used. I wouldn't mind someone going in there to give me a bit of feedback. I've got an agency that's supposed to look after the villa, but they don't seem to do very much apart from send bills. Also, my parents were there a few weeks ago and it looks as if some linen has gone missing. So, maybe you could stay there for a few weeks. You won't have to pay any rent. I'll tell the agency that you're friends of ours and you can give me a quick report. I need to check with hubby, though, but I know what he'll say. Do what you like.' She laughed. 'Anyway, have a think about it. I know you're still in Cotignac for a couple of weeks yet, so why don't we catch up in a few days? You seem nice enough people. I hope I'm not making a big mistake here. I haven't even met you properly. But hey, life's about taking risks.' She smiled.

'That's a shame,' I said. 'She seems really nice. First normal person we've spoken to in ages.' Debbie laughed. 'Look, you never know what we might find when we get there. The villa's on a private estate with hundreds of others, so you never know what we might pick up. And, if the agency is as useless as she says it is, we might get their work. Besides, we'll be back in familiar territory and if there is any work to be had, it's going to be round there. Fancy a game of Scrabble?'

Chapter 27

At the end of October, we left Cotignac and headed towards the villa in the hills behind Cannes where we'd agreed to meet a representative from the agency, who would give us the keys. Early one evening, we arrived at some large gates which we believed to be the entrance to the estate. Just outside there was a man standing next to a small van that we presumed to be his. I got out of our car and walked over to him. I took a scrap piece of paper with the villa's address on it and showed it to him. He shook his head, smiled and pointed up the road. Just then, the gates opened. The man jumped back in his van and drove through.

'It's somewhere up there apparently,' I said to Debbie, once back in the car, 'though I wouldn't hold my breath. Not really sure he knew what he was talking about.'

After a further fifteen minutes of driving in one direction and then the next, Debbie said, 'You'd better phone the agent. We're nearly half an hour late as it is.' A few minutes later, a quite stern chap in his thirties came to find us. Shortly after, we drove through the gates where we had met the man in the van and went round a few steep bends before stopping outside a villa with pale pink walls. We followed the unfriendly agent down some steps that had three orange trees to their left and on to the front door, which the agent opened. Inside it was pitch black. The agent reached to his right and pressed a button that caused all of the shutters to come up. He walked into the lounge which was to our right and opened a patio door that led onto a wooden terrace. Debbie and I followed. What was in front of us was simply spectacular. We were overlooking a bright blue Mediterranean Sea. There were a few speedboats zipping along not far from the shore and to our left we could see the islands of Saint-Honorat and Sainte-Marguerite. As I looked down, I saw there was an equally bright blue swimming pool.

'I don't bloody believe it,' I suddenly said to Debbie.

'What's up?' she asked, looking a bit worried.

'You couldn't make this up. You see that bloke there who's cleaning the pool. He's the one who was at the gates. It's that bloody idiot who sent us up the hill and made us late.' Debbie laughed.

'*Bonjour monsieur!*' I shouted.

'*Bonj…*' he said as he began to look up. Recognising us, he put his hand over his mouth, momentarily feeling a bit embarrassed. He then laughed, waved and continued to scoop some leaves out of the pool with his net. In one corner of the terrace was a spiral staircase that led down to the pool. Guss mastered it very quickly, unlike Debbie and I, who were slightly wary. There was one bedroom on the floor that we were on. There was also a fully equipped kitchen and a lounge that was both stylish and comfortable. Along the corridor was a set of stairs that led down to a hallway, to the side of which were three further bedrooms, each with patio doors that opened onto the swimming pool.

Debbie and I spent the next few days making lists of things that needed to be done before the summer when, hopefully, the villa would be rented out. We'd had Skype meetings with Sam, the owner, every few days and it was decided that it would be good for all concerned if we stayed a bit longer.

It was only a matter of weeks before talk turned to Debbie and I taking over from the agency and the possibility of us earning some commission if we were to get some bookings. Sam also felt quite certain that once word got around about us being on the estate, we would soon be snapped up by a lot of people and that there was every chance that we'd have to be turning some work away.

Debbie started to put the villa on some of the better-known holiday websites and, much to everyone's delight, within a few weeks she had got our first reservation.

'Cheers,' I said, having opened a bottle of Prosecco. 'Here's to the first booking. Well done, you.'

'Thanks,' Debbie replied, smiling awkwardly.

'What's the matter?' I asked.

'Well,' she began, 'the money's good but it's not until June. We need to be earning way before then, which is a shame because I really like it here. Timing as bloody usual.'

For the next few weeks, we did our best to put our financial concerns behind us and carried on with what we were doing. We were getting on really well with Sam, although at the same time we were looking for jobs in case we didn't pick up enough freelance work in the area. We put leaflets through most of the letterboxes on the estate, offering our services. We didn't get a single reply.

'The thing is,' Debbie said, rubbing her feet, which were aching, 'these are summer properties and most of the owners are away. If someone from an agency opens the letterboxes, what's the first thing they're going to do?'

'Put our leaflet in the bin.'

'Yep. Seemed like a good idea but, in hindsight, it was never going to work. We're going to have to keep looking, my love.'

Two weeks before Christmas, it happened. Debbie got a frantic call from an agency who said that our services were needed immediately.

'Great,' I said. 'Where?'

'Switzerland,' said Debbie.

'Switzerland? I'm not going to Switzerland. Are you mad?'

'What's wrong with Switzerland?'

'I'll tell you what's wrong with Switzerland. It's the most boring place on the planet. That's what's wrong with it. Even the Swiss don't like Switzerland.'

She laughed. 'You've never been there.'

'I haven't been to Afghanistan either, but…'

'Can you think of any real reasons why we shouldn't go?'

'We won't be allowed in,' I replied.

'Why so?'

'I can't play the Alpine horn, I don't own a pair of lederhosen, you're not called Heidi and I hate Toblerone. Apart from that, it's full of people sliding down the Cresta Run on tea trays. Why on earth would I want to go to Switzerland?'

'Maybe this?' replied Debbie, who printed off a copy of an email that had just arrived, detailing our salary.

'That's a week? Wow.'

'That's a week, which will be the most money we've earned since we left England. Not only that, they'll pay for all our food.'

'They'll pay for our food? That's a first. Surely it can't be that expensive out there – they only eat cheese fondues and chocolate. Anyway, what are we supposed to be doing when we get there? It's not likely I'm going to be doing much gardening is it? I can't see me planting a load of edelweiss in three feet of snow, can you?'

'Shut up for just one minute and listen please,' said Debbie. 'Look, I'm speaking to the Gertrude, the owner's daughter, on the phone this afternoon. I'll find out exactly what your role is then. Doesn't sound like she wants to speak to you, which, frankly, is just as well.'

'Go on then,' I said as Debbie hung up the phone later that afternoon. 'Do tell.'

'Well,' she began. 'She seemed a very nice woman from Belgium...'

'Belgium.' I interrupted. 'Another boring bunch of bastards. What have they ever done apart from invent the Duffel coat?'

'Will you be quiet? Seems like the couple they had booked let them down at the last minute.'

'Probably got offered a better job in Beirut.'

'I'm telling you, Brent. If you don't...'

'OK. I'm listening.'

So, your job. You're to make sure that the paths are clear of snow, keep the cars clean, do the airport runs, go shopping and help me in the kitchen.'

'Riveting.'

'I'm doing the usual housekeeping, preparing meals, serving drinks, et cetera.'

'So, how's it been left?'

'She needs an answer today and, if we agree, we need to be there on Monday. They'll pay our expenses.'

'Monday?' I said, slumping down onto the sofa. 'Monday? It's Wednesday now. That's not much notice.'

'I know, but look – they don't arrive until the twenty-seventh, so we'll have a couple of weeks to ourselves. We'll be on our own for Christmas. Just you, me and Guss. Not only that, we're getting paid for it. How good is that? So, what do you think? I'm quite excited.'

'In the absence of anything else, I think we should take it.'

'You're not really that much against it, are you?'

'No, not at all, but I was just beginning to enjoy it here. But, as you say, money doesn't talk, it screams, especially when you haven't got any. Who knows? I might be surprised. I doubt it, but you never know.' I took a coin out of my pocket and tossed it in the air. 'Heads or tails,' I said as it landed on the back of my left hand.

'This is for what?' Debbie asked.

'This is for who tells Sam.'

'Heads,' shouted Debbie.

'Bollocks.'

Having done my best to reassure Sam that we would be returning to Cannes at the beginning of March and that we could still market her villa, we set off on the Sunday morning. I tried to download a map of Switzerland but, unfortunately, as my GPS was so old, it was no longer capable of receiving any more information. So we bought a map. We had the choice of driving straight up through France or going via Italy. Having spoken to our friend James on the Thursday, we opted to go through France.

'There are an awful lot of long, dark tunnels to go through if you go via Italy,' he explained. 'Not the most pleasant of journeys, if I'm honest. If I were you, I'd stay in France.'

We packed what we needed into the back of our car and the rest I took down to Sam's garage. I'd put a big red circle in felt-tip pen around the town of Gstaad in the Obersimmental-Saanen region of Switzerland, which is where we were due to be working.

'Do you think the police in Gstaad are called the Gstaadpo?' I said to Debbie, barely before we'd got out of the estate. She didn't reply, so I took out her notebook to see what she'd written about where we were going. There was the usual list of duties and names of family members as well as their dietary requirements. At the bottom was a name and a phone number.

'Who's Hobair?' I asked.

'Hobair,' replied Debbie, 'is the name of the chap who keeps an eye on the property when the owners aren't there, apparently. He's due to show us around and give us the keys to the chalet when we arrive. He's a painter and decorator by trade so will probably be at work somewhere in the town when we get there. We have to give him an hour's notice before we get to Gstaad.'

'That's OK, but Hobair? What kind of a name is Hobair?'

'He's Swiss,' said Debbie as we joined the main road.

'That'd be right.'

We planned to stay overnight in the city of Annecy, about five hours' drive from Cannes, and then cross the border the following morning, hopefully arriving in Gstaad around two hours later. I looked at the outside temperature gauge on the car's dashboard. Even though it was December, when we left Cannes it read twenty-two degrees. The further north we drove, the lower the temperature became. Ten, nine, eight – and by the time we got to Annecy at just after three o'clock in the afternoon, it was a mere seven degrees centigrade outside.

'Bloody freezing,' I said as I got out of the car, which we'd parked in a small side street. I began to jump up and down.

'Put your coat on then, you big southern softy,' replied Debbie, who was wrapping her pink pashmina around her neck.

252

'Look at the way everyone else is dressed. You're not in the Côte d'Azur now.'

She had a point. I looked down at my lightweight, three-quarter-length trousers and training shoes. What was I thinking? Everyone else was dressed for the winter. Quickly, I ran to the back of the car and took out a jumper, my leather coat and a pair of jeans. I got changed in the passenger seat and then went to join Debbie, who was looking in some shop windows.

'That's more like it.' She smiled.

'This is really pretty,' she said as we walked arm in arm along the cobbled streets in the old part of the city. We strolled along the side of a canal that was flanked by quaint, pastel-coloured buildings. The small bistros and cafés were still busy, beautiful flowers adorned the small terraces in the apartments just above and the bakery had a queue of people waiting outside. We spent a few minutes admiring the huge lake before we went in search of a hotel for the night.

'I bet this place is heaving in the summer,' I said to Debbie.

'Not exactly quiet now,' she replied. 'Hardly surprising, though. It's amazing.'

We found a small, inexpensive hotel, where we stayed for the night. We also found a small bar and a nice restaurant. Having been well fed and watered that evening and promising to come back and visit Annecy properly one day soon, we retired to our room.

'Not long to go now,' Debbie said as we got into the car at ten o'clock the next morning. As we pulled out of the side street, she yawned. The temperature gauge read two degrees.

'Would you like me to put the heating on?' I asked. Debbie yawned again and pulled down the sun visor.

'No thanks. Not sure I'm fully awake yet. That'll just make me sleepier.'

'I'm cold.'

'Then I suggest you put your coat on.'

There was no one manning Customs as we crossed the border at Geneva.

We headed along Route 11, passing Montreux along the way. Soon after, we left the motorway and found ourselves driving along some country roads. With no GPS, we stopped every now and then to ask for directions. 'Not many signs round here,' said Debbie, who wasn't at all sure if we were going the right way.

'There's a good reason for that. No one ever comes here,' I replied, looking at the imposing mountains that surrounded us on all sides. Eventually, we passed a sign that told us that we were in Gstaad.

There was a small hotel at the entrance to the town. Next to that was a petrol station and a dry ski slope, which was busy.

'I'll go and ask in the hotel,' I said to Debbie as I picked up the piece of paper with the address of the chalet on it. We'd asked several times for the owner of the chalet to send directions but, for whatever reason, she hadn't bothered. Debbie parked next to one of the petrol pumps and I got out. I'd only just got out of the car when a taxi driver screeched to a halt at the side of the road.

He wound down his window and shouted, 'You can't park there, it's a petrol station!'

'I'm not parked here, you nosey old git,' I shouted back. 'I'm not the driver. It's a right-hand drive car.' This didn't seem to deter the taxi driver, who continued to shout, so I shouted back. It seemed that his English was about as good as my German, so in the end we exchanged hand gestures and the taxi driver drove off. *Welcome to Switzerland*, I said to myself as I walked into the hotel.

They had no idea where the chalet was, so I went back to the car. 'You'd better phone Hobair,' I said. 'Are you sure that's his name?'

'Yes,' replied Debbie quite firmly. 'You can listen if you like.' Debbie reached for her phone, which was in the pocket on the driver's side door. She put it on loudspeaker and dialled. '*Bonjour, est-ce-que c'est Hobair?*'

'*Oui*,' he replied.

Debbie looked at me and mouthed the words, 'I told you so.'

'It's OK, you can speak English if you like.' He laughed. Hobair then asked where we were and told us to stay put. He would be with us in about ten minutes.

254

'Told you,' said Debbie. 'You wouldn't have it, would you?' As we waited, we watched the people on the dry ski slope. Some waited patiently while others looked longingly at the sky in the hope that snow would soon arrive and they'd be able to head off into the mountains to ski. It was nearly Christmas and there was no snow in Switzerland – not where we were anyway, which suited me down to the ground.

Just then a white Volkswagen van pulled into the petrol station and flashed its lights in our direction, so we followed. We drove for about two miles along the main road and then turned onto a smaller road that was peppered with luxurious-looking chalets. We stopped outside the largest one of the ten or so that I could see. We all got out of our cars.

'Hello,' said a thin man in his early thirties, who was wearing a white boiler suit. 'I'll give you a very quick tour around the chalet but then I have to go. You can find your own way around your apartment.' He pointed to a small building to the left of the chalet. 'I'll be back later at about six o'clock and I'll show Brent the places he needs to know in the town.' Hobair punched some numbers into a keypad to the right of the front door and it opened. We found ourselves in the lobby, which was adorned with Christmas decorations. There were more in the lounge and the log fire was set. The kitchen was fully equipped with every modern gadget imaginable. Upstairs were five bedrooms with some very expensive-looking beds and furniture. The bathrooms were all lined with marble. In the basement there were rooms full of skiing equipment. There was also a wine cellar that was air-conditioned. Not only were there cases of fine wines, there were also bottles of spirits and upmarket tonic waters. The cellar also served as a second pantry as the shelves were stocked with jars of olives, bags of pretzels and crisps as well as peanuts and mixed dried fruits. On the floor were boxes of spare lightbulbs and batteries. Outside the chalet there was a small lawn, at the bottom of which was a waist-high gate.

At the end of the tour, Hobair asked if we had any questions. 'Just the one,' I replied. 'How do you spell your name?'

'Just like everybody else,' Hobair said, looking quite confused at my question. 'Why do you ask?'

'It's just that I'd never heard it before. That's all.'

'Really?' he replied, tilting his head and looking even more confused. 'It's a common enough name.'

'Would you mind writing it down for me?' I asked, taking a piece of paper out of my pocket and handing him a pen. 'It's only that Debbie's got your number, but I need to plumb it into my phone too.'

'Sure,' he said, clearly still finding it an odd request. As Debbie peered over my shoulder, he wrote R-O-B-E-R-T.

'Robert,' I said, pronouncing the T.

'Yes, Robert,' he replied, 'but we don't pronounce the T in French.'

'Oh, I see,' I said, looking at Debbie. 'And you're not Swiss?'

'No, I'm French. I drive over the border every day to work. I couldn't afford to live here. Right, I must go.' And with that, he ran hurriedly out of the front door and down to his van.

'I'll give you Hobair,' I said to Debbie, who just laughed. 'Didn't you ask Dirty Gertie or whatever her name is to spell it for you when you spoke to her on the phone?'

'Obviously not,' she replied as she began to open the kitchen cupboards. 'I did ask her twice and twice she said the same thing. In the end I thought it was me. Well I would, wouldn't I? I would have felt a right fool if I had to ask her for a third time. Anyway, look at this place, it's pristine. Not a bit of dust anywhere.'

'Not really surprising, is it?' I said.

'How do you mean?'

'Did you see his boiler suit? Not a speck of paint on it. He's a painter and decorator. Normally, after about five minutes, there's more paint on me than there is on the walls.' Debbie smiled.

'How did it go?' Debbie asked once I'd returned from my tour of Gstaad with Hobair.

'Well,' I replied, sitting down at the kitchen table in our small apartment, 'he's pointed out the bakery, the butchers, the two supermarkets and where the ski guide lives. He's quite important apparently. He showed me Saanen airport, where the family's private jet lands…'

'Wow, a private jet,' Debbie said, momentarily looking up from her cookery book. 'Properly rich then?'

'I guess so. He also showed me the chalet where he's working, in case I need to get hold of him urgently.'

'Is it nice?'

'There's a building site just outside town with about five or six chalets and guess what? You can have any style you like as long as it's exactly the same as the one next door. That's the thing about this place – it's like Groundhog Day. It's all the bloody same.'

Debbie laughed. 'Pretty, though.'

'It's all very chocolate box but it's characterless. Sterile, I'd say. Anyway, the town's pedestrianised, so we should go and have a proper look tomorrow. Didn't get chance to explore today.'

We parked in the Co-op car park the next morning and went for a walk around the town.

'There are some seriously wealthy people here,' said Debbie. 'Look at these shops. Louis Vuitton, Prada, and I wonder where that is,' she said, pointing to a Santa Claus who was standing outside a shop in the distance. We went to investigate. 'Cartier. Blimey.' Children of all ages were queuing to have their photos taken with the Santa Claus, who had his own designer costume. His red ermine coat was thick and neatly pressed. His belt buckle sparkled with diamonds and his white beard was magnificent and bushy. As he talked to the children, he waved a golden lantern containing a lit candle. Proud parents, clutching Cartier bags, looked on from the sides.

'I'll have that,' I said, spotting a Mclaren F1 in a shop window. We walked along a bit further and stopped at a large billboard with small red and green lights dotted all over it. 'What's that all about?' I asked Debbie.

'Ski slopes, I think,' she replied. 'Looks like the green lights are the ones that are open, and the red are closed.'

'Not many green,' I said. 'At least, not round here. Wow,' I said as we passed an estate agency. 'Six million Swiss francs for a chalet.'

'And that doesn't look the biggest either,' Debbie replied.

'We'd better have two then,' I said. Debbie smiled. 'There's some serious money round here.'

'You're not kidding.'

We put Guss into the back of the car and went shopping in the supermarket.

'Good grief,' said Debbie. 'You can see why they've offered to pay for our food. Twelve francs for two pork chops. It's about three in France. A chicken, twenty francs. This is madness. And this mince,' she said, putting the packet back in the fridge as if it was a hot coal, 'is about five times the price that it is in France.' For a few minutes we walked round the shop and made comparisons. I then left Debbie to finish shopping, got Guss back out of the car and went for a quick stroll.

'That was a real eye-opener,' said Debbie, who arrived back at the car half an hour later with two full carrier bags.

'Did you keep the receipt?'

'Too right I did. Nearly two hundred francs and I've got nothing. Unbelievable.'

Chapter 28

'Gertie and her family are not due for a week, are they?' I said to Debbie as she was unloading the shopping.

'No. Your point?'

'My point is, my love, that I think we should disappear back to Annecy for a night or two.'

'Why's that?' Debbie asked.

'I think we should stock up on provisions. It's just stupidly expensive in Gstaad and...'

'They're paying for our food,' Debbie interrupted.

'I know, but there are limits. And I doubt very much they'll pay for our wine. Besides, it's probably the only chance we'll get to break out of Dullsville before they get here.'

'That's true.'

On Tuesday morning, I phoned Hobair and told him that we were going away for a day, perhaps two. He said that he wasn't at all worried so long as we were back to pick up Gertrude and her family on the twenty-seventh. So, we spent two wonderful days in Annecy and began our return journey just after lunch on Thursday. This time, Customs was manned and we were pulled over by a very stern-looking, female Swiss official. The back of our car was filled to the brim and behind our seats, on the floor, were several boxes of wine. How much were we allowed to bring across the border? Was there a limit? I didn't know. Debbie wound down her window and as she did so, she looked at me even more sternly than the official and said, 'Don't say a word. Got it? Not one.' Feeling slightly aggrieved that somehow Debbie thought my mouth could get us into trouble, I folded my arms and did as I was told.

Debbie smiled at the official, who said, 'Forty francs. You must pay forty francs.'

'For what?' asked Debbie.

'For the use of the autobahn. Please go and pay,' she replied, pointing towards a kiosk. Debbie got out of the car and returned a few minutes later with a sticker, which I attached to the windscreen. As I looked round I noticed many other people forming a queue at the kiosk where Debbie had just been. The Customs officials didn't seem at all interested in the contents of people's cars – they were just there to collect money for the Swiss government.

We spent Christmas Day in Gstaad, where there was no snow whatsoever, although it was forecast later in the week. From my calculations, by the time I woke up on New Year's Day, the snow outside would be about two feet high. I'd found a way to walk Guss to the town via the forest, but how perilous that would become, I had no idea.

Whereas in the south of France towns were usually quite deserted at this time of year, in Gstaad people were arriving in their droves. Everyone was gearing up for the tourists, including the men in charge of the horse-drawn sleighs that were waiting in the town square. They'd often pass by on the road in front of our chalet and Guss would welcome them by standing on the lawn, jumping off the ground on all fours and barking as loudly as he could. The passengers in the carriage would look quite bemused, while Guss tended to be ignored by both the horses and driver. One afternoon, Debbie and I were walking in the town when I noticed the advertising banner on the back of the sleigh. I sniggered.

'What's so funny?' Debbie asked.

'I meant to tell you before. I looked it up the other day on Google Translate. There are some things that need no more explanation than the slogan itself,' I said.

'Meaning?'

'That, my love, is the German word for sleigh rides,' I said, pointing to the banner.

'*Schlittenfahrten?*' said Debbie, who then burst out laughing. 'You are kidding?'

'Nope.'

On the day of the owner's arrival I went down to the garage, where there were two cars, identical in make, model and colour. The only difference between the two was one digit on the number plates. The walls of the garage were lined with skiing equipment and the floor was clean enough to eat your food off. I set off to Saanen airport, which was only fifteen minutes away and where the private jets carrying the rich and famous came in to land.

I drove up to the barrier at the airport and waited. With no bell to ring, I felt fairly certain that someone would notice me. I waited five minutes and then tooted my horn. As soon as I did, an elderly gentleman looked out of a hut to my right and then came scuttling towards me.

'Not automatic, then?' I said.

'No,' he replied. I gave him the name of the owners, who he said were due to arrive in about ten minutes.

'I just wait in the car park. Is that how it normally works?'

'Oh, no,' the man said. 'They won't like that. Once the plane has come to a standstill, you drive up to it. I will help you with the luggage.'

I stood outside the car and waited. Suddenly, from over the mountains to my left, a small plane burst through the clouds. As it landed, the elderly gentleman came rushing out of the cabin and motioned for me to drive towards the plane. Hoping that I wasn't going to clatter one of the wings, I gingerly drove round to the right-hand side and waited. As I looked up, I could see the pilot, who was looking at me and laughing. He signalled for me to go round to the other side. It had never occurred to me, up until then, that the doors on most aircraft were on the left. How was I to know? I hadn't flown very much.

As the door opened, it seemed that the passengers had also found the whole episode quite amusing.

'Hello, I'm Gertrude,' said a heavily pregnant, blonde woman in her thirties. 'This is my mother, Countess Van Den Bosch,' she added, pointing to a woman who was coming down the stairs, 'and this is George, my husband,' who was carrying a young child that I guessed to be about two years old. 'And this is

Nanny,' she continued, introducing me to a woman in her early twenties.

Once the car was loaded, the countess pressed some notes into the hand of the elderly gentleman who had helped with the luggage and we left to go back to the villa.

'Have you been to Switzerland before?' asked the countess, who was sitting in the back seat next to her daughter.

'No, first time,' I replied.

'What do you think?'

'It's certainly different,' I replied.

'Isn't it?' the countess said enthusiastically. 'There's no place quite like it. We come here to relax. It's just amazing. I've really missed it.'

George, who was in the seat next to me fiddling around with his smartphone, said, 'No snow so far, Brent?'

'No,' I replied. 'According to the website that I use, it's not due until late New Year's Eve…'

'Then your website is wrong,' George snapped. 'I've spoken to my ski guide and he says it's coming down tonight. He's never wrong.' I didn't reply.

Once back, Guss introduced himself and his ball to the family. Soon after, they met Debbie, who was tasked with opening the family's bags and putting their clothes away.

'What are they like?' Debbie whispered to me after I'd carried the last of the suitcases upstairs.

'Didn't really speak to the women much but he seems a bit up himself.'

I was helping Debbie in the kitchen when George came in. 'Expenses,' he said. 'I've got some cash for you. Have you got your expenses?'

'I'll be right back,' said Debbie, who went over to our apartment and came back with some receipts that were attached an Excel spreadsheet.

George studied them on the centre console. 'Fine, fine, fine,' he said, 'except your expenses getting here. Four hundred euros?'

'Yes, it's all detailed,' I replied. 'Petrol, tolls…'

'I think it's fair that we pay half,' he interrupted, and he put a further two hundred euros on the console.

'That's not what the agency told us,' I said. Debbie turned round from the sink and frowned.

'I don't know about that,' said George. 'I haven't spoken to the agency. But I don't see why we should pay all the expenses.'

'Because that was what was agreed. The thing is…' I started to say.

'George, George,' a voice, which I recognised to be Gertrude's, interrupted.

'Coming,' he replied, leaving the kitchen and completely ignoring me.

'What a bastard,' I said. 'That wasn't what was agreed at all.'

Debbie threw down her tea towel and said, 'The agency warned me that since the countess's husband passed away last year, George thinks he's trying to fill his shoes, but he's also going about it the wrong way. That's what that's all about. They've lost a lot of good staff because of him, apparently. I'll write to the agency. See what they can do.'

Debbie did write to the agency, who replied saying there was nothing they could do because everything had happened so quickly that they didn't get anything in writing. We'd just have to 'suck it up,' as the agent helpfully put it.

That evening, Debbie prepared a meal for the family. There was a portion put aside for the nanny, who later took it up to the room where she was watching the sleeping baby.

'Would you open some wine, please, Brent?' asked George. 'A red and a white. You choose from the cellar. I'll be interested to see how good your wine-matching skills are.'

'Excellent choice,' said George as I brought two opened bottles into the dining room where he, the countess and Gertrude were sitting. I was just thinking that maybe he wasn't so bad after all when he piped up, 'Well I suppose they would be. After all, I order all the wine myself.' The countess and Gertrude laughed.

'Shut the door please, Brent,' said the countess as I left to go back to the kitchen. As instructed, I did so, though I was a bit confused. The dining room door was solid pine, so neither Debbie nor I would have any way of knowing when the family had finished their starters, short of standing outside the chalet and looking in through a window. I was just about to say what I thought of this arrangement to Debbie when one of my worst fears was realised – we heard the tinkling of a small bell coming from the dining room.

'Bastards,' Debbie said as she approached the door. 'Who do these people think they are? It's not Downton fucking Abbey.' She went into the dining room and was soon back.

Clearly angry, she asked, 'Can you get the bread basket out, please? I forgot the bread.' As Debbie began to carve a baguette, she explained to me, 'I noticed a small brass bell in the cupboard in the dining room earlier. I thought about telling you but knew you'd go mad if you actually thought they were going to use it.' The bell rang again. 'Coming!' Debbie bellowed at the top of her voice. 'They'll be wearing this dinner if they're not careful.'

The next morning George and I were to go in two cars to Saanen airport, where we'd collect Louis, Gertrude's brother, and his guests. 'No snow this morning then?' I said as we got out of our cars.

'I must have misheard my guide. Wasn't a very good line,' George said. 'I can see it now,' he said, looking at the screen on his phone.

'You can see what?' I asked.

'The plane – I'm tracking it. It's circling overhead. Can you hear it?' I nodded my head. 'Looks like we might have to go to Lausanne,' George said disappointedly. He sighed.

'Why's that then?'

'There's too much cloud. There's no way it can land.' Five minutes later, it landed.

On New Year's Eve, it snowed, and it snowed, and then it snowed some more. The lawn had turned from green to white and the paths had become mini ice rinks. I cleared what I could with the shovel and then went into the house and filled kettles with water which I had boiled. I had thought to use the bags of salt that were in the shed next to our apartment but, having done some research on the Internet, I learned that salt burns a dog's pads, so it was not an option.

Whenever I had the opportunity, I used to walk Guss into town via the forest. It wasn't so much the descent through the trees that became a problem for me but the footpaths. Once the snow had fallen it was impossible to see the ice underneath the snow, so I spent nearly as much time on my backside as I did standing up. None of this seemed to worry Guss, who would go running off in the distance. He'd wait for me just before we got to the main road and we'd go on from there. I'd check his pads, in which sometimes there was a solid piece of ice. I'd melt it using the warm bottle of water that I used to carry in my coat pocket.

By the beginning of February, with the chalet full of guests and not having had a day off since the Van Den Bosch's arrival, Debbie and I were beginning to feel the strain. Breakfast, lunch and dinner for up to ten people had become the norm. In between those times there was shopping to be done as well as making beds, cleaning bathrooms and doing the laundry. The baby's toys, which were regularly found either down the backs of cushions or under the sofa, had to be put away. Often, we'd finish work at ten or eleven o'clock at night and the only other chance we'd have to rest was between lunch and dinner service. Wherever possible, we'd try and get some sleep between three and five in the afternoon.

'Look at this,' I said to Debbie as I got back from the supermarket and walked into the chalet's kitchen. 'A bloody parking ticket. Can you believe it? Who dishes out parking tickets on a Sunday morning?' I asked.

'The Swiss, apparently,' Debbie answered, before yawning and rinsing out the cafetière.

'I was only there for ten minutes. I didn't see a warden. Must've been

265

hiding in the bushes. Anyway, you'd think on a Sunday it would be free. Forty francs. Forty bloody francs. Well, you know what they can do with that.' I made myself a coffee. 'Anything happen while I was out?'

'Only that you're taking Louis to Lausanne airport a bit later and you're bringing back Gertrude's best friend and her son.'

Just before eleven, I began to take Louis's cases, which he had left for me at the top of the stairs, down to the car and two hours after that I was at Lausanne airport. As I pulled up outside, Gertrude's friend, who was clearly known to Louis, began to wave. Louis got out of the car, kissed her on either cheek and started a conversation with her.

'I'll be back in a minute,' I said, rushing into the airport in search of the toilets. *One coffee too many*, I said to myself as I stood at the urinal. Once I got back to the car, I noticed that the boot still hadn't been unloaded.

'Hurry up, Brent,' Louis said. 'I'm late as it is.' I took the cases out and put them on a trolley, which I passed to him. 'I'll see you in a couple of weeks,' he said, before pushing his trolley towards the entrance to the airport.

We were back at the chalet two hours later. 'Would you like a hand with those?' I asked Gertrude's friend.

'No, you're all right, I can manage,' she replied, so I went up to our apartment and made myself a coffee. I'd just sat down and taken my first sip when there was a knock on the front door. Without waiting for a reply, Gertrude opened it and poked her head round the corner. 'Can you give us a hand with my friend's luggage please, Brent?' she said.

'She told me that she doesn't need a hand. She...'

'Well, I think she does,' Gertrude replied angrily. 'After all, that is what you get paid for, isn't it?'

'Give me five minutes, if you wouldn't mind,' I said wearily. 'I've just done a four-hour round trip without a break. I'll be there...'

Gertrude's face contorted in a way that I hadn't seen before. 'I suppose I'll have to fucking well do it myself!' she screamed, before slamming the door.

266

'Don't worry about it,' said Debbie when I saw her later. 'Hormones, I imagine. Anyway, we've got this evening off, at last. Thank God. I'm so tired.'

'Really?'

'Yes, really. I haven't been asked to cook, so maybe they've noticed we could do with a break. Are you doing the beers?'

Debbie and I had a bite to eat and shared a bottle of rosé. At just after five o'clock we went for what we hoped to be a nice long nap.

At seven o'clock the nap was interrupted by a loud banging on our front door. Debbie heard it but hardly stirred. I got up and went over to the front door, which I opened. On the other side was a furious Gertrude. 'What's happening for dinner?' she asked, snarling at me.

'I've got no idea,' I replied. 'You haven't asked for any.'

'It's not up to me to ask you – it's up to you to ask us,' she snapped. 'Communication.'

'Works both ways,' I snapped back. 'You're the boss. You're supposed to tell us.'

'So, what are we supposed to eat?'

'I don't know,' I replied, feeling my blood beginning to boil. 'Why don't you look in the fridge like any normal person?'

'Fuck you,' Gertrude said, before swivelling on her heels and marching back to the chalet.

'I got most of that,' Debbie said, who was now fully awake and getting dressed. 'Did I hear that correctly? She actually said, "Fuck you"?'

'She did.'

'Right, that's it. I'm not having that,' she said, hurriedly making her way to the door.

'Where are you going?' I asked.

'Over there,' she said angrily.

'You're not going to find them something to eat, surely?'

267

'Too bloody right, I'm not. I'm not having them speak to us like that. Cheeky bitch.'

'Are you sure that's a good…'

Debbie flew out of the door. Moments later, I could hear shouting. Within five minutes Debbie was back. She opened the bedroom cupboard, took out an empty suitcase and began to unzip it.

'You need to take the expenses over there now. We're leaving in the morning.'

'We've been fired?'

'No, I told them to go and fuck themselves. I also told her where she could stick her bell. Here,' said Debbie, handing me a piece of paper from the table next to the bed. 'And don't forget our travel expenses.'

'That was my fault,' I heard the countess say to her daughter as I gently opened the front door of the chalet. 'I forgot to ask them.' I walked through the small entrance hall and into the kitchen, where Gertrude and her mother were standing at the centre console. I passed our expenses to Gertrude, who briefly looked at the receipts and then picked up her purse that was beside her on the consoles. She counted out the cash in euros, which she asked me to check.

'Our travel expenses,' I said. 'You've only paid half of them.'

'I don't see why we should pay any more,' replied Gertrude.

'Because that is what you agreed when you spoke to the agency,' I snapped.

'I don't remember that conversation,' said Gertrude.

'Well, you wouldn't, would you? Look, I just want what's owed. Now, please.'

'Are you menacing me?' Gertrude asked.

'Do you mean, am I threatening you? No, I'm not. Are you going to pay us all of our travel expenses or not?'

'No.'

With that, I left and returned to our apartment.

'How did you get on?' asked Debbie, who was still packing.

'Only got half of the expenses, but otherwise OK.'

'I didn't really expect anything else,' Debbie replied. 'Are they still in the kitchen?'

'No, don't think so. Why do you ask?'

'I've left some store cupboard ingredients over there that we brought with us. Don't see why they should keep them. I'll be back in a minute. These two bags are ready to go. Could you get them into the car?' She went back across to the chalet.

By nine o'clock the car was packed. 'What time do you think we should set off?' Debbie asked when she got back.

'I've been thinking about that,' I replied. 'How about now? I'm not tired. If we stop over, we could be back in the south of France this time tomorrow. Maybe sooner.'

'Yes, OK. But I don't want to be driving all night. First place we see when we get to France, we stop. Agreed?'

'Agreed – on the condition that we can find somewhere open this time of night,' I replied.

Debbie looked at me suspiciously. She knew that I wouldn't be really happy until we were back in the south of France. Very quietly, we bundled Guss into the car. Debbie got into the passenger seat, reclined her chair and curled up. I noticed the parking ticket that I'd got in the Co-op and tore it into very small pieces. As we approached the Swiss border I opened my window and threw it out. *Snowing again*, I thought to myself as I watched the pieces of paper disappear behind the car.

'Where are we?' asked Debbie, who had just woken up at about one o'clock the following morning. She sat up.

'Just outside Grenoble.'

'I take it we haven't found a hotel then?'

'No, but I'm glad you're awake.'

'Oh really? Why?'

'We've got a decision to make. We go left, we head to Cannes. We go right, we go to La Grande Motte for a week or so. What do you reckon?'

'You decide,' I said as Debbie lay back down and yawned.

'Any regrets about leaving Switzerland?' I asked.

'Just the one,' she replied. 'I left my timer behind in the kitchen. I've had that for years. And you?'

'Swapping grey skies and the freezing cold for the south of France? Hardly.'

'Night night.'

A couple of hours later we pulled into a service station. I parked under a street lamp and reclined my seat. Guss and Debbie were both asleep and, shortly after, I joined them. I only managed to sleep for an hour and then we set off again.

As the sun started to stream through the window at about seven o'clock, Debbie asked where we were. 'La Grande Motte,' I said.

'Great. L'Ombrine,' said Debbie, referring to our favourite restaurant in France. She'd been wanting to go back there for a long time.

Soon after, I pulled into the car park of the Hôtel Saint Clair where we pleaded with the receptionist to let us check in early. Once we were in our room, we slept again until lunchtime.

At midday we were sitting outside L'Ombrine with a huge platter of fish and a bottle of rosé, watching the boats bobbing up and down in the harbour. We then went in search of an apartment that we could rent for a week before returning to the villa in Cannes.

Chapter 29

We'd been back at Sam's villa in Cannes less than a week when I got a phone call from Hélène, who'd left Paris and was back in Montauroux.

'I have just had a very strange visit,' she began. 'You remember Magnus and Frida, the people who replaced you at Mas des Collines?'

'I do,' I replied. 'What about them?'

'The thing is, they want to track you and Debbie down, so they came to ask me if I would give them your phone number. Obviously, I declined, but...'

'Why on earth would they want to track us down?' I interrupted. 'We haven't been there for over three years. Left all that behind a long time ago.'

'Well, the thing is, they've got a problem with Charles and want to know if you'd be prepared to help.'

'After what they did to us, not likely, is it? I can't believe they've actually got the nerve to ask. Wouldn't mind knowing what's happened though. What did they have to say?'

'They didn't tell me much except that it's already gone to court in Denmark.'

'Sounds serious.'

'Doesn't it?' Hélène laughed. 'Apparently, you and Debbie could be key witnesses.

'How can we be key witnesses?' I asked. 'We hardly spoke to them. Even when we did, it wasn't pleasant.'

'I don't know,' she replied, 'but don't you think it's at least worth finding out what's gone on? Could be quite intriguing.'

'Look, OK,' I said. 'I'm happy to meet up for a coffee but that's about it. Can you arrange that, Hélène?'

'Sure.'

'And please don't give them my phone number. Not yet, anyway.'

Hélène arranged the meeting and a few days later I was about to leave for Montauroux.

'You be careful,' said Debbie. 'And whatever you do, don't tell them where we are. Besides, we owe them nothing. I'm not really sure going there is the right thing to do, but anyway.'

'I've agreed for us to meet them at the café,' said Hélène as Guss and I arrived at her villa, which was only ten minutes by car from the town centre. 'You don't mind if I come, do you?'

'Of course not.' Hélène smiled and put her coat on.

We got into my car and we made the short journey up the hill into the town of Montauroux. We parked and walked across the small *pétanque* court to the café, where Magnus and Frida were waiting.

'It's been a long time,' Magnus began. 'I see you still have the dog,' he said, patting Guss on the head. 'I'm sorry to trouble you, but I'll come straight to the point. Our solicitor says that we really need your help. He wants you to be a witness in Denmark.' I smiled and shook my head. 'Don't worry, you don't have to go there in person. If you agree, you can do it by Skype.'

'I think you'd better tell me what's happened first,' I replied, just before we ordered our coffees.

'Yes, of course,' said Magnus. 'As you know, we took over from you when you left…'

'Left?' interrupted Hélène. 'They didn't leave. You helped to force them out,' she said quite firmly.

'Yes, I know. I'm sorry about that,' replied Frida, who was looking quite sheepish. 'Charles was very kind to us when we started…'

Magnus puffed out his cheeks and continued. 'When we started working for Charles we had a problem with a property that we had bought in Manchester. It developed some serious structural problems, so Charles agreed to give us a year's salary in advance – thirty-six thousand euros.'

'Wow. That sounds generous,' said Hélène, who had just lit a cigarette.

'Doesn't it?' I said. 'Except he wouldn't be paying any social charges on

272

top of that, which is about another sixty percent in France. That's why he agreed to give you the money up front.' I looked at Magnus and Frida. 'He's not stupid. So, where did it all go wrong?'

'Where it all went wrong,' Magnus replied, 'is when he got rid of us. He's now saying that the thirty-six thousand euros was a loan and not a salary and that he wants his money back.'

'Bloody hell,' I said. 'You're kidding.'

'I wish I was,' said Magnus. 'He's insane. He needs to be stopped.' This was something that Magnus kept repeating throughout our conversation.

'The problem is that he has won the first court case in Denmark,' Frida explained. 'We had emails to prove that he had employed us, but my computer broke down and we've only just managed to retrieve them, so it was our word against his. And he's a very convincing liar. He stood in that court and told lie after lie after lie. You can go to prison for that in Denmark. Up to four years. Why on earth would we work for nothing? It's a full-time job. Magnus landed up with two frozen shoulders with all that digging. I have never been so stressed in all my life. Charles said that we did the work so that we could use the place, but I have a nice villa in the village. We have our own pool. I don't need their house. They wanted us to stay there but we didn't want that either. We have a home. After the summer, when we had worked really hard, he asked us to send him photographs every day so that he could see what we'd been doing. I don't know why, but he didn't trust us anymore.'

'Sounds familiar,' I said. 'What I don't understand is why he's taken you to court in Denmark. You worked for Charles in France. What has Denmark got to do with anything?'

'I agree,' replied Frida. 'Maybe he doesn't believe that the French courts will believe him. There must be records of him employing people over here. Or perhaps he just wants to discredit us in our own country.'

'Also,' Magnus said, 'he has offices in Copenhagen, so perhaps he's got some advice from the people who work for him there. Look, the thing is, we need you to testify. You just have to say that you were employed, that's all.'

'I don't know,' I replied. 'I need to speak to Debbie…'

'But you were so mean to Brent and Debbie,' interrupted Hélène, who was not looking at all happy. 'They had to come to my house to do their washing. You locked them out of the laundry room and you stopped them getting their things out of the garage. Not only that, you spied on them. Why should they help you now?'

'Yes, I know,' Frida said. 'I'm sorry, Brent, we should have seen straight through it, but Charles was so convincing. He said that you had stolen a load of his wine and that you had destroyed his computer system. He also said that one day you were driving Belinda to the airport when the back door of the car flew open and she lost most of her luggage and all of her money.'

'That's rubbish,' I said. 'Firstly, he's been using AJ to look after his computer system, and as he'll tell you, I don't know one end of a computer from the other. Secondly, how I can manage to open the back door of a Land Rover from the driver's seat when travelling at seventy miles per hour is beyond me. And thirdly, one of the first things that Debbie and I did when we first arrived was a wine inventory, which we had to upload to a website so that Charles could keep a track of it. If I remember correctly, we overcounted some of it once, which Charles told us about, so he knew exactly what he had in the *pigeonnier* wine cellar. He didn't tell us at the time, but he'd got his own records somewhere. Anyway, if we had stolen it, why didn't he call the police? The man is a pathological liar.'

'I know. None of it makes sense now,' said Frida. 'For the first month when we took over and you and Debbie were still in the apartment, Charles made us sit in the *pigeonnier* at nine o'clock in the evening with a camera and wait for you to arrive. He's mad, but he had us believing him. I'm sorry, but you don't have a very good reputation in the village now…'

'Then I suggest you put that straight,' snapped Hélène. 'There's only one way that they could have got that reputation. That's due to you.'

'I know,' said Frida. 'Charles convinced us that you were bad people.

At first, I did think it was all a bit odd. I thought about coming to see you, Hélène, when we first arrived, to find out whether any of it was true. But Charles said that you and Alain were dangerous, so we shouldn't go anywhere near you.'

'Dangerous?' replied Hélène. She laughed.

'He just didn't want you speaking to them,' I said. 'You might have got the truth. And not just about us – about Pierre too.'

'What about Pierre?' Frida asked. 'He was the guardian before you, Brent, right?'

'Yes,' replied Hélène. 'He committed suicide in my house.' Frida looked shocked and put her hand over her mouth. 'You didn't know?' Frida shook her head. 'Of course, I can't blame Charles, but Pierre lost everything – his home, his job, his wife – who, by the way, had a gambling problem, which Pierre tried to sort out.'

'His wife had a gambling problem?' Magnus interrupted. 'Charles said it was Pierre.'

'You see? He just can't help himself,' I replied.

While Hélène told Pierre's story in more detail, I took out a piece of paper and wrote down the number of the solicitor that we used when we had had our problem with Charles.

'She may be able to help you,' I said. 'After all, this has happened in France, not in Denmark. I'd go and see her and have a chat if I were you. You never know. The only thing is, she doesn't speak much English.'

'That's a shame, because we don't speak any French,' said Frida, who then smiled.

'Thanks for the coffee,' I said to Magnus as he took out some coins to pay the bill. 'As I said, I'll speak to Debbie, but I can't make any promises. And if I can dig out any paperwork that might help in the meantime, I'll let you know.'

'Nice to see you again, Brent,' Frida said as Hélène and I got back into our car. 'Thanks for your help, Hélène.'

'What do you think?' I said to Hélène as we made our way back down the hill.

'Well,' she began, 'it's your decision but, if I were you, I'd stay well clear. It's not as if they were friendly to you when they were there.'

'They were apologetic.'

'Of course, they were apologetic – they want your help. If they hadn't fallen out with Charles, you would never had heard from them again. Anyway, denying you access to basic hygiene? I'm sorry, but their human instincts should have taken over, regardless of what Charles told them to do. I feel a bit sorry for them, but my advice is to stay out of it. Oh,' she continued as she wound down her window and lit a cigarette, 'if they ask me to go to Toulon with them to translate, the answer's no. You can tell them I'm travelling, which, actually, is not far from the truth. Did I tell you I'm off to Cadaques next week?'

As Hélène suspected, a few days later we received an email asking us if we thought Hélène would go to Toulon. They would be happy to pay for her time. I wrote back declining on her behalf. I also wrote to say that we wouldn't be prepared to testify, even via Skype, but this didn't deter Frida. She wrote two or three times over the coming weeks saying how important their solicitor felt that our evidence was. Again, we politely refused. Then came *la pièce de résistance*. We received one final email that was full of emojis with smiling faces and lucky clovers that asked us to go to Copenhagen to give evidence. Our flights and hotel would be paid for and we would have the chance to visit the beautiful city. We replied one last time, wishing Magnus and Frida the best of luck but saying we wanted no further involvement. We did, however, forward them a few emails that would prove that we were being paid a salary by Charles and Belinda. And that was the last we heard of them.

We'd been talking to Sam about the possibility of her withdrawing the maintenance contract from the agency, with whom she was becoming more and more frustrated. When confronted about some missing linen, the agent tried to blame it on Sam's parents, who had visited the property the week previously.

The agent was unable to provide receipts for the two thousand euros that were in the safe, which was supposed to have been set aside for emergencies. None of the tasks that Sam had asked to be done had happened, so she was ready to give the agency a month's notice.

'The thing is, Sam,' I explained, 'if we were to take over your contract we would still need work from another villa. We can't survive on just yours, so we'll have to wait.'

'Well, you may be in luck there,' Sam replied. I know a couple, Peter and Julie, who have a villa about five minutes from where you are now. They use the same agency as me and I know that they're not happy either. They're due to come over from England in a few weeks, so if you could hang on till then...'

While we were waiting, we applied for the few jobs that we had been sent by employment agencies. Hopefully, something would come up, but if it didn't we might be able to look after two villas and work for ourselves.

I had just made myself a cup of coffee at about eleven o'clock one morning when Debbie shouted from the dining room, 'I don't believe it. I don't bloody believe it!'

'What's up?' I asked, making my way from the kitchen and looking over Debbie's shoulder.

'What's up?' she replied, looking in disbelief at her computer. 'You're what's up. Normally, it's Guss who stops us from getting interviews, but this time it's you. I've just got an email from the agency.'

'I've never spoken to them. What's it got to do with me?' I asked.

'That job that we were put forward for. You know the one? Working on the estate with the vineyard in Bras.'

'Yes, what about it?'

'Well, the owner has googled you.'

'Has he now?' I said. 'I didn't feel a thing. Naughty boy.'

'Shut up. This is not funny.'

'Guess what he found?'

I shrugged my shoulders.

'I'll tell you then, shall I? What he found was *Cookham To Cannes*. He says, and I quote,' Debbie said, looking at the screen and shaking her head. '"Your candidate has written a book and it seems to be less than complimentary about the people that he has worked for in France so, regrettably, I won't be taking this application any further."' I'm telling you, Brent, you are a bloody liability.'

'That's a shame because I was really looking forward to that job. I…'

'You don't know anything about it,' Debbie interrupted. 'Thanks to you, we didn't even get as far as the interview stage. That's a first.'

'I know, but working in Bras. I've been fascinated with bras, or at least their contents, since I was a spotty teenager…'

'It's pronounced bra and the word *bras* is the French word for arm, as you well know,' Debbie said, who was still looking at the screen and shaking her head in disbelief.

'I know but think of the comedy value. I could have had so much fun with that. I could have written to people telling them that I was going to be spending the next few years of my life fumbling around in bras. Not only that, I'd be getting paid for it. How cool is that?'

Debbie sighed. 'Have you quite finished?' she said.

'No, not quite. One last thing.'

'I'm all ears.'

'Do you know the German word for bra?' I asked.

'No, but I'm sure you're going to tell me.'

'*Stoppem-floppen.*'

'Isn't it about time you took Guss for a walk?'

Two weeks later we met Julie and her husband Peter at their villa at the top of the estate. Julie, a very pretty woman in her forties, had the most infectious laugh I'd ever heard. She and Peter owned a construction company in the UK, although it soon became apparent that Julie's forte was interior design. The inside of the property was exquisite – something that her rental guests would comment on again and again in the future. Shortly after our meeting, we signed a contract to look after the villa. We'd be working on a self-employed basis, so all we needed to do was to find some accommodation to rent for ourselves. We'd no longer be living with and employed by lunatic control freaks with egos as large as their estates. And we did find some accommodation – a small apartment overlooking the sea in Cannes.

'Do you think we've finally managed to settle in France?' I asked one morning over breakfast in June 2016.

'Well,' Debbie replied, 'I think we'll be OK, provided the British public don't vote tomorrow to leave Europe. Then we might have a problem.'

'Can't see that happening, can you?'

Made in the USA
Monee, IL
08 May 2020